DATE DUE

GAYLORD			PRINTED IN U.S.A.

Occupational Choices and Training Needs

Leonard Abe Lecht

Published in cooperation
with The Conference Board

The Praeger Special Studies program—utilizing the most modern and efficient book production techniques and a selective worldwide distribution network—makes available to the academic, government, and business communities significant, timely research in U.S. and international economic, social, and political development.

Occupational Choices and Training Needs

Prospects for the 1980s

Andrew S. Thomas Memorial Library
MORRIS HARVEY COLLEGE, CHARLESTON, W. VA.

97193

Praeger Publishers New York London

PRAEGER SPECIAL STUDIES IN U.S. ECONOMIC, SOCIAL, AND POLITICAL ISSUES

331.1
L497o

Library of Congress Cataloging in Publication Data

Lecht, Leonard Abe, 1920-
　Occupational choices and training needs.

　(Praeger special studies in U.S. economic, social, and political issues)
　"Published in cooperation with the Conference Board."
　Includes bibliographical references and index.
　1. Vocational education—United States.
2. Minorities—Employment—United States.　3. Job vacancies—United States.　4. Manpower policy—United States.　I. Conference Board.　I. Title.
LC1045.L437　　　370.11'3'0973　　　76-24356
ISBN 0-275-23960-8

PRAEGER PUBLISHERS
200 Park Avenue, New York, N.Y. 10017, U.S.A.

Published in the United States of America in 1977
by Praeger Publishers, Inc.

789　038　987654321

All rights reserved

© 1977 by The Conference Board, Inc.

Printed in the United States of America

The activity that is the subject of this report was supported by the U.S. Office of Education, Department of Health, Education, and Welfare. However, the opinions expressed herein do not necessarily reflect the position or policy of the U.S. Office of Education, and no official endorsement by the U.S. Office of Education should be inferred.

PREFACE

This study seeks to expand the range of available occupational information by relating data on job openings to: information about the earnings of persons employed in different occupations, their educational attainment, and the opportunities individual fields are expected to offer to women and members of minority groups. The report presents historical data and projections to 1980 and 1985 which are consistent with the U.S. Department of Labor's economic growth model.

The significance of the study lies in the overview it presents of the many developments affecting occupational choices and training needs in the next decade. The report focuses on several key issues. First, it seeks to develop a better understanding of the growth rate through 1985 of 123 selected occupations in fields that do not usually require a college degree. Second, the study goes beyond a simple projection of growth to assess the economic returns to and the characteristics of the persons employed in these occupations. Finally, the study relates the occupational growth and characteristics of the fields considered to the actual and projected enrollments in vocational education. Since the vocational education system is the largest of all the public and private institutions concerned with occupational training, a successful transition from school to work for individuals, or success in recruiting and training in industry, is substantially affected by the progress made in planning in vocational education.

A study of so broad a scope is inevitably the product of the efforts of many people. Individuals in various agencies and organizations, public and private, have contributed ideas and raw materials. The study is indebted to the U.S. Office of Education for financial support and for cooperation in the execution of the project. Dr. Marc A. Matland has contributed to the study in many ways as principal investigator in the ongoing research; in particular, he has contributed to the preparation of the initial drafts on which this report is based. Richard J. Rosen has been responsible for most of the projections as well as for writing the appendixes dealing with methodology and the state-local projections. Diane Tullman typed and edited the manuscript, and contributed to the index together with Selina L. Wang, who also prepared several statistical tables. Needless to say, I am responsible for the errors of omission and commission in the book.

CONTENTS

		Page
PREFACE		vi
LIST OF TABLES		x

Chapter

1	AN OVERALL VIEW	1
	Introduction	1
	The Economic and Social Framework	4
	Job Openings: 1970 to 1985	7
	Occupations and Educational Attainment	11
	Prospects for Women and Nonwhites	14
	Vocational Enrollments, Social Changes, and Career Opportunities	18
	Notes	23
2	EMPLOYMENT, JOB OPENINGS, AND EARNINGS	24
	Sources of Job Openings	24
	Employment Growth and Replacement Demand	33
	Occupations and Earnings	37
	Notes	43
3	THE EDUCATIONAL ATTAINMENT INDICATORS	44
	Trends in Educational Attainment	44
	The Decline of the High School Dropout	46
	Educational Attainment and Earnings	54
	Occupational Training and Earnings	58
	Notes	61
4	WOMEN AND NONWHITES	62
	Equal Opportunity—Aspirations and Achievements	62
	Women in the Labor Market	67

Chapter		Page
	Nonwhites—Occupational and Income Shifts	71
	Notes	78
5	IMPLICATIONS FOR EDUCATIONAL AND MANPOWER PLANNING	79
	Labor-Force Indicators and Educational Planning	79
	Program Priorities in Vocational Education	80
	Enrollments and Earnings	84
	Women and Nonwhites in the Vocational Programs	87
	Pressures for and against Change	92
	Notes	95
APPENDIX A: THE NATIONAL PROJECTIONS Richard J. Rosen		97
	Introduction	97
	The Economic Framework for the Study	98
	Selecting the Occupations for Study	99
	Data and Data Sources	101
	Comparability of Occupational Data from Various Sources	101
	Projection Techniques	105
	Next Steps in Research	121
	Notes	124
APPENDIX B: REPLICABILITY OF THE NATIONAL PROJECTIONS FOR INDIVIDUAL STATES Richard J. Rosen		125
	Introduction	125
	The Economic Framework for State Projections	125
	Data, Data Sources, and Comparability	126
	Statistical Reliability of the Data	127
	Use of National Trend Data or Other Surrogate Measures for the State	130
	Deriving Benchmark Checks for the Projections	134
	Conclusions Regarding Feasibility of Preparing State Indicators	137
	Note	138

Chapter	Page
APPENDIX C: STATISTICAL TABLES	140
INDEX	199
ABOUT THE AUTHOR	205

LIST OF TABLES

Table		Page
1.1	Comparison of Occupations Included in Study with All Civilian Occupations, 1970	3
1.2	Selected Economic and Social Framework Variables, 1970 and Projected 1980 and 1985	5
1.3	Projected Average Annual Job Openings, 1970-85	8
1.4	Distribution of Employment in Occupations Studied, Grouped by Earnings, 1970	9
1.5	Distribution of Educational Attainment, 1970 and Projected 1985—Study Occupations	11
1.6	Projected Changes in the Civilian Labor Force by Sex and Race, 1970-85	14
1.7	Distribution of Employment by Sex and Race in Occupations Studied, Grouped by Earnings, 1970	15
1.8	Projected Vocational-Education Enrollments in 1977 and Average Annual Job Openings, 1970-85, Study Occupations	19
1.9	Distribution of Enrollment by Sex, Major Vocational-Program Areas—1971 and Projected 1977	21
1.10	Population Growth in Selected Broad Age Groups, 1960, 1970, and Projected 1980 and 1985	22
2.1	Employment in All Occupations and in Study Occupations, 1970 and Projected 1985	26
2.2	Projected Average Annual Job Openings, Major Occupational Groups and Larger Study Occupations, 1970-85	27
2.3	Estimated Changes in Employment by Region, 1970-85	32

Table		Page
2.4	Projected Large Increases and Declines in Employment, Study Occupations, 1970-85	34
2.5	Estimated Sources of Job Openings and Representation of Women in these Occupations Expected to Provide Large Numbers of Job Openings, 1970-85	36
2.6	Projected Average Annual Job Openings, 1970-85, and Employment Distribution in 1970 Grouped by Earnings in 1970	38
2.7	Median Earnings in 1970, and Projected Employment Growth, 1970-85, 10 Highest-Paid and 10 Lowest-Paid Study Occupations	40
2.8	Dispersion of Median Earnings in Study Occupations around Economy-wide Median for Full-Year Workers, 1970 and Projected 1985	41
3.1	Distribution of Educational Attainment, by Major Occupational Group, Study Occupations—1970 and Projected 1985	47
3.2	Years of Schooling Completed by All Workers and by Workers 16 to 34 Years Old, Selected Occupations, 1970	48
3.3	Distribution of Educational Attainment, Kentucky, New Jersey, and the Entire United States, 1970	49
3.4	Distribution of Educational Attainment, 1970, in Study Occupations with Projected Employment Increase of 100 Percent or More, 1970-85	51
3.5	Projected Changes in Representation of College Graduates in Selected Occupations, 1970-85	52
3.6	Distribution of Employment by Educational Attainment and Earnings, Study Occupations, 1970	55

Table		Page
3.7	Median Years of Schooling Completed, 1970, and Estimated Earnings in 1970 and 1985—Study Occupations Employing Largest Number of Men and Women	56
3.8	Median Earnings of Occupational-Training Completers and All Others by Educational Attainment and Occupational Group—All Occupations, 1970	59
4.1	Distribution of Employment, Nonwhites and Women, by Major Occupational Group, 1960 and 1974, All Occupations	64
4.2	Women and Nonwhites in 10 Highest-and 10 Lowest-Paying Study Occupations—1970 and Projected 1985	66
4.3	Employment of Women in "Female" Fields Included in Study Occupations, 1970 and Projected 1985	67
4.4	Estimated Changes in Employment and Representation Shifts for Women, Study Occupations, 1970-85	69
4.5	Representation of All Women in Work Force, 1970 and Projected 1985, and Representation of Women in under-35 Work Force, 1970, Selected Occupations	70
4.6	Changes in Employment and Representation Shifts for Nonwhites, Study Occupations, 1970-85	73
4.7	Projected Increase in Employment for Nonwhites, 1970-85, Selected Occupations	74
4.8	Representation of Nonwhites in Study Occupations with Projected Employment Increases of 100 Percent or More, 1970-85	76
4.9	Employment by Race, Workers Completing 12 to 15 Years of Schooling, Study Occupations—1970 and Projected 1985	77
5.1	Enrollment in Vocational Programs Per 100 Persons Employed in Related Study Occupations, 1970	81

Table		Page
5.2	Distribution of Enrollments in Vocational Programs, 1970 and Projected 1977; and Distribution of Employment in Study-Related Occupations, 1970 and Projected 1985	82
5.3	Enrollment-Employment Ratios in Programs Related to Occupations with High and Low Earnings, 1970	85
5.4	Distribution of Enrollments by Program Level in Vocational Programs Related to Occupations with High and Low Earnings, 1970	88
5.5	Distribution of Female Enrollments in Major Vocational Program Areas, 1970 and Projected 1977	90
5.6	Labor-Force Participation by Women—1960, 1973, and Projected 1985	91
5.7	Projected Annual Average Job Openings, 1970-85; and Representation of Women and Nonwhites in 1970, Selected Study Occupations	94
A.1	Data Sources and Information Obtained for Occupational Characteristics Study	102
A.2	Projecting the Distribution of Employment by Race in the 16-34 Age Group	108
A.3	Reconciliation of Employment Estimates by Sex and Race for Study Occupations with BLS Estimates of Total Employment—1960, 1970, and Projected 1985	111
A.4	Distribution of Women and Nonwhites in Selected Occupations—1970 Census, 1973 and 1974 Current Population Survey, and 1980 Projections	113
A.5	Reconciliation of Estimates of Employment by Level of Educational Attainment for Occupations Studied with BLS Estimates—1960, 1970, and Projected 1985	116

Table		Page
A.6	Industrial Sectors Supplying Productivity Benchmarks for Earnings Projections in Related Occupations	118
A.7	Median Earnings and Personal Income per Worker, United States, 1970, and Projected 1985	121
B.1	Data Sources and Information Obtained for Kentucky and New Jersey Projections	128
B.2	Educational Attainment of Workers in Kentucky, New Jersey, and the United States—Major Occupational Groups and Selected Occupations, 1970	131
B.3	Median Earnings of Full-Year Workers, New Jersey, Kentucky, and United States—Selected Occupations, 1970	133
B.4	Employment by Sex, Occupations Studied and All State Occupations for Kentucky and New Jersey—1960, 1970, and Projected 1980	135
B.5	Employment by Race, Occupations Studied and All State Occupations for Kentucky and New Jersey—1970 and Projected 1980	136
C.1	Selected National Economic Framework Indicators—1960, 1970, and Projected 1980 and 1985	140
C.2	Study Occupations and All Civilian Occupations, 1970, and Projected 1985	141
C.3	Median Earnings of Full-Year Workers in Study Occupations and Ratio of Occupational Median to Economy-wide Median—1970 and Projected 1980 and 1985	142
C.4	Employment in 1960 and 1970 and Projected 1980 and 1985, Study Occupations	149
C.5	Projected Average Annual Job Openings, 1970-85, Study Occupations	156

Table		Page
C.6	Employment by Sex, 1970 and Projected 1980 and 1985, Study Occupations	162
C.7	Distribution of Employment by Sex, 1970 and Projected 1980 and 1985, Study Occupations	168
C.8	Employment by Race, 1970 and Projected 1980 and 1985, Study Occupations	174
C.9	Distribution of Employment by Race, 1970 and Projected 1980 and 1985, Study Occupations	180
C.10	Distribution of Employment by Level of Educational Attainment, 1970 and Projected 1980 and 1985, Study Occupations	186
C.11	Vocational Programs Related to Occupations Included in Conference Board Study	190
C.12	Enrollment in Vocational Programs per 100 Persons Employed in Related Occupations, 1970, and Projected Average Annual Rate of Growth in Enrollment, 1970-77, and Employment, 1970-80	197

CHAPTER

1

AN OVERALL VIEW

INTRODUCTION

Vocational education is an educational program, a manpower program, and it has taken on many elements of a social program. Labor market information, as well as educational data, accordingly, is important in planning and decision making in vocational education. The manpower information that has received a high priority in planning in the past has been primarily concerned with future job openings and employment growth. Job-openings data are often an inadequate guide in planning. The openings may exist in occupations characterized by low earnings, formidable educational requirements, or difficult-to-breach barriers to entry by women or minority group members. This study seeks to expand the scope of the information available to educators, employers, and others by relating the job-openings data to information about other significant occupational characteristics, such as the earnings of the persons employed in different occupations, their educational attainment, and the opportunities individual fields are expected to provide for women and nonwhites. These considerations are important for students and educators, for employers and government officials concerned with job training, recruitment, and equal employment opportunity programs, and for persons generally concerned with manpower programs.

The occupational-characteristics indicators refer to 123 individual occupations. They include the occupations, or clusters of occupations, related to all the major federally supported vocational programs. They also include other occupations of prospective interest to educators or others concerned with occupational preparation in nonprofessional fields. These occupations have been selected on the basis of the earnings of the persons employed in them, their projected job openings in the 1970-85 period, and the educational attainment of their work force. All told, the occupations considered are expected to account for over 55 percent of the economy-wide job openings in the next decade. They are related to vocational programs which, according to U.S. Office of Education projections, will account for close to 85 percent of all enrollments in the federally-supported programs in 1977.

The relationship between the occupations considered and all occupations is summarized in Table 1.1 for 1970, the base year for the study.

The occupations considered in the study include a somewhat greater proportion of males than females, and a considerably greater percentage of whites than nonwhites. There is a smaller representation of professional and technical workers than in the overall labor force, and a larger proportion of craftsmen and salesworkers. College graduates are conspicuously underrepresented because of the choice of occupational fields. The median earnings of full-year workers in the 123 occupations in 1970 was an eighth less than the comparable earnings for the entire employed civilian labor force.

The overall findings that emerge from the study are summarized below:

1. About two-thirds of the job openings in the occupations considered in the 1970 to 1985 period are expected to arise from the replacement of attrition losses, and only one-third from employment growth. While many of the attrition-generated openings will represent opportunities to replace experienced and skilled workers, the bulk of the replacement demand will occur in less well-paid fields with a majority of female employees.

2. The vocational-education system typically prepares people for employment in fields that pay less than the median earnings for all occupations. In 1970, about two-thirds of the full-year workers in the occupations studied earned less than the median for all full-year workers.

3. If the trends of the past 15 years continue, the nation's commitment to equal employment opportunity will be accompanied by only modest changes in the occupational distribution for women and somewhat greater changes for nonwhites. As the largest of the publicly supported occupational-training programs, the vocational-education system is strategically situated to prepare more women and nonwhites for desirable careers in fields in which they have been poorly represented in the past.

4. The concentration of employment in occupations yielding low incomes is especially marked for women and nonwhites. Three-

AN OVERALL VIEW 3

TABLE 1.1

Comparison of Occupations Included in Study
with All Civilian Occupations, 1970

Indicator	Occupations Studied	All Occupations	Occupations Studied as Percent of All Occupations
Distribution of employment			
By sex (in thousands)			
Male	27,815	48,960	57
Female	15,585	29,667	53
By race (in thousands)			
White	39,888	70,182	57
Nonwhite	3,511	8,445	42
By years of schooling (in thousands)			
Less than 12	16,741	29,250	57
12-15	23,697	39,630	60
16 or more	2,961	9,750	30
By occupational group (in percent)			
Professional and technical workers	4.9	14.2	—
Salesworkers	10.6	6.2	—
Craftsmen	19.0	12.9	—
Laborers, except farm	1.5	4.7	—
Median earnings* (in 1973 dollars)	8,725	9,945	88

*Full-year workers only.
Sources: U.S. Department of Labor, Bureau of Labor Statistics; U.S. Department of Commerce, Bureau of the Census.

fourths of the women and over half of the nonwhite full-year workers in the occupations studied had earnings in 1970 that were approximately $2,000 or more below the national median for full-year workers.

5. While there will be many more college graduates in 1985 than at present, the more widespread changes are expected to stem from the sharp decline in the proportion of employed persons with fewer than 12 years of schooling. The reduction in the representation

of dropouts is projected to be greatest in the less skilled occupations in which they have traditionally been concentrated.

6. Although the vocational-education system has become more labor-market oriented in its planning, there are still significant divergences between the job openings and vocational enrollments anticipated in the next decade. There is a far larger proportion of enrollments than job openings in the agricultural field, and a considerably lesser proportion of enrollments than jobs in the health and distribution fields.

7. Demographic changes in the next decade can be expected to lessen the importance of the high school age group as the primary audience for vocational programs, and to increase the importance of adults with labor-force experience as the source of enrollment growth. As one indication of the dimensions of this demographic shift, the population of 14- to 24-year olds is projected to decline by 3.2 million between 1980 and 1985.

8. It is feasible to prepare most of the occupational-characteristics indicators presented nationally for individual states or the larger Standard Metropolitan Statistical Areas. However, because of the smaller population base and sample size, considerations of statistical reliability limit the degree of detail that can be provided in these estimates.

The occupations individuals choose have a major bearing on their income, their likelihood of becoming unemployed, and their opportunities for self-realization. Occupational choices, in turn, can influence the economy's growth by contributing to the development of manpower surpluses, which add to unemployment, or to manpower bottlenecks, which raise employers' costs. The information provided to students about occupations or used in educational planning must encompass the range of considerations that are relevant in making occupational choices. The information presented in this study can provide a first step in developing and improving a series of occupational-characteristics indicators to supply a more comprehensive overview of anticipated changes influencing the transition from school to work.

THE ECONOMIC AND SOCIAL FRAMEWORK

The changes in occupational characteristics projected for the 1980s reflect the economic, demographic, and social framework anticipated in 1980 and 1985. The strategic variables in this framework are summarized in Table 1.2 below.

TABLE 1.2

Selected Economic and Social Framework Variables, 1970 and Projected 1980 and 1985

Variable	1970	1980	1985	Average Annual Growth Rate (in percent)		
				1970–80	1980–85	1970–85
Population, 14 and over (in millions)	151.1	174.7	182.9	1.5	0.9	1.3
Civilian labor force (in millions)	82.7	99.8	105.7	1.9	1.2	1.7
Civilian employment (in millions)	78.6	95.8	101.5	2.0	1.2	1.7
Unemployment rate (in percent)	4.9	4.0	4.0	—	—	—
Gross National Product (in billions of 1973 dollars)	1,115	1,751	2,051	4.6	3.2	4.2
Gross National Product per worker (in 1973 dollars)	13,625	17,900	19,820	2.8	2.1	2.5
Average annual hours per worker*	1,968	1,920	1,888	-0.3	-0.3	-0.3

*Private economy only.

Sources: U.S. Department of Labor, Bureau of Labor Statistics; U.S. Department of Commerce, Bureau of the Census. Population projections based on Series E fertility assumption.

Occupational choices in the next decade will be made in an environment in which the labor force is expected to grow slowly. For example, the labor force increased by nearly 2 percent a year between 1968 and 1972, and a growth rate of this dimension is projected to continue in the 1970s. However, labor-force growth is expected to decrease to a 1.2 percent annual rate in the 1980-85 period because of declining birth rates 15 to 20 years earlier. The consequences of a slower growth in the number of persons available to produce goods and services show up in the anticipated slowing down of the Gross National Product (GNP) growth rate from an estimated 4.6 percent annually in the 1970s to a 3.2 percent average annual rate in the first half of the 1980s.

The slowly growing labor force in the next decade will reap the benefits of continuing technological change and productivity growth. These developments will frequently eliminate specific jobs, or reduce the numbers employed in them, or change their duties and skill content; in other instances, they will encourage the development of new occupations. The emergence of the computer programmer in the past two decades and the changes in employment in the printing trades are instances. Using growth in GNP per worker as a proxy for productivity increase, productivity is expected to grow at an average annual rate of 2.5 percent a year in the 1970-85 period. The productivity gains, together with changes in the occupational distribution of the work force, supply the basis for an anticipated increase in the earnings of full-year workers from $9,945 in 1970 to about $15,000 in 1985 (in 1973 dollars). Given the choice between larger earnings and more leisure, it is expected that, as in the past generation, Americans will assign a higher priority to earnings. Accordingly, annual man-hours per worker are projected to decrease only modestly, by an average of 0.3 of 1 percent a year. Over the entire 15-year period, however, this gradual decrease would represent the equivalent of an additional two weeks of leisure a year. As in the past, it is anticipated that the bulk of the reduction in hours will be taken in the form of more widespread and longer vacations rather than in reductions in the weekly hours of work.

The productivity gains, and their consequences for manpower utilization, are likely to be unevenly distributed between economic sectors. The gains in agriculture, for example, are projected to amount to double the average rate for the overall private economy. Slow growth in farm output coupled with continued high productivity increases are the basis for the anticipation that the farm occupations will constitute the one group in which employment is projected to decline, a decline estimated at almost a million between 1970 and 1985. The diminished share of the economy's output represented by agri-

AN OVERALL VIEW

cultural products will also set limits to growth in the broad spectrum of agribusiness occupations.

The projections of population and labor-force increase, productivity growth, GNP, and employment are consistent with the economic framework utilized in the U.S. Department of Labor's Bureau of Labor Statistics employment projections.[1] The basic employment and attrition estimates are also derived from Bureau of Labor Statistics sources. These estimates imply an unemployment rate of 4 percent in 1980 and 1985. This is a lesser rate than has been attained in the first half of the 1970s, and a substantially lesser one than the over 8 percent figure experienced in 1975. Changes in the makeup of the labor force will make it more difficult to attain a 4 percent rate in the next 10 years than a decade earlier because of the greater representation of the more unemployment-prone groups, such as nonwhites or women, in the work force. The restraints exerted on economic policy by fears of stimulating inflationary pressures can also be expected to compound the difficulties involved in attaining a 4 percent unemployment rate in the next 10 years. A higher unemployment rate than the one incorporated in the projections would reduce the job openings in most occupations to levels lower than those indicated in the projections, and lead to more modest changes in the representation of women and nonwhites in the better-paying fields than are shown in the projections. Slow growth and persistent high unemployment levels would also hasten the shift of college graduates into fields they have been reluctant to enter in large numbers in the past. It is impossible to predict what the unemployment rate will be five or ten years from now, and the projections of job openings must rely on assumptions about the economy's potential for a noninflationary minimum unemployment level in the coming decade. These assumptions are significant in that they underscore the importance of a dynamic economy as a critical variable in educational as well as manpower or business planning.

JOB OPENINGS: 1970 TO 1985

Three elements characterize the job openings in the fields considered in the study. One is the predominance of white-collar jobs in occupations that typically employ persons with some job skills but less than four years of college. Another is the importance of replacement demand as a source of job openings. The third is the concentration of earnings for persons employed in these occupations at levels below the median for the overall work force.

TABLE 1.3

Projected Average Annual Job Openings, 1970-85
(in thousands)

Occupational Group	Projected Job Openings
Professional and technical workers	204.0
Managers and administrators, except farm	344.2
Salesworkers	316.5
Clerical workers	794.7
Craftsmen and foremen	342.1
Operatives	307.5
Service workers	428.8
Laborers, except farm	20.3
Farm occupations	—
All Occupations	2,753.0

Note: Details may not add to total because of rounding.
Source: Conference Board projections.

The 123 occupations included in the study are expected to generate an annual average of 2.75 million job openings in the 1970-85 period. Sixty percent of the openings are projected to occur in white-collar fields. The distribution of the job openings by occupational group is described in Table 1.3.

The largest single group of job openings listed in the table are for clerical workers, a field overwhelmingly made up of female employees. The next largest are in a variety of more or less skilled service fields, including personal services, health services, and protective services. No figure is listed for the farm occupations since employment decline in this occupational group is expected to outweigh the replacement of attrition losses leading to a meaningless negative number for job openings.

Slightly more than 900,000 of the job openings anticipated annually between 1970 and 1985 are estimated to arise from employment growth, and the remainder, about 1.8 million, from the replacement of attrition losses. Individual occupations differ markedly in the relative importance of growth as compared with attrition. For example, three-fourths of the openings for engineering and science technicians, excluding subcategories listed separately, are expected to arise from employment growth. Nearly 80 percent of the projected openings for bookkeepers, to cite another instance, are projected to come about because of attrition. The occupations in which replacement demand dominates job openings tend to have a high representation of women who leave the labor force, at least temporarily, to rear children, and who usually retire at an earlier age than men. High replacement demand is also characteristic of slow-growth occupations, including a number of skilled crafts. Employment growth is typically the dominant element in new occupations, in occupations concentrated in rapidly growing industries, often public service industries, and in fields heavily influenced by technological advance. The fields in which the job openings are dominated by employment growth, especially the technical fields, include many of the better-paid occupations in which the earnings of full-year workers approximate or exceed the economy-wide median.

While a number of the occupations characterized by rapid employment growth frequently yield earnings greater than the overall median, close to two-thirds of the persons employed in the occupations studied who were full-year workers in 1970 earned less than the $9,945 median earnings (in 1973 dollars) for all full-year workers. Over two-fifths of the full-year workers in these fields earned $2,000 or more below the economy-wide median while only a fifth earned at least $12,000, approximately $2,000 more than the national average.

The distribution of employment by earnings in the occupations considered is described in Table 1.4.

TABLE 1.4

Distribution of Employment in Occupations Studied, Grouped by Earnings, 1970

Median Earnings of Occupations*	Distribution of Employment (in percent)
Less than $6,000	12.3
6,000-7,999	29.1
8,000-9,999	23.8
10,000-11,999	14.7
12,000-13,999	7.8
14,000 and over	12.4

Notes: Details may not add to total because of rounding.
Earnings refer to median earnings of full-year workers.
*In 1973 dollars.
Source: U.S. Bureau of the Census, Department of Commerce, Census of the Population, 1970.

Women and nonwhites are frequently overrepresented in the occupations paying substantially less than the national median. Low earnings are also characteristic of many slowly growing fields. These poorly paid occupations have often become relatively less well paid in the recent past as economic progress and productivity increases have led to more substantial increases in other fields. The median earnings for sewers and stitchers who worked a full year in 1970, for example, amounted to just under $4,900. This represented a decline from 58 percent of the national median for year-round workers in 1960 to 49 percent in 1970. Employment in some low-paid fields, often human-service occupations, is projected to increase rapidly in the 1970 to 1985 period. For instance, the median earnings for full-year health aides in 1970 was about $5,440. Employment in this occupation is expected to more than double in the 1970-85 period.

The better-paid occupations included in the study—those paying more than $12,000 a year for year-round workers in 1970—include semiprofessional fields, such as personnel workers and draftsmen, occupations related to finance and real estate, and a number of skilled craft and technician fields. Aside from the preponderance of white male representation in these occupations, they are also characterized by the high level of educational attainment of the persons employed in them. For example, only about a fourth of the employees in the occupations in the $12,000 and over group had finished less than twelve years of schooling and 15 percent had completed four or more years of college. At the other end of the occupational spectrum, in the fields in the less than $6,000 group, nearly 60 percent of the persons employed in them had completed less than a full high school education.

Economic growth and productivity gains are expected to increase earnings in virtually all occupations, an increase represented by escalation in the median earnings of full-year workers to approximately $15,000 by 1985. Growth is likely both to move up and increase the range of earnings in the occupations included in the study. The upgrading of earnings is expected to be especially significant in managerial and semiprofessional fields, and in technical occupations and skilled crafts, such as airplane mechanics.

The earnings data reflect the exclusion of the many professional occupations requiring at least four years of college for admission. They also reflect the widespread attitude that vocational education is education for "other people's children."[2] Accordingly, with many individual exceptions, the vocational programs have tended to cluster around the less well-paid occupations in our society.

AN OVERALL VIEW   11

OCCUPATIONS AND EDUCATIONAL ATTAINMENT

While economic and social mobility have come to be widely identified with a college education, the most striking change in educational attainment in the occupations considered is the sharp decline in the proportion of persons in the less skilled occupations with under 12 years of schooling. This change can be expected to outweigh the increase in the representation of college graduates in the largely nonprofessional fields included in the study. The greater supply of better-educated persons, especially young persons, is likely to reduce the scarcity value, and, accordingly, the economic return to the possession of educational credentials.

The changes anticipated in the level of educational attainment for the persons employed in the occupations studied are described in Table 1.5.

TABLE 1.5

Distribution of Educational Attainment,
1970 and Projected 1985—Study Occupations

| | Percent of Workers ||
Years Schooling Completed	1970	1985
Less than 12	38.6	22.8
12 to 15	54.6	68.1
16 or more	6.8	9.1

Source: Conference Board estimates.

The percentage of persons in the study occupations with less than 12 years of schooling is expected to decline by close to 16 percentage points in the 1970-85 period. This marked upgrading in educational attainment is concentrated among blue-collar and service workers. The upgrading is consistent with the increase in the educational attainment level of the overall labor force in the past decade. For example, between 1964 and 1974 the median number of years of schooling completed by all persons in the employed civilian labor force rose only from 12.2 to 12.5 years. The comparable median for blue-collar workers rose from 10.7 to 12.1 years.[3] For the 123 occupations included in the study, the upgrading of educational attainment in less highly skilled fields is illustrated by the service workers group. In 1970, close to half, 46.5 percent, of the service workers had less than 12 years of schooling. By 1985, this proportion is estimated to fall to 29.5 percent.

The upgrading of educational attainment in non-white-collar fields is most apparent among young workers, the age group that comprises the bulk of the new entrants into the labor force. In all of the occupations studied, in only five was the percentage of workers in the under-35 age group with less than 12 years of schooling as great as the proportion of all workers in this educational category in the occupation. The significance of the age differential is illustrated for males by farm owners and tenants, and, for females, by practical nurses. In 1970, almost three-fifths, 57 percent, of all farm owners and tenants had less than 12 years of schooling. The corresponding percentage for the under-35 group was slightly over a fourth, 27.5 percent. Of all practical nurses, 30 percent had less than 12 years of schooling. Only about 10 percent of the under-35 practical nurses were in the same educational attainment group.

The upgrading of educational attainment in the less skilled occupations has many ramifications for schools, for employers, and for the quality of life. The less skilled, more poorly paid, and generally less desirable occupations in the past had drawn their labor supply from persons with limited educational credentials. In the next decade the labor pool they will draw on will contain a proportion of high school graduates approximating the representation of high school graduates in more skilled fields. In addition, many more young people will have completed high school and be available to enroll in post-high school programs on a full or a part-time basis, a change likely to markedly increase the importance of postsecondary vocational education.

The authoritarian factory discipline, exemplified in the automobile assembly line of an earlier period, is likely to become less acceptable than it was in an earlier generation to a work force including a majority who have completed high school and frequently some college as well. A major ingredient underlying the recent concern with alienation from work, and the consequences of this alienation for productivity growth, has been the increase in educational attainment among the younger members of the industrial labor force.[4]

Recent studies suggest that a four-year college degree will become less important as the entrance requirement to middle-class status in the next decade than in the past one. The studies show, for

AN OVERALL VIEW

example, that the percentage of male new high school graduates going on to college has been diminishing. For instance, this proportion declined from 63 percent in 1968 to 50 percent in 1973. A major element underlying the shift has been a falling-off in the economic return from attending college. The falling-off is illustrated by a drop in the ratio of the income of male college graduates to high school graduates in the 25-to-34 age group from 1.39 to 1 in 1969 to 1.23 to 1 in 1973. The drop has been widely interpreted as a response to changes in market forces stemming from a more rapid increase in the supply of college graduates than in the demand for workers in the professional and managerial fields, which college graduates have typically entered in recent decades.[5]

It is unclear at present how much of the diminished attractiveness of the college degree represents a short-term response to the recession and high unemployment rates in the past few years, and how much represents a response to long-term economic and demographic changes. Declining enrollments in elementary and secondary schools underscore a reduction in opportunities for teachers in these fields, a reduction likely to continue for the next 10 years. The fluctuations in demand for engineers, on the other hand, mainly stem from changes in business conditions and shifts in national priorities—for example, the lesser priority assigned to the space program in the 1970s. For the coming decade, student reactions to a continued decline in the economic return from attending college can be expected to show up in two ways. One is a lesser rate of increase, or a decrease, in the number of college enrollments. The other is a greater representation of the college-educated population in occupations in which fewer college graduates had been employed in the past. The projections, reflecting the experience of the past 10 or 15 years, show only a modest percentage increase in the overall representation of college graduates in the occupations studied, an increase from under 7 percent in 1970 to slightly over 9 percent in 1985. The increase is expected to be concentrated in fields in which there is already a sizable proportion of persons with higher education—bank officials, stock and bond salesmen, or specialized computer programmers, for example.

For the vocational-education programs, a significant by-product of the slowing down of college enrollment growth will be the greater numbers of students with good learning ability who could be candidates for high school and post-high school vocational programs. In addition, in many semiprofessional, managerial, and technical fields, the vocational graduates will be competing with the larger number of college graduates seeking to enter the same fields. These developments suggest potentials for upgrading programs as the response of the vocational-education systems to the lesser economic return to college attendance.

PROSPECTS FOR WOMEN AND NONWHITES

Our society is committed to expanding employment opportunities for women and nonwhites through legislation, education, and affirmative action programs by employers. The historical record for the past 10 or 15 years shows many instances of breakthroughs into new occupational fields by women, and, somewhat more so, by nonwhites. Yet, if the trends of the recent past continue through the mid-1980s, the erosion of the barriers that frequently exclude women or nonwhites from the more desirable job opportunities will proceed at a slow pace. The projections raise questions about the role of the vocational-education system, as well as the role of government or employers, in breaking down the traditional stereotypes of "men's jobs" and "women's jobs" or in enlarging career prospects for blacks and other minority group members included in the Census "nonwhite" classification.

Women and nonwhites will make up a more rapidly growing component of the labor force than men or whites in the coming decade. The rate of labor-force growth is expected to be considerably more rapid for nonwhites than for women. These changes are described in Table 1.6.

TABLE 1.6

Projected Changes in the Civilian Labor Force by Sex and Race, 1970-85
(in thousands)

	1970	1985	Percent Increase, 1970-85
Total civilian labor force	82,715	105,716	27.8
Distribution by sex			
Male	51,195	64,057	25.1
Female	31,520	41,659	32.2
Distribution by race			
White	73,518	92,355	25.6
Nonwhite	9,197	13,361	45.3

Source: <u>Manpower Report of the President,</u> 1975, pp. 206, 207; 1985 projections are Conference Board estimates.

TABLE 1.7

Distribution of Employment by Sex and Race in
Occupations Studied, Grouped by Earnings, 1970
(in percent)

Median Earning of Occupation*	Distribution of Employment			
	Male	Female	White	Nonwhite
Less than $6,000	5.3	24.7	10.8	29.2
6,000-7,999	16.8	51.0	29.5	24.4
8,000-9,999	29.6	13.6	23.4	28.6
10,000-11,999	21.1	3.2	15.1	9.6
12,000-13,999	10.2	3.3	8.1	3.9
14,000 and over	17.0	4.2	13.2	4.3

Note: Details may not add to total because of rounding.
Earnings figures refer to median earnings of full-year workers.
*In 1973 dollars.
Source: Conference Board estimate.

Since women and nonwhites will make up a larger share of the labor force in 1985 than in 1970, members of these two groups would be more heavily represented in most occupations even if there were no changes in the kinds of jobs they held. Accordingly, in the coming decade measures that enlarge the opportunities open to members of the two groups will affect substantially more people, and a larger segment of the work force. Similarly, the economic, political, and social consequences of the persistence of discriminatory barriers will be more widespread than would have been the case in earlier periods when fewer persons were affected by these practices.

Women and nonwhites share similar problems in the labor market. Their unemployment rates are higher than those for men or whites. In 1975, to cite some recent history, the unemployment rate for women was 9.3 percent as compared with 7.9 percent for males, and the corresponding percentages by race were 13.9 percent for nonwhites and 7.8 percent for whites.[6] Because of their concentration in lower-paying occupations, members of the two groups who work for a full year earn considerably less than whites or males. Table 1.7 summarizes the earnings data by sex and race for persons who worked at least 50 weeks during the year in 1970 in the 123 occupations included in the study.

Three-fourths of the women and over half of the nonwhite full-year workers in 1970 were employed in occupations that paid about $2,000 or more below the economy-wide median for all year-round workers. Only 7 to 8 percent of the women or nonwhites were at work in fields that paid $2,000 a year or more than the median. Nonwhites fared somewhat better in their earnings record in the occupations considered than women. For instance, more than half the women but only about one-fourth of the nonwhites were employed in one of the low-paying groups, the $6,000 to $8,000 group. The predominance of women in the under $8,000 group was more than 3.5 times that of men while the proportion of nonwhites in this group was 1.3 times greater than the comparable figure for whites.

The 10 lowest-paying occupations among the 123 studied include many service fields, some operatives occupations, and farm laborers. Nonwhites made up slightly less than 11 percent of the total civilian employed labor force in 1970. They constituted more than 11 percent of the work force in eight of these ten fields. Women represented about three-eighths of the employed civilian labor force. They made up five-eighths or more of the persons employed in nine of the ten fields. Much of the low-earnings record of women is attributable to the high concentration of their employment in clerical fields, a white-collar group, rather than in the least skilled occupations. Of the women employed in the occupations considered, 41 percent were at work in clerical occupations in 1970 as compared with 6 percent for men. Greater-than-average educational attainment levels in clerical occupations are often associated with low earnings. For example, more than 90 percent of the secretaries employed in 1970 had completed high school or had some college education. Yet, the median earnings of secretaries who worked a full year were slightly less than $6,900 (in 1973 dollars), or about $3,000 less than the economy-wide median. Barriers to entry in better-paying occupations probably depress earnings in the occupations in which women or nonwhites are heavily represented by increasing the supply of persons seeking work in these fields.

There have been many breakthroughs in individual fields for women and nonwhites, and it is reasonable to anticipate that the breakthroughs will continue and accelerate in the decade ahead. More women are entering finance, managerial, and real-estate fields, while nonwhites are entering managerial, technical, and other white-collar occupations in larger numbers than ever before. About a sixth of bank officials and a third of real-estate brokers, for example, were women in 1970. The representation of women in the two fields is projected to increase to about a fourth for bank officials and well over two-fifths, 45 percent, for real-estate brokers by the mid-1980s. The changes

AN OVERALL VIEW

in the occupational representation of nonwhites are expected to be more extensive, in part because of the more rapid labor-force growth projected for nonwhites. To cite examples, the percentage of nonwhites employed as retail salespersons is expected to grow from 7.5 to 11.5 percent of the total, while the increase listed for scientific and engineering technicians is from about 5 to 9 percent.

Offsetting these evidences of change is a mass of data showing that the scope of the breakthroughs have typically been limited. This implies that if educational and employment practices continue changing in the next decade at a pace similar to the past one, the shifts in the occupational distribution in the 1970-85 period will generally be modest. For instance, 41 percent of the women in the occupations studied were employed as clerical workers in 1970. This is projected to grow to 42 percent by 1985. In 1970, about a fifth, 22 percent, of the nonwhites were at work in service fields. The comparable percentage for 1985 is 21 percent. The major change indicated in the projections is the sharp drop-off in the anticipated representation of nonwhites in two declining fields, the farm occupations and laborers' jobs.

Many of the significant developments in the affirmative action programs have taken place in the past few years. The 1972 Equal Employment Opportunity Act Amendments, or the Equal Employment Opportunity Commission (EEOC) guidelines on discrimination because of sex under Title VII of the Civil Rights Act, are instances. There is little evidence from the most recent and comprehensive data—the Current Population Survey reports for 1974—that these shifts have yet been substantially reflected in the pace of change in the occupational distribution for women or nonwhites. Continuing the experience of the 1960 to 1970 decade, the changes have been greater for nonwhites than for women. To cite instances, 98 percent of all secretaries were women in 1974, a proportion substantially identical with 1970. As in 1970, women made up 80 percent or more of the work force in the low-paid health service occupations.[7] However, illustrating the continued shift of nonwhites into white-collar fields, the percentage of blacks and other minority group members who were employed in all types of clerical work rose from 8.1 to 9.4 percent, a differential too large to be accounted for by sampling fluctuations.

By 1985, there are expected to be nearly 50 million women and male nonwhites in the labor force. The implications of the modest expansion in career opportunities indicated by the recent shifts in occupational representation, or the projections for 1985, point to a gap between aspirations and reality. Our aspirations stress increasing opportunities by substantially lessening, if not removing, discriminatory barriers based on sex or race. The reality is that the shifts have been slow, somewhat more so for women and less so for nonwhites.

The remedial measures to hasten the pace of change will involve the schools, and especially the vocational-education and guidance systems. However, the long-term prospects for training more women or nonwhites to prepare for more desirable job opportunities in new fields will be bounded by the willingness of employers to hire the graduates of the programs in fields related to their training.

VOCATIONAL ENROLLMENTS, SOCIAL CHANGES, AND CAREER OPPORTUNITIES

The 1968 Amendments to the Vocational Education Acts, like their predecessors, assign a high priority to the goal of "providing ready access to vocational training . . . which is realistic in the light of the actual or anticipated opportunities for gainful employment." The historical data and the projections show that the relationship between enrollments and job opportunities is often a loose one, suggesting that the vocational programs, especially in high school, serve a variety of exploratory and educational interests in addition to occupational training. The emphasis on "gainful employment" in the Amendments underscores the importance of a greater concentration on earnings in the occupations prepared for in program priorities and planning. Greater concern with earnings would lessen the tendency to enroll students, especially women, in programs leading to employment in poorly paid fields. Looking ahead, demographic changes and social pressures imply that the vocational programs in the next decade will include a smaller proportion of young people preparing to enter the labor market and a larger representation of adults with work experience.

The relationship between enrollments in the major program areas and the anticipated job openings provides an overall measure of the responsiveness of the vocational-education system to changes in job opportunities. Table 1.8 relates the U.S. Office of Education enrollment projections by major area in 1977 to the expected average annual job openings in the 1970-85 period.

By 1977, according to U.S. Office of Education estimates, the enrollments in areas other than agriculture, distributive education, and health should be roughly consistent with the job openings anticipated in related fields. The enrollments in distributive education and health, while they have been increasing, would still fall short of the projected job openings in these fields. As in the past, the major inconsistency between enrollments and job openings occurs in the field of agriculture. The percentage of total enrollments in agriculture would be 15 times the proportion of the expected job openings in the

AN OVERALL VIEW 19

TABLE 1.8

Projected Vocational-Education Enrollments in 1977 and
Average Annual Job Openings, 1970-85, Study Occupations
(in percent)

Program Area	Distribution of Enrollments in 1977	Distribution of Average Annual Job Openings, 1970-85
Agriculture	9.1	0.6*
Distributive education	8.7	25.2
Health occupations	3.9	9.5
Home economics (gainful)	5.9	5.4
Office occupations	31.0	29.2
Technical occupations	1.8	2.0
Trades and industry	39.6	23.3
Other	—	4.8

Note: Details may not add to total because of rounding.
*The figure listed for job openings related to agricultural programs in this table differs from the entry listed for farm occupations in Table 1.3 because it includes several other occupations directly related to agriculture, such as farm-implement mechanics. The occupations included are derived from U.S. Bureau of Labor Statistics, "Matching 1970 Census-Based BLS National-State Matrix Occupational Categories to Office of Educational Instructional Programs" (unpublished), 1974.
Sources: Derived from U.S. Office of Education, Trends in Vocational Education, Fiscal Year 1972, Vocational Education Information, No. 2, 1973; Conference Board projections of job openings.

fields that primarily make use of agricultural competencies. As in other program areas, and probably more so, vocational programs in agriculture serve as preparation for a family of occupations that are more or less closely related to the training offered. Including the jobs in closely related agribusiness fields, such as servicing or selling equipment and supplies to farmers, would raise the proportion of agriculture-related jobs from 0.6 percent of the total to 1.5 percent. This change would be insufficient to affect the substance of the enrollment-job openings differential. The magnitude of the differential suggests that, as in home economics, only a small part of the enrollment in the agricultural programs represents specific occupational preparation. Distinguishing between the agricultural programs that are intended as specific occupational preparation and those that contribute to other educational values or constitute a general introduction to the world of work would go far toward narrowing the large discrepancy between enrollments and career opportunities. Since agriculture is the one major field in which employment is projected to decline, this distinction would also highlight the importance of expanding the range of vocational-training options available to young people in the rural areas.

Vocational training that is realistic in the light of the expected job openings serves a limited social purpose if the occupations trained for provide little better than a poverty income to the persons employed in them. For example, health aides, other than nurse's aides, reported median earnings for full-year workers in 1970 of $5,440 (in 1973 dollars), while nurse's aides earned approximately $4,900. The poverty income-level for a four-person family in 1970 (again in dollars of 1973 purchasing power) was about $4,550. In the past, vocational training and other publicly supported programs trained persons for employment in these fields as part of the "new careers" movement emphasizing preparation for employment in paraprofessional human-service occupations related to health, education, and social welfare. Low earnings and absence of job security have been common features of many of the "new career" occupations. In these instances, concentration on job openings with limited consideration given to earnings has facilitated the establishment of programs more likely to perpetuate low incomes than to provide an escape from them.

Like concentration on the gross number of job openings, emphasis on gross enrollments obscures many important policy and planning issues in vocational education. In particular, the gross figures overlook the characteristics of the persons enrolled in the programs, including the distribution of the enrollments by sex and race.[8] Data on enrollments by race in individual program areas are generally unavailable. Recent studies report that the proportion of black males who had enrolled in high school vocational programs was similar to the percentage of white males in these programs, slightly less than a sixth. Data showing the distribution by sex in the major program areas are presented in Table 1.9. The table shows the actual enrollments in 1971 and the Office of Education enrollment projections for 1977.

The enrollment data indicate that the distribution of enrollments by sex follows the distribution of jobs. Five-sixths of the enrollments in the health field are female, to cite an instance, while women make up only about a tenth of the enrollments in the technical and trades

AN OVERALL VIEW   21

TABLE 1.9

Distribution of Enrollment by Sex,
Major Vocational-Program Areas—1971 and Projected 1977
(in percent)

	Distribution of Enrollment			
	1971		1977	
Program Area	Male	Female	Male	Female
Agriculture	96	4	92	8
Distributive education	55	45	54	46
Health occupations	12	88	17	83
Home economics	7	93	10	90
Office occupations	25	75	25	75
Technical occupations	92	8	91	9
Trades and industry	89	11	87	13
Total	44	56	43	57

Source: U.S. Office of Education, Trends in Vocational Education, Fiscal Year 1972, Vocational Education Information, No. 2, 1973.

and industry programs. The changes anticipated in the 1971-77 period show some modifications at the extremes. Slight declines are projected in fields in which women predominate—for example health occupations—and modest increases in fields in which women have been poorly represented, such as the trades and industry area. The historical data and the projections make it evident that the main drift of the vocational programs has been to maintain the existing pattern of "men's jobs" and "women's jobs." In part, this emphasis reflects the fear that training large numbers of young women for positions that, on the basis of past experience, may not materialize runs the risk of endowing the individuals trained with unutilized skills and frustrated aspirations. While the vocational-education systems, by themselves, cannot resolve the problems stemming from discrimination in the labor market, recognition of the implications of the present distribution of enrollments can constitute an important first step in planning to do more than extrapolate the experience of the past into the future.

    Planning and goal setting in education, including vocational education, in the 1960s and early 1970s took place in an environment characterized by growth in enrollments, in facilities, in finances, and in expectations. Much of this growth stemmed from a "one-time" rapid increase in the size of the basic high school and college population, the 14-to-24 age group. Because of the decline in birth rates in the recent past, growth in this age group will slow down in the 1970s and then decline in the 1980s. Table 1.10 summarizes the expected shifts in population, by broad age groups, in the 1960-85 period.

TABLE 1.10

Population Growth in Selected Broad Age Groups,
1960, 1970, and Projected 1980 and 1985
(in millions)

	Age Group		
	14 to 24	25 to 44	45 years and over
Population			
1960	27.3	47.1	52.9
1970	40.5	48.4	62.1
1980	44.9	62.3	67.5
1985	41.6	72.0	69.3
Growth in population			
1960 to 1970	13.2	1.3	9.2
1970 to 1980	4.4	13.9	5.4
1980 to 1985	-3.3	9.7	1.8

Source: U.S. Department of Commerce, Bureau of the Census.

The population in the 14-to-24 age group increased by over 13 million between 1960 and 1970. This was about as large as the increase in the 14-to-24 group in the preceding 70 years. Growth for this age group is expected to taper off by two-thirds during the 1970s, and growth would be followed by a decline of more than 3 million between 1980 and 1985. The 25-to-44 age group, which increased by only about one million during the 1960s, is projected to increase by about 23.5 million between 1970 and 1985.

The demographic shifts indicate that the vocational programs will grow slowly, or decline, if they continue seeking in much their present form to appeal to a student population similar to that served in the past two decades. The prospects for continued growth will lie in appealing to new groups, including many persons who are no longer full-time students. Part of this growth could come from drawing in more women or nonwhites or attracting a substantial part of the student body who in an earlier decade had gone on to college. New programs for adults will supply much of the growth potential, a potential underscored by the projected increase in the 25-to-44 age group. Likely prospects include married women seeking to reenter the labor market, unskilled workers attempting to upgrade their work skills, or older persons planning to embark on a second career. The appeal to these new groups of prospective students will be more successful if the programs available are concerned with meeting emerging manpower bottlenecks anticipated by employers, if they can realistically improve earnings, and if they contribute to the overall economic development programs, including manpower programs, undertaken by states and by local communities. Looking ahead, the demographic projections, like the manpower indicators, stress a larger role for vocational education as part of "lifetime learning" and a lesser role for the traditional schooling for the young.

NOTES

1. See U.S. Department of Labor, Bureau of Labor Statistics, The U.S. Economy in 1985, Bulletin No. 1809, 1974.
2. U.S. News and World Report, October 13, 1968, p. 45.
3. Manpower Report of the President, 1975, p. 269.
4. For an analysis of this problem, see S. A. Levitan and William B. Johnson, Work is Here to Stay, Alas (Salt Lake City: Olympus Publishing Co., 1973); U.S. Department of Health, Education, and Welfare, Work in America, 1972.
5. Richard B. Freeman, "Overinvestment in College Training," The Journal of Human Resources (Summer 1975): 287-311.
6. U.S. Department of Labor, Bureau of Labor Statistics, Employment and Earnings, January 1976, pp. 138-40.
7. "Employment Data for Detailed Occupations, 1974," Employment and Earnings, June 1975. Figures cited refer to all clerical occupations including those not receiving consideration in study.
8. L. A. Lecht, Evaluating Vocational Education—Policies and Plans for the 1970s (New York: Praeger, 1974), p. 21.

CHAPTER 2

EMPLOYMENT, JOB OPENINGS, AND EARNINGS

SOURCES OF JOB OPENINGS

The job-openings projections for the occupations included in the study show that two-thirds of the job opportunities in the 1970-85 period are expected to represent replacements for experienced workers, including poorly paid health-service and clerical workers and highly skilled and well-paid craftsmen and technicians. Over half of the replacement demand will occur in 10 occupations in which women make up a majority of the work force. Less than a third of the persons employed in the occupations studied were at work in fields in which the earnings of full-year workers in 1970 were at or above the median earnings for all year-round workers in that year. Eliminating the influence of replacement demand and concentrating on employment growth alone makes it apparent that rapid growth will take place both in many well-paid and in poorly paid occupations. However, these considerations based on national projections obscure the developments affecting career opportunities in the coming decade, because they overlook the marked divergences anticipated in regional patterns of economic and employment growth.

The job openings and earnings indicators for the 123 occupations are projections of past trends which have been modified in the light of recent experience. The basic employment, attrition, and productivity estimates are derived from U.S. Department of Labor sources.[1] They are substantially influenced by the expected slowdown in labor-force growth and productivity, and, consequently, slow growth in GNP in the number of younger workers in the 1980s coupled with a continued shift toward a more service-oriented economy.

EMPLOYMENT, JOB OPENINGS, AND EARNINGS

Although the occupations considered generally exclude fields in which a majority of the work force possesses a four-year college degree, they include a large proportion of the economy's professional, technical, and managerial workers. Growth in the representation of white-collar and service employment in the study occupations and the decline in farm and blue-collar jobs between 1970 and 1985 is expected to parallel the changes taking place in the employment distribution for the overall economy. The relationship between the changes in the occupational makeup of the entire labor force and the study occupations is described in Table 2.1.

White-collar employment in professional, technical, managerial, sales, and clerical occupations is approximately the same in both groups, slightly less than half the total in 1970 and slightly more than half in 1985. However, a larger share of the white-collar workers in the study occupations are clerical or sales personnel. Relatively more skilled craftsmen and foremen and fewer less skilled operatives are included in the occupations singled out for consideration. In the least skilled fields, the laborers' jobs and private household work, the study occupations include either a smaller proportion of the total employment, or, as in the case of private household workers, they are unrepresented. The 1970 to 1985 trends in both the overall labor force and the study occupations reflect the movement to a more technologically oriented, postindustrial service economy in the United States.

The importance of employment growth and attrition as sources of job openings varies considerably in different occupations. Rapid employment growth is often characteristic of skilled occupations whose job content is closely linked with technological advance. High growth rates also frequently come about from growth in demand for services from government or the private sector which are provided in large part by less skilled workers. The nonprofessional health-service fields are an instance. The predominance of attrition as the source of job openings in clerical occupations reflects the predominance of women in the clerical work force. The projections of job openings for major groups and individual occupations for which job openings in the 1970-85 period are expected to average 10,000 or more annually are listed in Table 2.2.

The job-openings projections show the impact of many forces, including greater automation and mechanization, changes in national priorities, and the GNP growth rate assumed in the projections. Greater use of automated data processing can be expected both to increase and to decrease skills and manpower requirements in many fields. As bookkeeping and record keeping have become automated, employment in clerical fields, such as bookkeeping, has grown slowly

TABLE 2.1

Employment in All Occupations and in Study Occupations, 1970 and Projected 1985
(in percent)

Census Occupational Classification	Distribution of Employment			
	1970		1985	
	All Occupations	Study Occupations	All Occupations	Study Occupations
Professional, technical, and managerial workers	23.5	18.1	26.5	20.4
Salesworkers	6.4	10.6	6.5	10.7
Clerical workers	17.5	18.8	19.5	20.7
Craftsmen and foremen	13.2	19.0	13.0	18.6
Operatives	17.0	15.9	15.1	14.5
Farm managers and owners	2.2	4.0	0.9	1.6
Service workers, excluding household workers	11.4	10.0	12.3	11.7
Private household workers	1.7	0.0	1.0	0.0
Laborers, including farm laborers and foremen	7.1	3.6	5.2	1.8

<u>Note</u>: Details may not add to totals because of rounding.

<u>Source</u>: U.S. Department of Labor, Bureau of Labor Statistics, Occupation-by-Industry Matrix (unpublished), 1974. These data differ from published data pertaining to the same occupational groups in the <u>1975 Manpower Report of the President</u>, in part because of changes in occupational classifications and definitions that have been incorporated in the matrix estimates.

TABLE 2.2

Projected Average Annual Job Openings, Major Occupational Groups and Larger Study Occupations, 1970–85

	Average Annual Job Openings, 1970–85		
		Openings due to:	
Occupation	Total	Growth	Attrition
Professional and technical workers	204,000	108,700	95,300
Computer programmers	12,300	7,600	4,700
Drafters	17,000	11,300	5,700
Electrical and electronic-engineering technicians	13,300	10,900	2,400
Engineering and science technicians, n.e.c.	29,700	22,300	7,400
Personnel and labor-relations workers	29,100	17,600	11,500
Registered nurses	70,300	21,300	49,000
Therapists	12,600	6,400	6,200
Managers and administrators, except farm	344,200	143,300	200,900
Bank officials and financial managers	30,300	13,700	16,600
Buyers, wholesale and retail trade	11,800	7,100	4,700
Managers and administrators, n.e.c.	247,500	102,300	145,200
Managers and superintendents, building	13,000	4,900	8,100
Restaurant, cafeteria, and bar managers	22,300	5,500	16,800
Sales managers and department heads, retail	18,900	10,200	8,700
Salesworkers	316,500	100,000	216,500
Insurance agents, brokers, and underwriters	23,700	10,900	12,800
Real-estate agents and brokers	26,900	8,900	17,900
Sales representatives, manufacturing	16,800	6,600	10,200

(continued)

(Table 2.2 continued)

	Average Annual Job Openings, 1970–85		
		Openings due to:	
Occupation	Total	Growth	Attrition
Sales representatives, wholesale	31,200	13,500	17,700
Salesclerks, retail trade	175,500	42,300	133,200
Salesworkers, retail trade	21,400	7,700	13,700
Salespeople, service and construction	14,000	6,600	7,400
Clerical workers	794,700	228,200	566,500
Billing clerks	16,500	6,500	10,000
Bookkeepers	117,000	24,000	93,000
Computer equipment operators	14,400	9,300	5,100
Keypunch operators	13,900	-3,900	17,700
Payroll and timekeeping clerks	14,300	4,200	10,100
Secretaries	364,800	113,400	251,400
Shipping and receiving clerks	15,100	4,400	10,700
Statistical clerks	22,200	5,600	16,600
Stock clerks and storekeepers	27,300	11,600	15,700
Typists	111,600	28,500	83,100
Miscellaneous clerical workers	50,200	20,100	30,100
Craftsmen and foremen	342,100	161,500	180,600
Air-conditioning, heating, and refrigeration mechanics	12,200	9,000	3,200
Auto mechanics	29,000	14,200	14,800
Carpenters	40,100	14,300	25,700
Electricians	23,100	13,300	9,800
Excavating, grading, and road-machine operators	15,300	9,300	6,000

Foremen	51,800	20,000	31,800
Heavy-equipment mechanics, including diesel	31,100	16,500	14,600
Machinists	15,200	6,900	8,300
Painters, construction and maintenance	14,200	3,000	11,200
Plumbers and pipefitters	18,300	9,700	8,700
Operatives	307,500	95,300	212,200
Assemblers	44,500	10,400	34,100
Bus drivers	13,800	5,700	8,100
Checkers, examiners, and inspectors, manufacturing	35,300	9,300	26,000
Cutting operatives	11,400	3,900	7,500
Delivery and route workers	27,100	12,700	14,400
Sewers and stitchers	64,700	8,100	56,600
Truck drivers	38,000	16,600	21,400
Welders and flame cutters	26,000	15,500	10,500
Service workers	428,800	155,500	273,300
Bartenders	10,200	3,100	7,100
Cooks, except private household	52,300	11,900	40,300
Childcare workers, except private household	43,500	13,800	29,700
Firefighters	11,700	8,900	2,800
Food-service workers, except private household	31,300	8,200	23,100
Hairdressers and cosmetologists	49,100	12,100	37,000
Health aides, except nursing	22,000	9,800	12,200
Housekeepers, except private household	12,700	4,500	8,100
Nursing aides, orderlies, and attendants	97,200	35,100	62,100
Police and detectives	19,300	13,300	6,000
Practical nurses	69,300	31,000	38,300

(continued)

(Table 2.2 continued)

	Average Annual Job Openings, 1970–85		
		Openings due to:	
Occupation	Total	Growth	Attrition
Laborers, except farm	20,300	-1,900	22,200
Gardeners and groundskeepers, except farm	21,900	1,200	20,700
Total, all occupations studied	2,753,000	905,000	1,848,000
Total, all U.S. occupations	4,946,000	1,524,000	3,422,000
Occupations studied as a percent of all U.S. occupations	56	59	54

Notes: For complete occupational listing see Appendix C, Table C.5.
Details may not add to total because of rounding.

Sources: Derived from U.S. Department of Labor, Bureau of Labor Statistics, Tomorrow's Manpower Needs, Supplement No. 4, Estimating Occupational Separations From the Labor Force for States; and sources in Table 2.1.

or declined, while requirements for the more highly skilled computer operators, programmers, and repairmen have increased. In other instances, the changes toward use of more complex technology are likely to reduce skill requirements. Examples include the introduction of cash registers that compute the change due customers and relieve the cashiers of the need to possess the skills required to undertake this operation.

Shifts in national priorities can also influence job opportunities. Achieving goals in pollution abatement similar to those in the Air Quality Act or the Water Quality Act would significantly increase expenditures for capital goods and for the pollution-control equipment used in motor vehicles. This spending would increase requirements for factory operatives in the industries producing the equipment, and for engineers, designers, technicians, and mechanics who design, operate, and repair the equipment.[2] A high priority assigned to offsetting the rising price of imported petroleum by developing new energy sources within the United States—by obtaining oil from shale rock, for example—would change the regional as well as the occupational and industrial distribution of employment. The high priority given to making health care more readily available to Americans, a priority illustrated by Medicare, Medicaid, and the expansion of employers' group health programs, contributes to the large increases anticipated in job openings for nonprofessional health therapists and aides of many kinds. Enactment of some version of national health insurance in the next 10 years, together with efforts to seek more efficient ways of providing health services, could increase requirements for health personnel considerably beyond those anticipated in the projections and change occupational requirements to include more technicians to operate automated diagnostic and other testing equipment.

The projections assume a GNP growth rate of 4.6 percent a year in the 1970s, followed by a decline to 3.2 percent in the 1980-85 period. The decline stems from the expected slowing down in labor-force growth following the falling-off in birth rates in the 1960s. It is also affected by continued growth in the importance of service industries, industries whose productivity, as conventionally reckoned in output per man-hour, is less than in goods-producing industries. The recession characterizing 1974 and 1975, if it were to continue or recur, would outmode projections based on the expectation of substantial economic growth in the 1970s. The unemployment-prone groups—nonwhites, teenagers, and women—would be most affected by a slowing down in economic activity in obtaining jobs and in penetrating into new and more desirable fields. The unemployment rate for blacks and other nonwhites, for example, was 13.9 percent in 1975 compared with 7.8 percent for whites. Averaging job openings over the 1970-85 period tends to diminish the influence of cyclical fluctuations which can cause the projections at a particular time to be wide of the mark. In addition, slow GNP growth typically affects employment growth more heavily than replacement demand. The importance of replacement demand in the job-openings projections makes them less sensitive to changes in the pace of GNP growth than would be the case for employment projections alone.

National manpower projections can sometimes be misleading because they overlook developments in individual regions and states, which often follow a different pattern from the national one. Young people entering the labor force typically obtain jobs, at least their first full-time job, in their local area. With the passage of time, the availability of more attractive opportunities elsewhere will attract persons from areas of slow growth to more rapidly expanding states and regions. The occupational and industrial makeup of employment in the rapidly growing areas frequently diverges from the national pattern, reflecting the weight of rapidly growing industries contributing to the high growth rates. The aerospace and electronics industries in California in the 1960s supply instances. The differences in the anticipated patterns of economic growth by region are summarized in Table 2.3.

The areas where the more rapid employment growth is anticipated are concentrated in the western states, especially in the mountain areas and the Pacific Coast. Many young people now in school

TABLE 2.3

Estimated Changes in Employment by Region, 1970-85
(in percent)

Region	Change, 1970 to 1985
New England	21
Middle Atlantic	25
Great Lakes	22
Southeast	29
Plains	26
Southwest	31
Mountains	36
Far West	38

Source: National Planning Association, Regional Economic Projections: 1960-85, Report No. 73-R-1, 1973, Table 1, p. S-3.

in New York or Rhode Island or Nebraska, to cite instances, at some stage in their careers are likely to move to these areas of rapid growth. The recent decline in manufacturing jobs in the New York metropolitan labor market area underscores the importance of regional, state, and local differences in employment growth in assessing the relationship of occupational-training programs to career opportunities for their students or to the economy's future manpower needs.*

EMPLOYMENT GROWTH AND REPLACEMENT DEMAND

Although rapid growth can be anticipated in many occupations, employment growth will be considerably less important than the replacement of attrition losses as a source of job openings in the coming decade. Employment growth will contribute significantly to job openings in technician and health-service fields. However, over half of the job openings are expected to take place in 12 large occupations characterized by a preponderance of job openings arising from replacement needs. Women make up over half of the work force in 10 of these 12 fields.

In a dynamic economy, employment in some fields will be increasing in response to economic, social, and technological changes while employment in others is declining. The economy-wide employment level is expected to grow by 29 percent between 1970 and 1985. Employment growth in many of the occupations included in the study is projected to amount to more than 29 percent, in some instances to more than 50 or 100 percent. Other occupations list decreases, although there are fewer decreases than increases and the percentage decreases are generally smaller.

Table 2.4 summarizes the strong cases of employment growth and decline in the study occupations. The table lists the occupations for which the employment is expected to at least double together with those for which the decline is projected to be greater than a third.

Three of the eight fields listing increases of 100 percent or more are health occupations. The other five are technical specialties requiring knowledge of modern technology, especially electronic and

---

*While employment in manufacturing in the United States grew by 4.8 percent between 1965 and 1972, employment in manufacturing in New York City declined by 21.6 percent in the same period. (See D. Puryear and R. Bahl, "Economic Problems of a Mature Economy," Maxwell School, Syracuse University, 1975.

TABLE 2.4

Projected Large Increases and Declines in Employment,
Study Occupations, 1970-85

Occupation	Employment (in thousands)		Percent Change in Employment, 1970 to 1985
	1970	1985	
Increases of 100 percent or more			
Therapists*	82	178	117
Practical nurses	370	835	126
Health aides, except nursing	133	280	111
Electrical and electronic-engineering technicians	154	317	106
Other technicians, except health	37	95	157
Data-processing machine repairers	36	93	158
Engineering and science technicians, n.e.c.	190	525	176
Air-conditioning, heating, and refrigeration mechanics and repairers	130	265	104
Declines of 34 percent or more			
Farm owners and tenants	1690	867	-49
Farm laborers, wage workers	897	401	-55
Tabulating-machine operators	9	3	-67
Stenographers	128	78	-39
Carpenter helpers	117	70	-40
Printing-trades apprentices, except pressmen	6	3	-50
Solderers	42	24	-43
Total employment, all U.S. occupations	78,600	101,500	29

*Includes various medical-technical specialties, such as inhalation therapists, occupational therapists, and so on.
Source: U.S. Department of Labor, Bureau of Labor Statistics, Occupation-by-Industry Matrix Projections for 1985 (unpublished), 1974.

electrical technology. The decreases in employment stem primarily from continued technological change. The declines in employment are especially marked in the farm occupations. The smaller number of farmers and farm laborers projected for the 1980s reflects the anticipation of continuing high productivity increases in agriculture resulting from mechanization and growth in corporate farming. These developments are reinforced by the tendency for the consumption of farm products to rise at a less rapid rate than GNP. The large decline for stenographers comes about from the widespread acceptance of dictating equipment in everyday office use.

The lesser role of rapid employment growth in generating job opportunities is illustrated by the occupations in which employment is expected to at least double or more in the 1970-85 period. All told, these fields are projected to supply only about 5 percent of all job openings in the occupations studied. By comparison, over half of the job openings would take place in 12 large established occupations which are estimated to provide an average of 50,000 or more job openings a year. They include both rapidly growing health fields and occupations expected to show only modest growth, such as bookkeeping. These 12 large occupations are characterized by the importance of attrition in their prospective job openings and the high representation of women in their work force. The occupations are described in Table 2.5.

Attrition exceeds employment growth as a source of job openings in these fields by an average of 2.2 to 1. Women make up over half of the work force in 10 of the 12 occupations in the table. The high rate of attrition for retail salesclerks or secretaries results mainly from the predominance of female employees who leave the labor force for reasons of marriage or childrearing and later frequently return. Significantly, employment growth makes up a larger percentage of the job openings for craftsmen than for any other nonprofessional group. While the average age in many skilled crafts is high, leading to substantial replacement requirements, this is offset by the sizable employment growth anticipated in individual crafts, especially those concerned with the maintenance and repair of air conditioning or communications equipment, or with electrical and electronic equipment of many kinds. For much the same reasons, rapid employment growth is also expected to outweigh attrition in many nonmedical technician and semiprofessional occupations.

Women are expected to make up a larger share of the labor force by 1985, to increase by 32 percent between 1970 and 1985 as compared with 25 percent for men.[3] With the present attrition rates for women, replacement demand would make up a more important source of job openings in the next decade than in the past one.

TABLE 2.5

Estimated Sources of Job Openings and Representation of Women in these Occupations Expected to Provide Large Numbers of Job Openings, 1970-85

Occupation	Average Annual Job Openings, 1970-85			Women as Percent of Work Force, 1970
	Total	Openings due to		
		Growth	Attrition	
Secretaries	364,800	113,400	251,400	97.6
Managers and administrators, n.e.c.	247,500	102,300	145,200	11.6
Salesclerks, retail trade	175,500	42,300	133,200	64.8
Bookkeepers	117,000	24,000	93,000	82.1
Typists	111,600	28,500	83,100	94.2
Nurse's aides	97,200	35,100	62,100	84.6
Registered nurses	70,300	21,300	49,000	97.4
Practical nurses	69,300	31,000	38,300	96.3
Sewers and stitchers	64,700	8,100	56,600	93.8
Cooks, except private household	52,300	11,900	40,300	62.8
Foremen	51,800	20,000	31,800	8.0
Miscellaneous clerical workers	50,200	20,100	30,100	64.5
Total, 12 occupations	1,472,200	458,000	1,014,100	
Percent of all job openings in study occupations	53.5	50.6	54.9	

Source: See Table 2.2.

Continuation of the recent tendencies toward smaller families, later age of marriage for women, and greater availability of childcare facilities would reduce female attrition rates. Continued emphasis on early retirement for men and women would increase replacement demand, although frequently the replacement would be for a less well-paid worker who had been upgraded to fill the vacancy created by the retirement of older and more experienced persons. Since estimates of replacement demand are based on rates of withdrawal from the labor force for different age and sex groups derived from past experience, they are subject to change. Changes in the status of women, in retirement practices, or changes in mortality in the coming decade could be expected to influence attrition rates and replacement demand in the 1980s.

Projections based on replacement demand and the expected employment growth are incomplete representations of future job openings. They exclude large elements of labor turnover which fluctuate too markedly with changes in business conditions or even in the weather to be taken into account in the projections. Employees may quit their jobs in search of more desirable positions, or move to another area, and be replaced by other persons. They may be laid off because of cyclical downturns in business conditions and other persons hired when economic conditions improve. Seasonal changes in the weather will often cause construction workers to be without employment, and others may replace them when construction is resumed. Since these components of turnover are subject to wide fluctuations that cannot be anticipated in advance, they are omitted from the estimates of replacement needs. Accordingly, the job-openings projections based on employment growth and withdrawals from the labor force have a built-in bias toward underestimating future job opportunities because of the great uncertainty surrounding a major component of employee turnover.

OCCUPATIONS AND EARNINGS

The projections of job openings point to the need to expand the range of occupations for which vocational training is available if the tendency to prepare students for low-paying careers is to be minimized in the coming decade. Rapid growth in some low-paying fields, together with replacement demand in these occupations, contributes to a concentration of job openings at the lower end of the earnings distribution. However, eliminating the effects of replacement demand and concentrating on employment growth makes it apparent that the spread of earnings away from the economy-wide median for persons employed in the occupations considered will be greater in the mid-1980s than in 1970. Many of the more highly paid occupations will be in technical specialties, in finance and real estate, and in management or personnel work.

Nearly 70 percent of the job openings in the occupations considered are in occupations that paid less than the economy-wide median of slightly under $10,000 for full-year workers in 1970. While this concentration reflects the exclusion of many professional fields, it also stems from the high attrition rates in many low-paid positions. Because of the high replacement demand, the job openings anticipated in these occupations in the 1970-85 period make up a considerably larger percentage of the total than was the case with the employment in these fields in 1970. The high turnover in poorly paid occupations can make them appear as attractive candidates for educational or manpower training programs because of their large number of job openings often difficult to fill.

Table 2.6 highlights the importance of replacement demand in creating job openings in low-paying occupations by comparing the job openings distribution grouped by the 1970 median earnings with the comparable distribution of employment in that year.

TABLE 2.6

Projected Average Annual Job Openings, 1970-85, and Employment Distribution in 1970 Grouped by Earnings in 1970

Median Earnings of Occupations in 1970*	Average Annual Job Openings, 1970 to 1985 (in percent)	Employment in 1970 (in percent)
Under $6,000	15.5	12.3
6,000-7,999	34.9	29.1
8,000-9,999	19.1	23.8
10,000-11,999	12.4	14.7
12,000-13,999	6.9	7.8
14,000 and over	11.3	12.4

Note: Details may not add to totals because of rounding.

*Refers to median earnings in 1973 dollars of persons who worked 50 weeks during the year.

Source: Derived from U.S. Department of Commerce, Bureau of the Census, 1970 Census of Population, Subject Report, Occupational Characteristics.

Half of the job openings are listed in the under $8,000 group of occupations. Only slightly more than two-fifths, 41 percent, of the persons employed in these positions in 1970 earned less than this amount. In the fields paying more than $8,000 to full-year workers in 1970, the percentage of persons employed in each income group was greater than the proportion of job openings. Accordingly, the frequent availability of large numbers of job openings in low-paying fields—for example, sewers and stitchers—often reflects high turnover for a largely female work force rather than the presence of desirable career opportunities.

While the rapidly growing fields in which attrition is less important include many well-paid occupations, they also include many poorly paid jobs. The high national priority placed on health, for example, makes for rapid growth in employment in low-paid nonprofessional health-service fields, a growth frequently accompanied by comparably high attrition. Rapid expansion in employment in other occupations— technicians, for instance—can provide well-paid and attractive career prospects. The loose association between employment growth and earnings is illustrated by Table 2.7, showing the 10 most highly paid and the 10 most poorly paid fields among those considered in the study.

The high-paying occupations are typically expected to grow more rapidly than the low-paying ones, and none is projected to undergo an employment decline. Five of the ten are estimated to increase by 50 percent or more between 1970 and 1985. The low-paying fields, by comparison, include both the largest percentage increases, for practical nurses and health aides, and the two instances of declining employment, for farm laborers and dressmakers and seamstresses. As many of the low-paying fields are listed to increase by at least 50 percent as the high-paying occupations—five in each group. While educational achievement levels clearly differentiate high- and low-paying jobs, it is significant that in only one of ten better-paying fields was the work force in 1970 made up of a majority of persons with four or more years of college. The single exception were the stock and bond sales agents. The high-paying fields, therefore, can offer appropriate potentials for vocational training, often in postsecondary institutions.

Eliminating the influence of replacement demand makes it apparent that more of the persons at work in the study occupations in the mid-1980s will be employed in fields that pay either considerably more or considerably less than the economy-wide median for year-round workers. As the reverse side of this distribution, a smaller percentage will be at work in fields in which earnings are relatively close to the national figure. The increase in the dispersion of earnings follows from the anticipated greater-than-average growth in the highly paid and the poorly paid occupations.

The greater dispersion of earnings is also influenced by the expected tendency for earnings in the better-paying occupations to increase as a percentage of the national average, and for the income received in poorly paid fields to decline relative to other occupations.

TABLE 2.7

Median Earnings in 1970, and Projected Employment Growth, 1970-85, 10 Highest-Paid and 10 Lowest-Paid Study Occupations

Occupation	Median Earnings, 1970*	Percent Increase in Employment, 1970-85
10 highest paid		
Stock and bond sales agents	23,070	49
Managers and administrators, n.e.c.	16,770	35
Bank officials and financial managers	15,990	62
Sales representatives, manufacturing	15,540	25
Real-estate appraisers	15,450	58
Designers	14,260	48
Personnel and labor-relations workers	13,820	92
Sales representatives, wholesale	13,690	32
Computer programmers	13,600	64
Mechanical-engineering technicians	13,430	50
10 lowest paid		
Practical nurses	5,870	126
Hairdressers and cosmetologists	5,770	38
Cooks, except private household	5,470	22
Health aides, except nursing	5,440	111
Nurse's aides	4,890	63
Sewers and stitchers	4,880	13
Farm laborers	4,750	-55
Dressmakers and seamstresses	4,390	-6
School monitors	3,870	85
Childcare workers	3,840	61

*Earnings data refer to earnings in 1973 dollars of full-year workers.

Sources: U.S. Department of Commerce, Bureau of the Census, 1970 Census Report, Occupational Characteristics; U.S. Department of Labor, Bureau of Labor Statistics, Occupation-by-Industry Matrix Projections (unpublished), 1974.

For instance, in the 10 highest-paying fields listed in Table 2.7, earnings for full-year workers in six positions are expected to increase as a ratio to the national median and to undergo a relative decline in only three. In the ten lowest-paid occupations, earnings are projected to decrease relative to the economy-wide average in six, and to increase in two. To cite an illustration drawn from the highly paid occupations, the annual earnings of sales representatives, manufacturing, are projected to increase from $15,540 in 1970 to $26,110 in 1985. Expressed as a percentage of the economy-wide median, this represents a change from 156 to 171. The comparable earnings for nurse's aides, a low-paying field, are estimated to rise from $4,890 to $6,940. This constitutes a decline from 49 percent of the national average in 1970 to 45 percent in 1985. While the changes in the earnings in high-and low-paid fields relative to the national median are generally small, the shifts in position emphasize the tendency for occupations at both ends of the earnings distribution to depart further from the average in the next decade.

Table 2.8 summarizes the increase in the dispersion of earnings by comparing the distributions in 1970 and 1985.

Between 1970 and 1985 the median earnings of full-year workers in all occupations are projected to rise from $9,945 to $15,260, an increase of slightly more than half. The growth in earnings stems from the expected GNP and productivity growth together with the nation-wide shifts in the occupational makeup of the labor force toward

TABLE 2.8

Dispersion of Median Earnings in Study Occupations around Economy-wide Median for Full-Year Workers, 1970 and Projected 1985

Deviation from Economy-wide Median[a]	Percent Distribution of Employment		Earnings Range (in dollars)	
	1970[b]	1985	1970	1985
25 percent greater or more	17.0	21.4	12,431 or more	19,075 or more
Within 25 percent in either direction	50.1	42.2	7,460- 12,430	11,446- 19,074
25 percent below median or more	33.0	36.4	7,459 or less	11,445 or less

Notes: Details may not add to total because of rounding.

Economy-wide median was $9,945 in 1970; it is projected at $15,260 in 1985.

[a]Refers to median earnings in 1973 dollars of persons who worked at least 50 weeks during the year.

[b]Source: See Table 2.6.

a greater representation of the more skilled and better-paying fields. The major change in the occupations studied is the greater concentration of employment at both extremes away from the national median. For example, half of the persons employed in these positions in 1970 were at work in fields that paid full-year workers within 25 percent of the national median in either direction. This proportion is projected to decrease to slightly more than two-fifths, or 42 percent, by 1985. Earnings levels are expected to increase in virtually all occupations in the 1970-85 period so that persons earning 25 percent below the national average could still be receiving as much as $11,445 a year. The percentage of employees under this figure, or receiving 25 percent or more below the national median, is estimated to increase from 33 to over 36 percent. The percentage receiving at least 25 percent more than the economy-wide average, or over $19,000, is estimated to rise from 17 to nearly 21.5 percent. The spread of earnings in the study occupations in 1970, or in projected earnings levels in 1985, highlights the broad range of earnings in the occupations that are typically filled by graduates of vocational-training programs or are prospective candidates for these programs.

The earnings estimates for 1985 represent "surprise-free" projections based on recent relationships between changes in earnings in individual occupations and changes in productivity in the industries employing the bulk of the persons at work in these positions. This relationship builds in the interplay between changes in productivity, in the "human capital" represented by differences in skill levels and educational attainment, in the strength of collective bargaining, and other factors that affect the supply and demand for labor in particular fields.* Even more than projections of employment, anticipations of future earnings contain an element of uncertainty because the relationships they assume from past experience are sometimes unstable, and they may undergo unanticipated changes in the future. The projections, therefore, can be regarded as points on a scale that illustrate what would happen if the relationships between earnings and productivity in the past 10 or 15 years were to continue through the coming decade. A marked change in productivity growth or in the supply of persons seeking to enter a particular field, or manpower bottlenecks generated by sharply rising demand for the output produced by specific groups of workers, could shift earnings above or below the points represented by the projections. These changes, however, would be less likely to

---

*For a discussion of the procedures used in making the earnings projections, see Appendix A.

narrow substantially the range of earnings in the occupations typically involving skill or training of a type different from what is represented by a four-year college degree.

The employment, job-openings, and earnings data identify alternatives for expanding the career options open to persons who differ in their aspirations, their abilities, their educational achievements, and their interests. Some individuals, because of limited academic abilities, or from personal preference, may seek employment in low-paying fields in which many job openings are anticipated in the next decade. Employment in these occupations, as in the health-service fields, frequently serves important economic and social needs. It is reasonable to expect that a majority of persons receiving occupational training will be attracted to fields offering good prospects of increasing their earnings potential. The projections make it evident that there are large numbers of occupations offering better-than-average earnings that are suitable candidates for vocational training.

NOTES

1. Sources: U.S. Department of Labor, Bureau of Labor Statistics, The U.S. Economy in 1985, Bulletin 1809, 1974; Tomorrow's Manpower Needs, Supplement No. 4, Estimating Occupational Separations from the Labor Force for States, 1974; Occupation-by-Industry Matrix (unpublished), 1974.

2. See L. A. Lecht, I. Gutmanis, and R. Rosen, Assessing the Impact of Changes in National Priorities on the Utilization of Scientists and Engineers in the 1970s (Washington, D.C.: National Science Foundation, 1974).

3. Manpower Report of the President, 1975, pp. 203, 309.

CHAPTER

3

THE EDUCATIONAL ATTAINMENT INDICATORS

TRENDS IN EDUCATIONAL ATTAINMENT

Three tendencies stand out in characterizing the changes in educational attainment in the largely nonprofessional occupations included in the study. One is the continued sharp decline in the proportion of persons employed in them with less than 12 years of schooling, a decline most pronounced in the less skilled fields. Another is the relatively modest penetration of college graduates into fields in which few college graduates had been employed in the past. A third is the persistence of the association between educational attainment and earnings, an association less apparent for groups such as women than for the overall labor force.

The increase in the size of the group who are high school graduates or have some college education in the study occupations is expected to outweigh substantially the increase in the representation of college graduates. For example, the increase in the number of workers with 12 to 15 years of schooling in the 1970-85 period is projected to amount to almost seven times the growth in employment of persons with a full college education. The projections also suggest that the anticipated oversupply in some fields in which the college degree is typically a requirement for admission—for example, teaching—is likely to be accompanied by a greater representation of college graduates in managerial, sales, finance, and technical positions already employing large numbers of college graduates. Less than 3 percent of the work force in blue-collar or service fields in 1985 is expected to be made up of persons with four or more years of college.

THE EDUCATIONAL ATTAINMENT INDICATORS 45

The historical data and the projections underscore the association between educational attainment and earnings. The economic advantage of the group with 16 or more years of schooling is apparent in the distribution of employment by earnings. Nearly three-fifths of the persons in 1970 in the occupations receiving consideration with this level of educational attainment were in fields yielding $12,000 or more to full-year employees. Approximately three-fourths of the high school dropouts were employed in occupations providing earnings less than the economy-wide median of $9,945 for year-round employees. Occupational training in or out of the public schools represents an important form of education. A 1970 Census survey of vocational training shows that individuals other than college graduates who had completed a formal occupational-training program had higher earnings than those who had never participated in or completed such a program.[1] The differential was apparent in all occupational groups.

The data dealing with educational attainment indicate broad trends marked by numerous exceptions. For instance, while the educational attainment level for the entire work force has undergone a marked upgrading in the past two decades, rapid growth in employment in some occupations characterized by low levels of educational achievement is likely to increase the number of dropouts employed in these fields. Examples include nurse's aides, construction-machine operators, and many food-service fields. And, while the proportion of college graduates entering the better-paid nonprofessional white-collar fields is expected to increase, it is projected to decline in several of these occupations. Recreation workers and personnel and labor-relations workers are instances. Although higher educational attainment and greater earnings generally go together, many women with 12 to 15 years of schooling were in the relatively low-paid $6,000-$8,000 earnings group in 1970. Research and national policy have emphasized the economic penalty attached to becoming a high school dropout. Yet in some fields the lifetime earnings of persons who did not complete high school are greater than those who graduate. To cite illustrations, the earnings foregone by completing a fourth year of high school by white male students who later became electricians or linemen were sufficient to reduce the present value of their lifetime earnings at age 17 by over $2,000 as compared to persons with less education in the same fields.[2] These offsetting tendencies do not negate the general directions apparent in the historical data and the projections. They do suggest that the educational attainment data, like like other manpower information, are compatible with a range of policy options adapted to the needs of individuals who differ in their aspirations, their abilities, their interests, and their labor-market circumstances.

THE DECLINE OF THE HIGH SCHOOL DROPOUT

The continued rise in the level of educational attainment implies that the high school diploma will become more of a minimum requirement for employment in most occupations in the 1980s than it has been in the recent past. Over three-fourths of the employment in the study occupations in the mid-1980s, to cite a summary statistic, is projected to occur in fields in which persons with 12 to 15 years of schooling will make up three-fifths or more of the work force. This represents an increase from 30 percent in 1970. In many nonprofessional white-collar occupations, employees with a high school diploma or junior college credentials will face increasing competition from college graduates. This competition may be less severe than is often anticipated because of the decline in the proportion of high school graduates entering college beginning in the late 1960s.

Allowing for a sizable increase in the supply of college graduates, the most striking change in the projections is the growth in the number of high school and postsecondary graduates. The growth reflects a major falling-off in the size of the group who do not complete high school, a decline most marked in the less skilled operative, laboring, farm, and service occupations.

The anticipated changes in educational attainment are summarized in Table 3.1. The table refers to the persons employed in the 123 occupations included in the study.

In 1970 the high school dropout population in the labor force was still an important group. In that year over half of the persons in the study occupations employed as operatives, laborers, or in the farm occupations had less than four years of high school. Nearly half of the craftsmen were in the same educational group. By 1985, persons lacking a full high school education are expected to constitute a majority only among the laborers. Part of the sharp decline in employment for persons with limited education stems from the anticipated steep decline in the employment of farm laborers, one of the least well-educated and most poorly paid employee groups in the economy. The increases in the representation of college graduates in the occupations considered are modest. They are projected to grow from less than 7 to slightly more than 9 percent of the work force in the 123 occupations.

The age distribution has an important bearing for the educational attainment level in individual occupations. Younger workers, the newer entrants into the labor force, have typically attended school for a longer time than older workers, who completed their schooling at a time when less attention was paid to educational credentials in hiring. The significance of the age factor is illustrated by selected

TABLE 3.1

Distribution of Educational Attainment, by Major Occupational Group, Study Occupations—1970 and Projected 1985
(in percent)

Occupational Group	1970 Educational Attainment			1985 Educational Attainment		
	Less than 12 Years	12-15 Years	16 Years or More	Less than 12 Years	12-15 Years	16 Years or More
Professional and technical workers	9.9	68.7	21.4	5.8	71.3	22.9
Managers and administrators, except farm	25.4	54.5	20.1	10.9	62.0	27.1
Salesworkers	29.5	58.2	12.2	16.1	68.7	15.2
Clerical workers	16.4	78.6	5.0	8.1	86.2	5.7
Craftsmen and foremen	49.6	48.5	1.9	32.3	65.2	2.5
Operatives	59.5	39.8	0.7	44.0	55.0	1.0
Service workers	46.5	51.5	2.0	29.5	68.1	2.4
Laborers, except farm	71.2	27.4	1.5	57.9	39.4	2.2
Farm occupations	64.1	33.1	2.8	44.1	51.1	4.8
Total, all study occupations	38.5	54.8	6.7	22.7	68.5	8.8

Note: Details may not add to totals because of rounding.

Sources: U.S. Bureau of the Census, 1970 Census of Population, Subject Report, Occupational Characteristics; U.S. Department of Labor, Bureau of Labor Statistics, Occupation-by-Industry Matrix Projections (unpublished), 1974; The Conference Board.

TABLE 3.2

Years of Schooling Completed by All Workers and by
Workers 16 to 34 Years Old, Selected Occupations, 1970
(in percent)

Occupation	School Years Completed		
	Less than 12	12-15	16 or More
Practical nurses			
All ages	30	69	1
16-34	11	88	1
Bookkeepers			
All ages	16	78	5
16-34	10	85	5
Auto mechanics			
All ages	57	42	1
16-34	45	54	1
Carpenters			
All ages	60	38	1
16-34	35	63	2
Machinists			
All ages	46	53	1
16-34	30	69	1

Note: Details may not add to totals because of rounding.
Sources: U.S. Bureau of the Census, 1970 Census of Population, Subject Report, Occupational Characteristics; Special Tabulations, 1970 Census Public Use Tapes.

instances drawn from the study occupations. They are summarized in Table 3.2. The "all ages" group includes the 16-to-34-year-olds, so that the presence of many younger workers in an occupation tends to increase its educational level. The occupations included in Table 3.2 illustrate the shift in nonprofessional occupations toward a considerably greater emphasis on completion of high school, and, frequently, some post-high school education as well. Although age has only a minor bearing on the proportion of college graduates in the occupations listed, it has a major bearing in other educational levels. While the occupations selected are strong cases, the trends they illustrate are generally evident, to a greater or lesser extent, in other fields. In only 5 of the 123 occupations considered was the percentage

THE EDUCATIONAL ATTAINMENT INDICATORS

of workers in the under-35 age group with less than 12 years of schooling in 1970 as great as the representation of this group in the overall occupational work force.

The distribution of educational attainment, like the anticipated growth in employment, varies considerably from state to state and from region to region. The variations grow out of differences in the occupational makeup along with dissimilarities in the age, race, and sex composition of the area's work force. The resources available to the educational systems as illustrated by the per pupil expenditure in elementary and secondary schools are also probably a factor. The importance of the regional differences are illustrated in Table 3.3, which compares Kentucky, a state with a large rural sector, and New Jersey, primarily an industrial state, with the entire United States. The comparison refers to all occupations rather than to the 123 receiving special consideration.

Nearly half of the employed persons in Kentucky in 1970 could be classified as high school dropouts, as compared to three-eighths for the entire United States and slightly more in New Jersey. There were considerably more college graduates in New Jersey than in Kentucky and somewhat more than in the entire United States. Current per pupil expenditures in the public elementary and secondary schools were higher, nearly $1,300 in New Jersey as compared to over $700 in Kentucky. If educational attainment can be regarded as an indicator of a type of investment in human capital embodied in individual persons, the investment is greater in industrial and wealthier states like New Jersey than in more heavily rural and less wealthy states like

TABLE 3.3

Distribution of Educational Attainment, Kentucky,
New Jersey, and the Entire United States, 1970
(in percent)

Years of Schooling Completed	Distribution of Employed Work Force		
	Kentucky	New Jersey	United States
Less than 12	48.2	39.5	37.2
12 to 15	41.8	46.2	50.4
16 and more	10.0	14.4	12.4

Note: Details may not add to totals because of rounding.
Source: See Table 3.2.

Kentucky. While personal income levels are affected by many elements other than education, per capita personal income in New Jersey in 1973 was about 45 percent greater than in Kentucky, approximately $5,750 in New Jersey and $4,000 in Kentucky.[3]

Nationally, the occupations included in the study in which employment is expected to increase especially rapidly are largely fields in which a greater-than-average proportion of the work force possesses a full high school or some college education. The educational achievement level of the rapidly expanding fields is illustrated by the occupations in which employment is projected to increase by 100 percent or more between 1970 and 1985 (see Table 3.4).

The rapidly growing fields listed in the table, other than the health-service occupations, are among the higher-paid occupations considered, although their earnings are often less than in managerial, financial, or specialized sales positions. In six of the eight occupations listed, the percentage of high school cropouts was less and persons completing 12 to 15 years of schooling was greater than the overall average. In one of the two exceptions, the medical therapists, the representation of high school graduates was low because a majority of the persons employed had completed four or more years of college. In most of these fields, however, there were relatively fewer college graduates employed than in the overall group. The rapidly growing and better-paid fields have frequently become the special concern of post-high school occupational education, education often provided by community colleges.

There has been widespread concern in the past few years that an oversupply of college graduates in the coming decade will lead to greater competition by college-educated persons for positions previously filled mainly by high school or postsecondary graduates. For example, the Department of Labor's projections of job openings for college graduates indicate that there will be a total demand for 9.6 million new college-educated workers between 1970 and 1980. Over a fourth of this demand, or 2.6 million job openings, is expected to come about because of educational upgrading as college graduates seek employment in many fields in which fewer of them had been employed in the past.[4] Much of the educational upgrading will take place because of the sharp decline anticipated in requirements for teachers. The Carnegie Corporation Commission on Higher Education estimates that requirements for new teachers will decrease from the equivalent of 35 percent of the college graduates in 1963 and 26 percent in 1968 to between 12 and 15 percent in 1980.[5]

Recent studies show that the economic return to a four-year college education has been diminishing since the late 1960s as the supply of new graduates has come to exceed the growth in demand in the oc-

TABLE 3.4

Distribution of Educational Attainment, 1970, in Study Occupations with Projected Employment Increase of 100 Percent or More, 1970-85
(in percent)

Occupation	Distribution of Educational Attainment in 1970		
	Less than 12 Years	12-15 Years	16 Years or More
Therapists	6.3	38.3	55.4
Practical nurses	29.9	69.1	1.0
Health aides, except nursing	38.0	57.7	4.3
Electrical and electronic-engineering technicians	11.5	83.0	5.5
Engineering and science technicians, n.e.c.	14.3	72.7	13.0
Other technicians, except health	12.1	72.3	15.6
Data-processing machine repairers	6.1	88.5	5.4
Air-conditioning, heating, and refrigeration mechanics and repairers	47.9	50.8	1.3
All study occupations	38.5	54.8	6.7

Note: Details may not add to totals because of rounding.
Source: See Table 3.1.

cupations in which these persons had typically been employed in the past. With this change in supply-demand relationships, the estimated discounted lifetime earnings of male graduates of four-year colleges at age 22 is reported to have decreased from $99,200 in 1969 to $95,100 in 1972. The corresponding earnings for persons with four years of high school in this period increased from $87,100 to $88,100. The consequences of these labor-market changes show up in a decline from 63 percent in 1968 to 50 percent in 1973 in the proportion of new male high school graduates entering college.[6]

The projections imply that the increase in representation of college graduates will primarily take place in white-collar technical, managerial, and specialized sales fields. These occupations already employ many persons with 16 or more years of schooling. The penetration of the college graduate population in clerical, service, or blue-collar occupations, including the skilled crafts, is expected to be slight.

The changes in the representation of college graduates in selected individual occupations which illustrate the shifts are described in Table 3.5. The changes for major groups are listed in Table 3.1.

TABLE 3.5.

Projected Changes in Representation of College Graduates in Selected Occupations, 1970-85
(in percent)

Occupation	Completing Four or More Years of College	
	1970	1985
Computer programmers	41.7	53.3
Personnel and labor-relations workers	39.1	35.3
Recreation workers	32.0	22.4
Registered nurses	15.9	19.4
Bank officials and financial managers	35.7	52.5
Stock and bond salesmen	53.2	71.3
Sales representatives, manufacturing	27.1	34.9
Police and detectives	6.1	7.9
All study occupations	6.8	9.1
All occupations	12.4	19.0

Sources: See Table 3.2; The Conference Board.

The sizable increases in the representation of college graduates are expected to occur in white-collar and technical fields, such as computer programmers, bank officials, and stock and bond salesmen. Lesser increases are anticipated in other occupations seeking to attain a more professional status, such as registered nurses or police and detectives, or in areas in which earnings are relatively large, such as manufacturers' sales representatives. The shifts are in both directions since in some semiprofessional fields, the proportion of persons with a full four-year college education is projected to decrease. Recreation workers or personnel and labor-relations workers are instances.

It is unclear at present how far the penetration of college graduates will increase in nonprofessional fields in the next decade or to what degree the growth in college enrollments will slow down. Part of the diminished attractiveness of the college degree represents a short-term response to the recession and high unemployment rates characterizing the past few years, and another part constitutes a reaction to longer-term economic and demographic changes. While the decline in requirements for teachers is linked with the drop in birthrates in the past 10 or 15 years, fluctuations in demand for engineers and related technicians stem mainly from changes in economic activity and shifts in national priorities. A national commitment to massive energy research and development programs, for example, would probably lead to considerably expanded requirements for engineers and enrollments in colleges of engineering. Moreover, the reactions to the economic environment can sometimes be the opposite of what appeared reasonable in an earlier period. For example, the depressed labor market in 1975 has probably prompted an increase in college enrollment, a rise encouraged by the absence of desirable job opportunities as the alternative to attending college. [7]

If the version of the future represented by the anticipations of declining enrollment growth in higher education were to materialize, a significant by-product would be a greater number of students with good learning ability who would be candidates for occupational education leading to employment in white-collar but nonprofessional fields. Allowing for some slowdown in the growth of college enrollments in the next 10 years, it is apparent that the overall educational level in the occupations studied will continue to increase, although at a less rapid pace than in the past. Two major developments can be expected to follow from the greater educational achievement—one economic and the other social. The economic change would take the form of an increase in productivity beyond what would otherwise occur because of the greater human capital represented by the rising educational level of the work force. This increment in productivity could, to some extent, offset the slowing down of productivity growth projected in the 1980s, primarily because of the greater weight of the services sector in the economy. The social change concerns the shift in the makeup of the persons available to fill the less well-paid lower-level occupations in the United States in the 1980s. A generation ago the less skilled operative, laborer, and service jobs were usually filled by persons with limited schooling, often with eight years or less of formal education. The work force with these limited educational achievements included many recent migrants from the rural South, from depressed areas such as Appalachia, or from Puerto Rico or Europe. In many European nations that underwent rapid economic growth during the 1960s, the lower-level occupations were again filled by migrants, generally individuals with less education who came from southern

Europe or North Africa. The comparable positions in the United States in the next 10 or 15 years will be filled by persons usually born in the United States, brought up in metropolitan areas, and with a high school education and sometimes better.

EDUCATIONAL ATTAINMENT AND EARNINGS

Americans have historically regarded education as one of the most important means for bringing about greater economic and social mobility. The significance attached to these consequences of upgrading educational attainment is evident in the compensatory education programs adopted in the 1960s and in such efforts as the Open Admissions program in the New York City colleges. Recent studies such as the Jencks report at Harvard University have questioned the contribution of education to economic mobility.[8] The evidence from the occupations included in the study indicates an association between educational attainment and earnings, an association most evident at the extremes of the earnings and the educational distributions. However, the association exists side by side with numerous exceptions, especially among disadvantaged groups in the labor market, most notably women.

The relation between educational attainment and earnings is evident for persons with less than a full high school education in the lowest and highest earnings groups, and for persons with four or more years of college at all earnings levels. These relationships are summarized for 1970 in Table 3.6.

The high school dropout group was overrepresented in the two lowest earnings groups and underrepresented in the two highest groups. There were fewer high school graduates in the lowest income group, the under $6,000 group, and a larger percentage in each of the above-average income groups beginning with the $10,000 level. However, a larger proportion of the 12-to-15-year group was in the relatively low $6,000 to $8,000 bracket than among the persons with less than a high school education. The economic advantage of the group with 16 or more years of schooling was apparent in both the high- and low-income classifications.

The data on the overall relationships between educational attainment and earnings are somewhat misleading because they obscure the differentials in earnings based on sex or race. The differential is evident in the heavy representation of individuals in the 12-to-15-year educational achievement group in the $6,000 to $8,000 earnings bracket. This concentration is largely attributable to lower earnings for women—often clerical workers—than for men with similar educational credentials. The educational attainment of men and women in all occupa-

THE EDUCATIONAL ATTAINMENT INDICATORS

TABLE 3.6

Distribution of Employment by Educational Attainment
and Earnings, Study Occupations, 1970
(in percent)

Median Earnings of Occupations in 1970*	Educational Attainment		
	Less than 12 Years	12-15 Years	16 Years or More
Less than $6,000	18.7	9.0	2.2
6,000-7,999	24.5	33.9	15.4
8,000-9,999	30.5	20.7	11.6
10,000-11,999	13.5	15.9	11.2
12,000-13,999	5.5	8.2	17.4
14,000 and over	7.3	12.3	42.2

Note: Details may not add to totals because of rounding.
*Refers to median earnings in 1973 dollars of workers employed for at least 50 weeks during the year.
Sources: U.S. Bureau of the Census, 1970 Census of Population, Subject Report, Occupational Characteristics, Special Tabulations, 1970 Census Public Use Tapes.

tions in the United States in 1970 as represented by the median number of years of schooling completed was identical, 12.4 years for both. But the economic returns to educational achievement for women has been consistently less. The discrepancy is illustrated in Table 3.7 by the 10 occupations receiving consideration in the study employing the largest number of males and the 10 employing the largest number of females. The earnings projections for 1985 in the table suggest that if the relationship between earnings and productivity characterizing the past 10 or 15 years continues through the coming decade, the differentials in earnings based on sex will remain and in some instances increase.

The earnings disadvantage in the fields employing large numbers of women is evident in the table. The educational achievement level in the mainly female occupations exceeded the economy-wide median of 12.4 years of schooling in 1970 in 7 of the 10 fields. The comparable figure in occupations employing large numbers of males was four. One of the occupations with a greater-than-average educational level, salesclerks in retail trade, is among the largest employers of both men and women. Full-year workers earned less than

TABLE 3.7

Median Years of Schooling Completed, 1970, and Estimated Earnings in 1970 and 1985—Study Occupations Employing Largest Number of Men and Women

Occupation	Median Years of Schooling Completed, 1970	Median Earnings of Full-Year Workers*		Percent Change 1970-1985
		1970	Projected 1985	
Employing largest number of men				
Auto mechanics	10.5	9,070	13,270	46
Carpenters	9.7	9,720	14,390	48
Deliverymen	11.7	9,060	12,720	40
Farm owners and tenants	10.5	7,780	15,910	104
Foremen	12.7	12,320	19,160	56
Heavy-equipment mechanics	11.1	10,300	15,070	46
Managers and administrators, n.e.c.	13.8	16,770	26,040	55
Salesclerks, retail trade	12.7	6,470	9,480	47
Sales representatives, wholesale	13.8	13,690	21,030	54
Truck drivers	9.0	9,640	16,160	68
Employing largest number of women				
Bookkeepers	13.7	6,530	9,600	47
Cooks	9.1	5,470	8,570	57
Hairdressers and cosmetologists	13.0	5,770	8,650	50
Nurse's aides	11.8	4,890	6,940	42
Practical nurses	13.2	5,870	8,910	52
Salesclerks, retail trade	12.7	6,470	9,480	47
Secretaries	13.9	6,860	10,100	47
Sewers and stitchers	8.5	4,880	6,970	43
Registered nurses	14.2	8,090	11,970	48
Typists	13.7	6,070	8,890	46
All U.S. occupations	12.4	9,945	15,260	53

*In 1973 dollars.

Sources: U.S. Bureau of the Census, Department of Commerce, Census of the Population, 1970; Conference Board projections.

$8,000 in all but one of the fields listed in the female group, the exception being the registered nurses. The occupations listed in the male group were in this low-earnings category in only two instances. One was the retail salesclerks included in both groups. In the three clerical fields listed, all with 1970 earnings of less than $7,000, the predominantly female work force had close to two years of post-high school education. Between 1970 and 1985, the differentials in earnings for the two groups of occupations are projected to increase. The average (unweighted) increase in the fields in the male group is estimated at 56 percent, and increases of 50 percent or more are projected in 5 of the 10 fields. The average increase in the female group is estimated at under 48 percent, and increases of 50 percent or more are anticipated in only three fields. The increases in educational attainment for both men and women in the labor force, according to Department of Labor sources, are expected to be virtually identical in the next 10 years, a rise by 1985 to 12.7 for men and 12.6 years for women.

Comparable information on the association between educational achievement and earnings in the occupations employing large numbers of blacks or other nonwhites would lack significance because far fewer fields are predominantly nonwhite. These occupations are overweighted with unskilled and poorly paid positions, and many nonwhites are employed in other and more desirable jobs in which they make up a small percentage of the work force. Large differences in earnings for similar levels of educational achievement are apparent. In 1972, for example, the median income of black and other nonwhite families in which the family head had completed four years of high school was $8,893. The income for white families whose head had completed the same number of years of schooling was $12,426, or 40 percent greater.[9]

The association between educational attainment and earnings would be greater if discriminatory barriers based on sex or race did not diminish the economic gains from education for persons in groups with a disadvantaged labor-market status. The fact of an association need not imply that increased exposure to schooling, by itself, is the cause of the higher earnings. More education can increase work skills or improve the ability to read and write, to communicate, and to work together with people. In an economy in which educational credentials are often regarded by employers as a surrogate for ability to learn, or for potentially good work habits and motivation, absence of the appropriate credentials may constitute a formidable obstacle to entrance into many desirable jobs. As the high school diploma becomes characteristic of the work force in most fields, especially among younger workers, possession of a full high school education will become more of a standard minimum qualification for employment than in the past. The high school diploma, however, is unlikely to provide the same assurance of employment or job mobility it did several decades earlier, as persons with only a high school education come to find themselves increasingly in competition with job seekers possessing the same or higher educational qualifications.

OCCUPATIONAL TRAINING AND EARNINGS

The relation between educational attainment and earnings is usually considered in terms of the association between years of schooling completed and earnings. But education can take place in many types of programs, only some of which involve the established educational institutions. Since occupational education, in particular, is often provided outside of high school or postsecondary schools, many types of institutions provide education in the expectation that it will have an influence on earnings. A 1970 Census survey of occupational-education programs indicates that a majority of the persons in virtually all occupational groups have learned their skills from sources other than a formal occupational-training program. But program completers, excepting the graduates of four-year colleges, had higher earnings than the others in all occupational groups. The differentials were especially significant for persons with less than 12 years of schooling.

Occupational education—for purposes of the Census survey—included formal vocational programs in the public schools, or in a business, nursing, or trade school, or technical institute, in apprenticeship programs, and training received in the Armed Forces or in the Job Corps. Correspondence courses, on-the-job training, and basic or officer military training were excluded. The programs included in the Census study, therefore, take into account the types of training offered by the public vocational-education system and they extend beyond it.

The largest representation of completers was among the professional and technical workers with 12 to 15 years of schooling, and the craftsmen and foremen in the same educational classification. Approximately half the persons in both groups were included among the completers. While the persons who enrolled in but did not complete one of the programs may have derived an economic benefit from their participation, the earnings of the completers who were not college graduates were greater than those who had never enrolled or finished in every occupational group. The college graduate group is

TABLE 3.8

Median Earnings of Occupational-Training Completers and All Others by Educational Attainment and Occupational Group—All Occupations, 1970
(in dollars)

	Median Earnings of Workers			
	Less than 12 Years Schooling		12 to 15 Years Schooling	
Occupational Group	Completed Occupational Training	All Others	Completed Occupational Training	All Others
Professional and technical workers	7,999	6,622	8,532	8,219
Managers and administrators, except farm	9,275	7,980	10,399	10,001
Salesworkers	6,450	5,173	7,644	7,095
Clerical workers	5,888	5,439	5,937	5,550
Craftsmen and foremen	8,737	7,503	9,659	8,729
Operatives, except transportation	6,622	5,550	7,365	6,407
Transportation-equipment operatives	7,307	6,981	7,897	7,820
Laborers, except farm	6,008	5,501	6,854	6,667
Farm occupations	4,218	3,573	5,841	5,698
Service workers, except private household	4,554	3,779	5,398	4,744
Private household workers	1,513	1,158	1,523	1,223
All occupations	6,868	5,642	7,756	6,943

Note: "All Others" category includes persons who did not enroll in or complete a formal occupational-training program. Data are for persons 25-64 years old.

Source: U.S. Bureau of the Census, 1970 Census of Population, Subject Report, Vocational Training, 1973.

excluded as a special case since persons in this group generally receive their occupational education in other types of programs.

The differentials in earnings between the program completers and the others are described in Table 3.8.

Both high school graduates and high school dropouts who finished a formal training program had greater earnings than those who did not participate in or complete such a program. The average earnings differential in all occupations between the completers and the others in the group that had never completed high school was considerably greater than the corresponding difference in the group with 12 to 15 years of schooling, approximately $1,200 in the dropout group as compared to slightly more than $800 for the high school graduates. In the group with less than 12 years of schooling, the gains favoring those who finished the programs were greatest for white-collar workers, other than clerical employees. The differential among high school graduates was largest for craftsmen and for operatives, excluding the transport operatives. The large differential in earnings favoring the program completers who lacked a high school diploma suggests that a formal training program often serves as a substitute for a full high school education in imparting work skills and habits or in obtaining a credential which can facilitate entrance into many desirable positions.

The Census survey is suggestive rather than conclusive. It does not attempt to allow for factors other than program completion that may affect earnings. It is likely that differences in motivation, learning ability, and socioeconomic status between the completers and the others contribute to the differentials in earnings. The Census data do not make it possible to distinguish between the increase in earnings attributable to the acquisition of work skills and those attributable to the possession of a credential permitting access to better jobs. The large number of persons in the nonprofessional occupations who had never completed a formal vocational program indicates that completing these courses is seldom a prerequisite to employment. However, the consistency, as well as the magnitude, of the differential favoring the completers supports the contention that the persons finishing the programs derive an economic benefit from their participation.

The median years of schooling completed by the employed civilian labor force has increased from 10.9 years in 1952 to 12.1 in 1962 and to 12.4 in 1970.[10] This long-term rise in educational attainment is important because of its bearing on earnings and because of its implications for human relations and the organization of authority within industry. In the late 1960s and early 1970s there was considerable concern that alienation from work was becoming translated into slower rates of productivity growth. While the extent of the alienation was difficult to assess, it was evidently a factor in recent major labor disputes in the automobile industry. Sar Levitan, an authority on the labor force, evokes the problem in the title chosen for one of his recent works, <u>Work is Here to Stay, Alas</u>.[11] Work <u>is</u> here to stay, of course; but it is reasonable to anticipate that the conditions under which it is performed will differ for a work force typically made up of persons with at least a high school education from those prevailing when the labor force was predominantly composed of high school dropouts.

NOTES

1. U.S. Bureau of the Census, <u>1970 Census of Population, Subject Report, Vocational Training</u>, 1973.
2. S. O. Schweitzer, "Occupational Choice, High School Graduation, and Investment in Human Capital," paper presented at hearings, Joint Economic Committee of Congress, Subcommittee on Economy in Government, National Priorities, June 1970.
3. <u>Statistical Abstract,</u> 1974, pp. 130, 380.
4. <u>Manpower Report of the President,</u> 1972, p. 114.
5. The Carnegie Commission on Higher Education, <u>College Graduates and Jobs</u> (New York: McGraw-Hill, 1973), p. 70.
6. Richard B. Freeman, "Overinvestment in College Training," <u>The Journal of Human Resources</u> (Summer 1975): 287-311.
7. <u>New York Sunday Times</u>, December 13, 1975, Section 4.
8. C. Jencks, <u>Inequality: A Reassessment of the Effect of Family and Schooling in America</u> (1972). While the Jencks study is concerned with inequality rather than economic mobility, the historic rationale has been that education enhances equality of opportunity by increasing the mobility of persons from low-income backgrounds.
9. <u>Statistical Abstract,</u> 1974, p. 386.
10. <u>Manpower Report of the President,</u> 1975, p. 269.
11. S. A. Levitan, and W. B. Johnston, <u>Work is Here to Stay, Alas</u> (Salt Lake City: Olympus Publishing Co., 1973).

CHAPTER 4

WOMEN AND NONWHITES

EQUAL OPPORTUNITY—ASPIRATIONS AND ACHIEVEMENTS

    The social and political changes since the early 1960s have brought about far-reaching changes in expectations about the economic role of women and nonwhites. These changes are symbolized by the civil rights movement, the women's movement, the equal employment legislation adopted by Congress and in many states, and the affirmative action programs introduced by large numbers of employers. Translating expectations into achievements hinges to a large extent on expanding the range of job options available to women or to blacks and other members of minority groups. While women and, even more, nonwhites have improved their economic status in the past decade, the changes to date have generally been modest. A continuation for another decade of the trends of the past 10 or 15 years in gradually modifying the occupational distribution for the two groups can be expected to generate a gap between aspirations and reality, with significant consequences for the educational system, government, labor organizations, and private employers.

    The drive for equal employment opportunity for women reflects underlying demographic, economic, educational, and social changes. Later age at marriage, declining birth rates, the greater prevalence of divorce, and more widespread educational opportunity have all reinforced the effects of changing social attitudes in increasing participation in the labor force by women. The impact of inflation in raising costs of living since the late 1960s has intensified these tendencies. Accordingly, the proportion of women in the 25-to-54 age group who are in the labor force has increased from 37 percent in 1950 to 54 percent by 1974. By 1974, over two-fifths, 43 percent, of the married women whose husbands were present were in the labor force.[1]

Since approximately 90 percent of the persons classified as "nonwhite" in the occupational statistics are blacks, the job experience of blacks dominates this group. Much of the economic progress, and many of the labor-market problems, facing blacks in the past generation represent the consequences of massive migration from the South to other parts of the nation. In the course of this movement, the black population has changed from a primarily rural to a primarily urban group, a change indicated by the increase in the urban component from 34 percent of the total black population in 1920 to 81 percent in 1970.[2] Absence of skills in demand for nonwhites shows up in high unemployment rates as well as in low and decreasing labor-market participation by nonwhite males. Unemployment rates for nonwhites have been approximately double or more the white rate for the past decade. More than a third of the male nonwhite teenagers and over three-eighths of the females were unemployed in 1975.[3]

Slightly over half (53 percent) of all women who were employed in 1970 and over two-fifths of the nonwhites were at work in the 123 occupations considered in the study. While evidence of change is apparent in these fields, many of the occupational shifts involving the two groups have taken place in other areas omitted from consideration either because of educational requirements, usually involving a full college education, or, at the other end of the occupational spectrum, an absence of job skills sufficient to minimize their potential for vocational-training programs. The changes in the distribution for nonwhites and women in all occupations between 1960 and 1974 are summarized in Table 4.1.*

The occupational shifts for nonwhites, as indicated by the major groups, have been more extensive than those for women. One of the most striking changes for both groups has been the sharp falling-off in employment in private household work, a field dominated in the past by black women. Growth in employment in white-collar occupations, especially in professional and technical and clerical fields, constituted a major change for nonwhites. All told, the percentage of nonwhites employed as white-collar workers doubled between 1960 and 1974, increasing from a sixth to nearly a third of the total employment. The decline in employment in the farm occupations for both women and nonwhites was greater than the drop in overall em-

---

*For a different analysis of the occupational participation of women and black workers, see S. Garfinkle, "Occupations of Women and Black Workers," <u>Monthly Labor Review</u>, November 1975, pp. 25 ff.

TABLE 4.1

Distribution of Employment, Nonwhites and Women, by Major
Occupational Group, 1960 and 1974, All Occupations
(in percent)

	Distribution of Employment			
	Women		Nonwhites	
Occupational Group	1960	1974	1960	1974
White-collar workers	55.3	61.6	16.1	32.0
Professional and technical workers	12.4	14.9	4.8	10.4
Managers and administrators, except farm	5.0	4.9	2.6	4.1
Salesworkers	7.7	6.8	1.5	2.3
Clerical workers	30.3	34.9	7.3	15.2
Blue-collar workers	16.6	15.5	40.1	40.2
Craftsmen and foremen	1.0	1.5	6.0	9.4
Operatives	15.2	13.0	20.4	21.9
Laborers, except farm	0.4	1.1	13.7	8.9
Private household workers	8.9	3.6	14.2	5.1
Other service workers	14.8	17.8	17.5	20.0
Farm occupations	4.4	1.4	12.1	2.7

Note: Details may not add to totals because of rounding.
Source: Manpower Report of the President, 1975, pp. 226, 228.

ployment in this field. Continuing past trends, the proportion of women employed as clerical workers increased between the two years.

Allowing for many individual instances of occupational breakthroughs, a continuation of the experience of the past 10 or 15 years in the fields considered in the study would result in the bulk of the employment increases for women taking place in occupations in which females already predominated. The largest single increase between 1970 and 1985 would take place in clerical occupations, a growth in employment estimated at 3.4 million. The changes anticipated for nonwhites would represent a more general upgrading of occupational skills, especially in white-collar, service, and skilled craft fields. Part of this shift would be concentrated in less well-paid white-collar positions with higher social status. For example, the largest single increase in representation projected for nonwhites in the occupations studied is for secretaries.

Because of their limited access to the more desirable job opportunities, women and nonwhites share common problems of low earnings. In 1970, for instance, over three-fourths of the women and more than half of the nonwhites employed in the study occupations were at work in fields that paid full-year workers under $8,000 a year, or approximately $2,000 or more below the median earnings for all year-round workers in that year (see Table 1.7). The common problem of access to opportunity is illustrated by the representation of women and nonwhites in the 10 highest-paying and the 10 lowest-paying occupations, according to their 1970 earnings, among the 123 considered in the study. Their actual representation in 1970 and the projected representation in 1985 are summarized in Table 4.2.

The projections show that if the developments of the past 10 or 15 years continue, women would be better represented by the mid-1980s in most of the higher-paying fields. A larger proportion of the stock and bond salesmen, to cite an instance, would be females, and women would make up a larger percentage of the bank officials, designers, or mechanical-engineering technicians. The representation of blacks and other nonwhites is expected to increase in all of these fields. Offsetting this evidence of progress toward greater equality of opportunity, the percentage of women or nonwhites in all of the higher-paying fields in 1985, as in 1970, would be less than their representation in all the study occupations or in the overall employed work force. Similarly, women would be overrepresented in nine of the ten low-paying fields in the 1980s and nonwhites in eight. If more detailed breakdowns were available, it is likely that they would show the least-favored group to be made up of the individuals with a double labor-market disadvantage—nonwhite women.

The historical data and the projections dealing with nonwhites and women point to a problem and a challenge rather than presenting a forecast of what the future must hold. The problem arises from the gap between the social and political goals that have enlarged aspirations and the slow progress in translating the aspirations into greater opportunity in the labor market. In this sense, the projections reflect the implications of recent developments, and they would become outmoded as the educational system, employers, and government proceeded to transform the aspirations into a closer approximation to reality.

TABLE 4.2

Women and Nonwhites in 10 Highest-and 10 Lowest-
Paying Study Occupations—1970 and Projected 1985
(in percent)

Occupation	Female		Nonwhite	
	1970	1985	1970	1985
10 highest paid				
Stock and bond sales agents	8.6	12.5	2.2	3.7
Managers and administrators, n.e.c.	11.6	11.0	2.8	4.0
Bank officials and financial managers	17.4	23.5	2.5	4.2
Sales representatives, manufacturing	8.5	5.7	1.8	3.2
Real-estate appraisers	4.1	8.7	2.0	2.2
Designers	23.5	30.3	4.4	7.7
Personnel and labor-relations workers	31.2	28.7	6.4	8.8
Sales representatives, wholesale	6.4	9.9	2.0	3.4
Computer programmers	22.7	18.7	5.5	7.5
Mechanical-engineering technicians	2.9	7.3	3.0	5.6
10 lowest paid				
Practical nurses	96.3	97.8	23.5	30.4
Hairdressers and cosmetologists	90.4	92.4	8.3	5.6
Cooks, except private household	62.8	60.4	22.3	18.6
Health aides, except nursing	83.9	79.2	20.8	22.5
Nurse's aides	84.6	88.9	26.5	28.5
Sewers and stitchers	93.8	93.5	12.1	21.3
Farm laborers	13.2	17.4	22.6	14.3
Dressmakers and seamstresses	95.7	94.2	12.2	17.0
School monitors	91.2	95.8	8.0	10.0
Childcare workers, except private household	93.2	88.4	16.6	20.0
All study occupations	35.9	40.5	8.1	10.3
All occupations	37.7	39.0	10.7	12.4

Source: See Table 2.7.

WOMEN IN THE LABOR MARKET

Job opportunities for women in the next 10 years are more likely to arise out of employment growth and replacement needs in fields in which women are already well represented than from large-scale penetration into new fields. Much of the basis for this anticipation stems from the tendency for younger women—the newer entrants into the labor force and the group most affected by the recent changes in social attitudes—to enter the same or similar fields as do all women.

The employment of women is concentrated in a small number of occupations. In the occupations considered in the study, close to half of the women workers, 45 percent, are expected to be employed in 5 fields in 1985, seven-tenths in 13 fields, and five-sixths in 34. This tendency toward concentration of employment is illustrated in Table 4.3. An occupation is considered "female" for the purposes of the table if 50 percent or more of the persons employed in it are women.

The "female" occupations include such fields as nursing and health-service jobs, most clerical positions, retail salesclerks, operatives jobs—such as dressmakers or sewers and stitchers—and service occupations connected with personal care, childcare, or food service. Barriers to entry in many occupations together with the persistence of stereotypes defining what are appropriate "men's jobs" and "women's jobs" lead women to seek employment in a relatively narrow range of occupations. Overcrowding in these fields serves to increase the supply of qualified workers, and, in this way, to depress

TABLE 4.3

Employment of Women in "Female" Fields Included in Study Occupations, 1970 and Projected 1985

	1970	1985
Total employment of women in occupations studied (in thousands)	15,585	23,191
Employment of women in "female" occupations (in thousands)	12,195	19,186
Percent of female employment in "female" occupations	78	83
Number of "female" occupations	31	34
Total number of occupations studied	123	123

Source: See Table 2.7.

earnings. The availability of large numbers of women with better-than-average educational credentials—for instance, secretaries or bookkeepers—often leads employers to stress educational qualifications as a weeding-out device in hiring. Because women leave the labor force more frequently than men, typically to rear young children, a common feature of the predominantly "female" occupations is a high ratio of job openings arising from replacement needs as compared with employment growth.

The changes projected in the occupational distribution for women in the 1970-85 period can be illustrated by the representation shifts projected in different fields. These shifts consist of the part of the employment growth expected to arise because of an increase in the proportion of women in the occupations studied. All told, representation shifts are estimated to account for about a seventh of the total employment growth for women in the occupations considered in this period. The representation shifts are described for major occupational groups in Table 4.4.

Women can be expected to increase their representation in most fields in the next 10 years because they will make up a larger share of the labor force. The largest single employment gains are listed for the clerical occupations. Over two-fifths, 44 percent, of the total employment increase for women is projected to arise in this one field. Women will typically make up a slightly larger percentage of the work force in most clerical fields in the mid-1980s. Their representation is expected to increase in the few clerical fields that had predominantly employed males in the past. Shipping and receiving clerks or stock clerks are examples. Offsetting these instances, 97.6 percent of the secretaries were women in 1970 as were 94.2 percent of the typists. These percentages are expected to grow to 98.6 percent by 1985 for secretaries and to decline to 93.2 percent for typists. Aside from the clerical occupations, women would increase their representation in operatives jobs, such as bus drivers, especially those employed in driving school buses. A somewhat smaller proportion of women would be at work in managerial fields—buyers in department stores, for example. But women would make significant representation gains in individual managerial and administrative positions—as bank officials and financial managers, for example. Representation shifts make up over two-thirds of the employment increase listed for the skilled crafts. However, after allowing for many individual breakthroughs by women in these fields, the increase in female penetration in skilled crafts, such as auto mechanics or electricians, would be small. To cite an instance, employment for women as air-conditioning, heating, and refrigeration mechanics is projected to increase by 400 percent between 1970 and 1985. This would represent a growth from about

TABLE 4.4.

Estimated Changes in Employment and Representation Shifts for Women, Study Occupations, 1970-85
(in thousands)

Occupational Group	Employment 1970	Employment 1985	Change in Employment, 1970-85	Change due to Representation Shifts, 1970-85
Professional and technical workers	968	1,595	627	26
Managers and administrators, except farm	881	1,152	271	-68
Salesworkers	1,759	2,530	771	221
Clerical workers	6,363	9,733	3,370	307
Craftsmen and foremen	306	568	262	177
Operatives	2,163	2,725	562	231
Service workers	2,924	4,745	1,821	157
Laborers, except farm	18	28	10	11
Farm occupations	200	116	-84	18*
Total	15,585	23,191	7,606	1,080

Note: Details may not add to totals because of rounding.
*Although employment for women in the farm occupations is expected to decline between 1970 and 1985, there is a positive representation shift for women in this field because the proportion of the total employment made up of women is projected to increase from 7.5 to 8.7 percent.
Source: See Table 2.7.

1,000 to 5,000 women at work in an occupation employing 130,000 persons in 1970. Overall, slightly less than 3 percent of the growth in employment projected for women in the study occupations represents growth as craftsmen or foremen.

Part of the explanation for the modest representation shifts for women is that the newer entrants into the labor force tend to enter the same fields that all women have been employed in for the past few decades. The significance of the tendency for younger women to perpetuate the prevailing occupational distribution by entering what are already predominantly female fields can be summarized with reference to the 10 occupations included in the study in which women made up 90 percent or more of the employed work force in 1970 (see Table 4.5).

TABLE 4.5

Representation of All Women in Work Force, 1970 and Projected 1985, and Representation of Women in under-35 Work Force, 1970, Selected Occupations
(in percent)

Occupation	Women in Work Force, 1970	Women in under-35 Work Force, 1970	Women in Work Force, 1985
Registered nurses	97.4	97.2	97.2
Secretaries	97.6	98.4	98.6
Calculating-machine operators	90.8	84.4	80.3
Stenographers	93.4	98.0	90.1
Typists	94.2	94.1	93.2
Dressmakers and seamstresses	95.7	91.5	94.2
Sewers and stitchers	93.8	93.0	93.5
Childcare workers	93.2	92.2	88.4
Hairdressers and cosmetologists	90.0	90.6	92.4
Practical nurses	96.3	96.0	97.8

Note: Women made up more than 90 percent of school monitors in 1970. This occupation has been omitted because of apparent inconsistencies in the data.

Sources: U.S. Bureau of the Census, <u>1970 Census of Population, Occupational Characteristics</u>; Special Tabulations, 1970 Census Public Use Tapes.

The comparison between women under 35 and all women is a gross one, since women under 35 made up close to two-fifths of the total female labor force in 1970. Yet, the pervasiveness of the tendency for younger women to continue in the fields regarded as "female" is evident in the table. In nine of the ten occupations listed, at least 90 percent of the work force under 35 was female. As the younger entrants into these fields continue to enter the "female" fields, they increase the likelihood that similar patterns will prevail in the next decade. Accordingly, women are projected to make up 90 percent or more of the work force in eight of the ten occupations in the mid-1980s and at least 80 percent in the other two. The fields in which women are heavily overrepresented are typically characterized by low earnings. The propensity of younger women to continue in the steps of their predecessors helps to perpetuate low earnings by assuring a steady stream of new entrants added to the supply of labor in these occupations.

Women already in the labor force frequently lack either the skills or the credentials to enter new and better-paying fields. For example, married women over 35 have typically left the labor force to rear a family. They then seek to return after an absence in which their job skills have often become obsolete or suffer from disuse. Moving away from the traditional stereotypes of women's jobs and reversing the process that embodies the stereotypes in the prevailing occupational distributions would involve creating new types of institutions and programs geared to the needs of adult women in the labor force. They would place a greater emphasis on "lifetime learning" in the schools, on counseling for second careers, and on company and publicly supported training and upgrading programs for adults who are locked into a narrow range of job skills and options.

NONWHITES—OCCUPATIONAL AND INCOME SHIFTS

The manpower indicators for nonwhites, like the experience of the past 10 or 15 years, suggest more extensive occupational shifts in the coming decade than do the comparable indicators for women. In addition, the stereotype of the nonwhite labor force as largely made up of high school dropouts will come to represent a marked departure from reality as nonwhites achieve a rough parity with whites in the extent to which their employment becomes concentrated in occupations with a work force largely composed of high school graduates. Allowing for the occupational shifts and the greater educational attainment, continuation of the trends of the recent past imply that a sizable majority of the nonwhites will be employed in low-paying fields. The anticipation of slow progress in changing the distribution of earnings reflects several considerations. One is the expectation that nonwhites will continue to be overrepresented in less skilled fields. Another are the indications that much of the upgrading in occupational status for nonwhites will be unaccompanied by comparable increases in earnings.

For instance, the largest amount of upgrading will take place in the clerical area, a relatively low-paid white-collar field.

Blacks and other nonwhites will be more heavily represented in most occupations in the coming decade because they will make up a larger share of the labor force. The civilian-labor-force increase projected for nonwhites in the 1970-85 period, for example, amounts to 45 percent as compared to 26 percent for whites. About 8 percent of the persons employed in the study occupations were nonwhites in 1970; the comparable proportion for 1985 is slightly over 10 percent. These figures are less than the representation of nonwhites in total civilian employment, owing to the substantial representation of nonwhites in many unskilled fields and in some professions not included among the occupations considered in the study.

Employment for nonwhites in the study occupations is projected to grow by nearly 2.4 million between 1970 and 1985. Two types of effects are associated with the employment growth. One, more far-reaching, will take the form of an increased representation in most of the fields considered. Close to three-fifths, 57 percent, of the employment growth in this period is expected to take the form of representation shifts. The other, a less marked change, will make itself evident in a change of the occupations in which nonwhites are employed so that the nonwhite occupational distribution will come to approximate the white distribution more closely.

The representation shifts for nonwhites are especially evident in the clerical and sales fields, and among skilled craftsmen. The shifts are described in Table 4.6.

The increase in employment in the occupations considered, about two-thirds, is greater than the projected 45 percent growth in the nonwhite labor force in the 1970-85 period. This suggests that in the coming decade a larger percentage of the nonwhites will be employed in fields in which the vocational-education system offers preparation, or in nonprofessional occupations involving some degree of skill. Many of the largest representation shifts are projected to take place in fields—typically low paying—in which nonwhites have historically been represented in excess of their proportion in the overall labor force. Nurse's aides, practical nurses, and sewers and stitchers are instances. Some of the other occupations with marked representation shifts—for example, clerical positions—are low-paying white-collar positions whose occupational and social status is relatively high. The greater representation in craftsmen and foremen positions underscores a growth area characterized by greater-than-average earnings and also by an upgrading of occupational status. Both the number and the proportion of nonwhites employed in two low-skilled and poorly paying fields, nonfarm and farm laborers, is expected to decline.

TABLE 4.6

Changes in Employment and Representation Shifts for
Nonwhites, Study Occupations, 1970-85
(in thousands)

Occupational Group	Employment 1970	Employment 1985	Change in Employment, 1970-85	Change due to Representation Shifts, 1970-85
Professional and technical workers	145	380	235	128
Managers and administrators, except farm	176	338	162	95
Salesworkers	164	342	178	126
Clerical workers	553	1,180	627	401
Craftsmen and foremen	522	980	458	314
Operatives	792	1,232	440	282
Service workers	761	1,245	484	56
Laborers, except farm	141	122	-19	-12
Farm occupations	257	64	-193	-56
Total	3,511	5,879	2,368	1,338

Note: Details may not add to totals because of rounding.
Source: See Table 2.7.

Over half of the employment increase for nonwhites, and many of the major representation shifts, are projected to take place in 11 occupations. Seven of these fields paid full-year workers under $8,000 or approximately $2,000 or more below the economy-wide median for these employees in 1970 (see Table 4.7).

The largest employment increase listed for nonwhites in any of the individual fields considered is for secretaries, and the next two largest are for nurse's aides and practical nurses. Sizable growth is also projected in two more highly paid occupations—miscellaneous managers and administrators and foremen. However, the miscellaneous managers category includes many dissimilar types of positions with large differences in earnings so that the median earnings figure for the entire occupation may be misleading for any one group. Three of the occupations in the table are clerical fields, and one, registered nurses, reflects greater penetration in a professional occupation in which nonwhites have been well represented in the past. Overall, the

TABLE 4.7

Projected Increase in Employment for Nonwhites,
1970-85, Selected Occupations

Occupation	Expected Increase in Employment, 1970-85 (in thousands)	Median Earnings, 1970*
Registered nurses	67	8,090
Managers and administrators, n.e.c.	113	16,770
Salesclerks, retail trade	106	6,470
Bookkeepers	74	6,530
Secretaries	201	6,860
Typists	126	6,070
Foremen	83	12,320
Sewers and stitchers	111	4,880
Welders and flame cutters	67	9,640
Nurse's aides	167	4,890
Practical nurses	167	5,870
Increase in 11 occupations	1,282	—
Increase in all study occupations	2,368	—
Increase in 11 occupations as percent of increase in all study occupations	54	—

*In 1973 dollars.
Source: See Table 2.7.

expected areas of growth underscore the prospect of an upgrading in occupational status accompanied by less rapid changes in earnings levels.

The expected increases and decreases in employment for nonwhites parallel those for whites, but the percentage changes are generally considerably larger for members of minority groups. For instance, employment for white craftsmen and foremen in the study occupations is expected to increase by a fourth between 1970 and 1985. The comparable increase for nonwhites is seven-eighths. But, after allowing for the more rapid growth for nonwhites, about a sixth of the blacks and other nonwhites would be at work as craftsmen and foremen in the 1980s, as compared with nearly a fifth for whites. Within the skilled crafts, nonwhites would be well represented in less specialized or heavy construction crafts such as brick and stonemasons, bulldozer operators, or painter apprentices; there would be relatively few at work as electricians, photoengravers, plumbers, or structural-metal craftsmen.

For nonwhites in the labor force, isolation from the mainstream of the more desirable jobs is one of the underlying reasons for low incomes. This isolation helps explain the presence of millions of "working poor" or near-poor in periods of full employment. The earnings from some full-time jobs in which blacks are overrepresented are little more than could be obtained by family heads without working from welfare-assistance programs. In terms of the study occupations, the effects of isolation are evident in the figure showing that 30 percent of the nonwhites at work in these fields in 1970 were employed in occupations paying under $6,000 to persons who worked 50 weeks or more during the year (see Table 1.7). Several developments in the coming decade are likely to diminish, although probably not eliminate, the isolation. One is the declining proportion of nonwhite workers, those under 35, entering many of the least skilled and most poorly paid fields. This development contributes substantially to the expected decline in the proportion of nonwhites employed as laborers or farm laborers (see Table 4.6). On an economy-wide basis, the tendency of the younger nonwhites to avoid the least desirable fields also helps to explain the sharp falling-off since 1960 in the employment of blacks and other minority group members as private household workers (see Table 4.1).

Rapid growth in occupations offering attractive career prospects can also be important in creating opportunities for lessening the concentration of nonwhites in the less desirable jobs. Discriminatory barriers are less formidable and well established in most expanding fields and most, especially the technical and equipment repair positions, provide better-than-average earnings to the persons employed in them. Nonwhites are expected to increase their representation in all of the most rapidly growing fields, those in which increases in employment of 100 percent or more are projected between 1970 and 1985 (see Table 4.8).

The concentrations of nonwhites in the high-growth occupations are expected to remain high in health-service fields characterized both by rapid growth and low earnings. However, nonwhites are projected to increase their representation in many of the rapidly growing technical specialties to approximately their overall proportion in the study occupations. The rapidly growing fields related to technological advance or medical-technical therapies are expected to offer many

TABLE 4.8

Representation of Nonwhites in Study Occupations with
Projected Employment Increases of 100 Percent or More, 1970-85
(in percent)

Occupation	Nonwhite Employees	
	1970	1985
Therapists	8.4	10.4
Practical nurses	23.5	30.4
Health aides, except nursing	20.8	22.5
Electrical and electronic-engineering technicians	5.2	8.2
Engineering and science technicians, n.e.c.	5.2	9.1
Other technicians, except health	7.5	10.5
Data-processing machine repairers	3.1	3.7
Air-conditioning, heating, and refrigeration mechanics	4.6	7.6
All study occupations	8.1	10.3

Source: U.S. Department of Labor, Bureau of Labor Statistics, Occupation-by-Industry Matrix Projections for 1985 (unpublished), 1974.

opportunities to members of minority groups, as well as others, with the education and training to enter them.

The occupations in which most nonwhites were employed in the past were characterized by low educational attainment, a condition frequently associated with unskilled work and low earnings. This characterization had become less than an accurate description by 1970, and it will be even less valid by 1985. The projections indicate that by 1985 more than 70 percent of the nonwhites will be employed in occupations in which more than a majority, at least three-fifths, of the work force will have completed between 12 and 15 years of schooling. This compares with less than a fourth in 1970. By the mid-1980s nonwhites will have achieved parity with whites in their representation in the generally more skilled fields in which 80 percent of the work force are high school graduates but with less than a full college education. The anticipated changes in the educational makeup of the occupations in which whites and nonwhites are employed are summarized in Table 4.9.

The projections show both the influence of occupational upgrading for many nonwhites in the coming decade and the overall advance in the educational attainment level of the work force. By the mid-1980s, blacks and other nonwhites will have made substantial inroads in the occupations in which most workers have a high school education or more. However, the shifts toward greater parity in educational attainment are unlikely to be accompanied by a comparable advance toward greater parity in earnings, since much of the occupational upgrading will take the form of greater employment in jobs in which high educational attainment and relatively low earnings go together. Clerical fields and professional nursing are instances. In addition, increases in educational attainment have been especially marked in the occupations involving minimum skill, and, in the past, a high representation of high school dropouts. Many operative, service, and laborer jobs are examples. These occupations have provided the bulk of the employment for nonwhites. Accordingly, for nonwhites, as for women, the economic return for more schooling has frequently been less than for white males.

TABLE 4.9

Employment by Race, Workers Completing 12 to 15 Years of Schooling, Study Occupations—1970 and Projected 1985

Percent Completing 12-15 Years of Schooling	1970		1985	
	White	Nonwhite	White	Nonwhite
Under 20	0.0	0.0	0.0	0.0
20-39.9	22.6	36.3	2.9	4.4
40-59.9	45.6	40.3	19.7	24.2
60-79.9	19.2	13.9	51.8	45.8
80-100.0	12.6	9.5	25.6	25.6

Note: Details may not add to totals because of rounding.
Sources: U.S. Bureau of the Census, 1970 Census of Population, Occupational Characteristics; U.S. Department of Labor, Bureau of Labor Statistics, Occupation-by-Industry Matrix Projections for 1985 (unpublished), 1974.

Concern with equality of opportunity for nonwhites and women has focused on three areas: assuring equal pay for the same work, reducing the high unemployment rates characterizing both groups, and eliminating discriminatory barriers in employment. Shifting the occupational distributions for the two groups in the coming decade is an underlying issue in all of these areas. Equal pay for the same work would represent scant improvement if most women and nonwhites continue to be confined to occupations at the lower end of the earnings distribution. To a considerable extent, the high unemployment rates for the two groups are a consequence of the concentration of their job prospects in less skilled, poorly paid, and unemployment-prone fields. The objective in eliminating discriminatory barriers in hiring and upgrading is to open up new and more desirable types of job opportunities previously closed. The criterion of success of education or training, or equal employment programs, for members of groups with a disadvantaged labor-market status, therefore, is the extent to which they succeed in changing past trends of the occupational distribution of employment.

NOTES

1. Manpower Report of the President, 1975, p. 57-58.
2. Manpower Report of the President, 1974, p. 90.
3. U.S. Department of Labor, Bureau of Labor Statistics, Employment and Earnings, January 1976, pp. 134-35.

CHAPTER 5

IMPLICATIONS FOR EDUCATIONAL AND MANPOWER PLANNING

LABOR-FORCE INDICATORS AND EDUCATIONAL PLANNING

The overriding significance of the manpower indicators lies in their implications for priorities and planning in vocational education. The present vocational programs are educational programs, manpower programs, and social programs. A greater emphasis on one of these objectives is likely to be accompanied by a lesser emphasis on the others. However, it is the manpower orientation of vocational education that distinguishes it from other educational programs.

The federally supported vocational-education system is only one, although the largest, of a number of channels by which training can be acquired for occupations that do not usually require a four-year college degree. For persons already employed, much training is acquired on the job, often in company-sponsored programs. Apprenticeship programs are an important training resource in many skilled crafts, particularly in the building trades. The continued existence of private vocational schools is a testimonial to the desire of large numbers of people to gain specific occupational training through a formal program. In recent years, community colleges have greatly expanded the scope of the occupational training they offer. The massive growth of the federal government's remedial manpower-training programs for adults in the past decade underscores the importance attached by the nation to programs for enhancing earning capacity and employability as a remedy for the poverty of persons who are, or who could readily be, in the labor force. The specific feature differentiating the vocational-education programs is that they offer occupational instruction provided by professional educators in a school context mainly, but not exclusively, to young people not yet in the labor force.

Vocational education is often regarded as "career preparation," with the implication that an individual attending school is preparing for a specific lifetime career, to enter the first rung of a well-defined career ladder. While this preconception is often valid in skilled craft, technical, and professional occupations, it overlooks the large elements of flexibility and interoccupational mobility characterizing the work force. For example, beginning with the first position held for at least six months, the typical member of the labor force without a college education, to cite one study, holds 12 different jobs during a 46-year working life. Only one man in five in this group can anticipate remaining in the same major occupational category for his entire life.[1] The education and training that is significant for these people would stress increasing the options available to individuals in a changing society rather than primarily training them for a first or a second job. Occupational education, from this perspective, is important because it imparts skills and techniques, including communication skills, and an orientation to the world of work. In an increasingly mobile and impersonal society, vocational education also provides the entrance credentials needed to qualify for a job. Possession of the credentials, according to a noted European labor-market authority, Nils Kellgren, has come to mean "placing a label on a person." With this label, "he is invited to the working life and is accepted."[2] These considerations emphasize the special role of vocational education in bridging the gap between school and work.

PROGRAM PRIORITIES IN VOCATIONAL EDUCATION

Continuation of the recent program priorities in vocational education in the coming decade would imply that the system remain an important source of trained employees in some fields, such as office occupations, and a lesser source in many of the better-paid white-collar and technical fields. While the anticipated increases in enrollment in the coming decade are frequently roughly similar to the expected changes in employment, the projections indicate imbalances between enrollments in the programs and job opportunities in closely related fields in such areas as distributive education and the agricultural programs.

The relationship between enrollment and employment in the occupations studied can be expressed in terms of the "penetration rate," a ratio showing the enrollment per 100 persons employed in the occupations related to the different vocational-education program areas.

IMPLICATIONS

TABLE 5.1

Enrollment in Vocational Programs per 100 Persons Employed in Related Study Occupations, 1970

Program Area	Enrollment per 100 Persons Employed in 1970
Agriculture	23
Distributive education	3
Health occupations	7
Home economics (gainful)	6
Office occupations	22
Technical occupations	20
Trades and industry	10
All areas	11

Sources: U.S. Office of Education, Trends in Vocational Education Fiscal Year 1972, Vocational Education Information, No. 2, 1973; U.S. Bureau of Labor Statistics, "Matching 1970 Census-Based BLS National-State Matrix Occupational Categories to Office of Education Instructional Programs" (unpublished), 1974.

The data for 1970 underscore the marked differences in penetration in individual areas (see Table 5.1).

An average of 11 persons were enrolled in vocational programs in 1970 for every 100 persons employed in the related occupations. However, the enrollment ratio was only 3 in the distributive education programs, courses often regarded as preparation for employment in the merchandising field, while the rate was 22 in the office occupations programs and 23 in the agricultural programs. The penetration rate was also high in the technical programs, courses that frequently prepare young people for employment in various technical specialties, such as electronics.

Interpretation of the penetration-rate data or other enrollment figures in the federally supported vocational programs requires qualification on several grounds. In many fields, such as secretarial work or computer programming, private institutions are an important source of supply and their contribution must be taken into account in appraising the enrollment data in the public vocational programs. Community colleges provide vocational instruction in many of the better-paid white-collar and technical areas without receiving federal support. The vocational programs also differ considerably in the extent to which their programs constitute preparation for employment in specific fields closely related to the training. According to a recent study of occupational education in the public postsecondary schools and in private proprietary institutions, only a fifth of the graduates of the accounting programs obtained jobs as accountants or in related fields. Less than a fourth of the graduates of the computer-programming courses were employed in programming or in closely related areas. Most of the persons receiving training as dental assistants, secretaries, or cosmetologists, on the other hand, took positions related to their training.[3] Moreover, in interpreting these data, allowance must be made for the fact that graduates of such programs as accounting or computer programming may obtain employment in entry-level occupations considerably below the skill level for which they have been trained, and, in this way, obtain the necessary experience to qualify for employment more closely related to their training at a future date.

Another way of assessing priorities in vocational education as they relate to manpower considerations is to compare the anticipated changes in enrollments with the projected changes in employment. Consideration of changes over time is important because shifts in priorities usually require the passage of time to become implemented, since existing facilities, equipment, and tenured faculty must be directed to new fields. The anticipated changes in enrollment are evident in the historical information for 1970 and the projections for 1977. The 1977 data are Office of Education projections. They refer to enrollments in the vocational programs related to the occupations considered in the study, about 85 percent of the total vocational enrollments projected for 1985. The employment data indicate the actual employment in these occupations in 1970 and the anticipated employment in 1985 (see Table 5.2).

The most striking increase in the projections is the growth in enrollments in the trades and industry programs. These are courses preparing persons for employment, largely in private industry, in fields such as metal working, electrical or electronic trades, or in the building trades. More rapid growth in enrollments in this program area than in the employment in related fields suggests a marked increase in the enrollment-employment ratio in the coming decade. Enrollments in distributive-education courses preparing young persons for employment in jobs relating to merchandising, although increasing, would still be relatively less important in the next five or ten years than the job openings in these fields. The decline in the share of enrollments in the office education programs would repre-

TABLE 5.2

Distribution of Enrollments in Vocational Programs, 1970 and
Projected 1977; and Distribution of Employment in Study-
Related Occupations, 1970 and Projected 1985
(in percent)

Program Area	Distribution			
	Enrollment		Employment	
	1970	1977	1970	1985
Agriculture	15.8	9.1	7.4	3.4
Distributive education	6.5	8.7	26.0	27.0
Health occupations	3.1	3.9	4.8	6.3
Home economics (gainful)	2.7	5.9	4.5	4.3
Office occupations	40.8	31.0	19.4	21.7
Technical occupations	2.5	1.8	1.3	2.1
Trades and industry	28.7	39.6	29.3	28.7
Other	—	—	7.3	6.5

Notes: The vocational program enrollments listed in the table relate only to the occupations included in the study.

Details may not add to totals because of rounding.

Sources: See Table 5.1 and U.S. Bureau of Labor Statistics, "Occupation-by-Industry Matrix Projections" (unpublished), 1974.

sent a falling-off to a proportion still greater than but more nearly equal to the projected job openings in the field.

A large and complex imbalance exists between enrollments in the agricultural programs and the related employment. The percentage of vocational enrollments in the agricultural courses is projected to fall off significantly between 1970 and 1977, indicating a change in the priority given to this area. With this relative decline, enrollments in the agricultural programs would be 50,000 larger in 1977 than in 1970. The employment concept used in the comparison refers directly to the farm-related occupations. Expanding the concept to include the entire agriculture industry would raise the projected employment level by slightly less than 20 percent. However, employment in the agriculture industry is expected to fall from 3,450 in 1970 to 1,900 in 1985.[4] Including the closely related agribusiness occupations would increase the employment figures further.* However, the expectation that a growing number of students in the agricultural programs will obtain employment in the agribusiness field selling supplies or repairing equipment, in the dairy industry, or distributing farm products, requires tempering in the light of the expected decline in the share of GNP originating in agriculture in the coming decade. While output in agriculture will probably continue to increase slowly, the percentage of the Gross National Product originating in this sector of the economy is projected to decline, according to U.S. Department of Labor sources, from 3.5 percent of the total in 1970 to 2.1 percent in 1985.[5] The decline in the relative importance of agriculture in the economy, together with the high rates of productivity growth in this area, imply that employment in fields closely related to agriculture will provide jobs for a smaller segment of the labor force in the next decade than in the past one.

ENROLLMENTS AND EARNINGS

The relationship between the expected enrollment changes and job openings indicates an effort, with some exceptions and inconsistencies, to bring enrollments and job openings more closely into balance in the coming decade. The program concentrations also suggest a need for giving consideration to earnings prospects equivalent to that given to job openings in determining program priorities.

The emphasis on earnings in program planning is illustrated by the penetration rates in 1970 in programs related to the occupations included in the study with high and low earnings. These data are presented in Table 5.3.

There are more programs related to occupations that yield below-average earnings than there are programs offering preparation for jobs in fields with above-average earnings. Enrollments in the low-paying fields are generally a larger proportion of the employment in related occupations than in the high-paying fields. For instance, in the finance and credit programs offering training leading to employment in financial institutions, the vocational programs enrolled only four students for every 100 persons employed in these fields. The

---

*For a presentation of the agribusiness occupations, see National Committee on Employment Opportunities and Training Needs in Agribusiness, <u>Employment in Agriculture and Agribusiness Occupations</u>, Economic Research Service, U.S. Department of Agriculture, 1974.

TABLE 5.3

Enrollment-Employment Ratios in Programs Related to
Occupations with High and Low Earnings, 1970

	Enrollment per 100 Persons Employed in Related Occupations in 1970
Programs Related to High-Earnings Fields	
Finance and credit	4
General merchandising } Apparel and accessories	2
Hardware and building materials } Industrial marketing	1
Personnel, training, and related programs	3
Programs Related to Low-Earnings Fields	
Agricultural production	22
Landscaping	9
Practical nursing	16
Nurse's assistant	6
Medical assistant	3
Care and guidance of children	8
Clothing management } Dressmaking } Home furnishings	8
Accounting and computing	17
Stenography and secretarial	16
Typing	57
Cosmetology	8
Quantity food preparation	2
All programs studied	11

Note: "High" refers to occupations in which the median earnings of full-year workers in 1970 were at least 25 percent above the corresponding median for all occupations. "Low" refers to these with a 1970 median at least 25 percent below the national figure.

Source: See Table 5.1.

enrollment ratios were often several times greater in the programs preparatory to employment in occupations with below-average earnings. The two highest penetration rates were in the typing and agricultural production programs, suggesting that these programs serve a variety of interests in addition to training for the specific occupations directly related to them. The low penetration rates in the higher-paying, largely white-collar, fields imply a reluctance by the vocational-education system in the past to assign a heavy emphasis to programs whose graduates would frequently compete for jobs with persons possessing more elaborate educational credentials. However, the projections of enrollment and employment growth indicate an increase in enrollment-employment ratios in both well-paying and poorly paying fields. If both the enrollment and the employment projections were to materialize, much of the shift in enrollments would be from programs related to occupations with earnings significantly below the overall median to occupations more closely approximating the national average.

In the rapidly growing occupations, fields largely concerned with technological advance and health services, the penetration rates of the vocational programs are typically high with the exception of some of the health fields (see Table 2.4). Enrollment ratios are expected to grow in the fields in which employment is projected to increase by 100 percent or more during the 1970-85 period. The increases indicate that the vocational programs are likely to increase their share of the market in these high-growth fields in the coming decade. Aside from the courses training practical nurses and health aides, two rapidly growing fields with below-average earnings, the earnings in the high-growth fields are typically greater than the national median.

Although the federally supported vocational-education programs are concentrated in the high schools, they offer extensive training to persons beyond the normal high school leaving age. These courses are offered in postsecondary programs, often in community colleges or technical institutes, and in special adult programs. High school students made up approximately half, postsecondary close to a sixth, and adult students a third of all enrollments in the early 1970s. In terms of enrollments, accordingly, the vocational programs are involved with large numbers of persons who are, or could readily be, in the labor force.

The postsecondary and adult programs are concentrated in the health, technical, and trades and industry program areas. They made up three-fifths or more of the total enrollment in 1970 in the programs related to the study occupations in each of these areas. The programs intended for students who have left high school are frequently more

IMPLICATIONS

closely geared to specific occupations than are the high school programs. The better-paying fields, which typically require higher levels of education and occupational preparation, are often important in the programs for the more adult students. It is also apparent that a number of the programs offered to persons who are no longer in high school lead to careers with poor earnings and that, in some instances, the high school programs provide training for careers in the better-paying fields.

The concentration of the different program levels in areas related to high- and low-paying occupations is illustrated in Table 5.4.

Postsecondary and adult programs accounted for two-thirds or more of the enrollment in three of the four high-paying fields listed in Table 5.4. They also made up two-thirds or more of the enrollment in four of the low-paying occupations. The high school programs were less well represented in the high-paying areas. But they also constituted two-thirds or more of the enrollment in only three of the fields with low earnings. Two tendencies stand out in the distribution of enrollments by educational level in Table 5.4. One is the greater representation of the post-high school programs in the better-paid fields. The other is the substantial representation of both the high school and the post-high school enrollments in the poorly paid fields. Educational level, accordingly, is a poor discriminator of the earnings prospects associated with the different program levels.

WOMEN AND NONWHITES IN THE VOCATIONAL PROGRAMS

The responses of the vocational-education system to changes in the larger society are illustrated by the participation of women and nonwhites in the vocational programs. In both instances, social changes have generated pressures to increase the enrollment of students from these groups and to upgrade the occupational preparation available to them as a means for overcoming their disadvantaged status in the labor market.

Women and nonwhites make up two of the most rapidly growing segments of the labor force. Women are expected to constitute over two-fifths of the growth in the civilian labor force between 1970 and 1985, and nonwhites close to one-fifth.[6] The weight of the numbers involved, as well as the social and equity issues, suggest that decisions as to future directions in dealing with students from the two groups will have an important bearing on the role of vocational education as a change agent in implementing the nation's commitment to equal opportunity goals.

TABLE 5.4

Distribution of Enrollments by Program Level
in Vocational Programs Related to Occupations
with High and Low Earnings, 1970
(in percent)

Program	Distribution of Enrollments		
	Secondary	Postsecondary	Adult
Programs Related to High-Earnings Fields			
Finance and credit	20.7	7.2	72.1
General merchandising } Apparel and accessories	53.5	15.2	31.2
Hardware and building materials } Industrial marketing	29.4	19.5	15.1
Personnel, training, and related programs	16.5	32.1	51.4
Programs Related to Low-Earnings Fields			
Agricultural production	57.8	0.9	41.2
Landscaping	73.8	9.5	16.7
Practical nursing	8.7	70.6	20.7
Nurse's assistant	30.7	18.2	51.1
Medical assistant	12.0	58.5	29.5
Care and guidance of children	37.0	37.9	25.1
Clothing management } Dressmaking } Home furnishings	33.6	9.9	56.5
Accounting and computing	60.9	21.4	17.7
Stenography and secretarial	62.5	16.5	21.0
Typing	72.4	4.5	23.1
Cosmetology	66.5	23.6	9.9
Quantity food preparation	50.8	15.9	33.3
All programs related to study occupations	52.2	14.9	32.9

Notes: "High" and "low" are defined as in Table 5.3.
Details may not add to totals because of rounding.
Source: U.S. Office of Education, Enrollment in Vocational Education Occupational Programs, Vocational Education Information, No. 2, 1971.

Data on enrollments by race are unavailable for individual vocational programs. Office of Education reports indicate that blacks, American Indians, and Orientals accounted for a sixth of the overall vocational enrollments in 1972. A survey in the late 1960s reported that in their sample, the same proportion of black males as white males, 16 percent, had taken a high school concentration in the vocational program.[7] These data indicate that nonwhites are substantially represented in vocational programs. In the absence of more detailed information, the implications of the global figures on nonwhite participation are obscure. Increasing nonwhite enrollment in programs to enhance their work skills and earning capacity has received widespread support. Some blacks and others have dissented from this approach on the grounds that emphasis on vocational education as possessing a special significance for them has represented an effort "to increase the individual's labor value . . . within the context of second class citizenship."[8]

Recent court decisions spelling out the applicability of equal employment legislation to women imply that concern with expanding occupational choices for members of disadvantaged groups will become a more important issue in the next decade than in the past one.* The distribution of the vocational enrollments for women in 1970 and in the Office of Education projections for 1977 is summarized in Table 5.5. The table deals with enrollments in all programs, since data dealing only with the programs related to the occupations considered in the study are unavailable.

The information in Table 5.5. shows that planning in vocational education is concerned with increasing the occupational choices open to women in the next five or ten years. More women would be participating in trade and industry programs in 1977 than in 1970, and fewer would be enrolled in office occupation courses. These changes would take place in a setting in which the vocational enrollments in the past had been heavily concentrated in programs preparing women for jobs in the traditional female occupations. The preponderant concentration for women has been in programs preparing them for employment in clerical jobs. While the enrollment projections for women indicate an intention to give a lesser priority to this area, over half of the women in vocational programs intended as preparation for gainful employment in 1977 would still be enrolled in this one area.

---

*For a discussion of these changes, see Ruth G. Shaeffer, <u>Nondiscrimination in Employment, 1973-1975,</u> The Conference Board, Report No. 677.

TABLE 5.5

Distribution of Female Enrollments in Major Vocational
Program Areas, 1970 and Projected 1977
(in percent)

Program	Distribution of Female Enrollments	
	1970	1977
Agriculture	0.8	1.9
Distributive education	12.1	11.5
Health occupations	7.8	12.7
Office occupationa	68.8	59.1
Technical occupations	1.3	1.2
Trades and industry	9.2	13.6

Note: Home economics (gainful) has been omitted from this list because of the unavailability of detailed projections of enrollment by sex in 1977. In 1970 an estimated 5.9 percent of the female vocational enrollments were in gainful home economics programs related to the occupations considered in the study.

Source: U.S. Office of Education, Trends in Vocational Education, Fiscal Year 1972, Vocational Education Information, No. 2, 1973, and unpublished U.S. Office of Education data on enrollments by sex.

Encouraging women to prepare for employment in fields historically regarded as "women's jobs" eases the problem of placement for women in the vocational programs after they have left school. Since the traditionally female occupations provide earnings below the economy-wide median, preparation for employment in these fields typically prepares persons for jobs in the less well-paid areas. For example, based on the 1970 enrollment information in programs related to the study occupations, about 55 percent of all female vocational students were in programs offering training for employment in occupations in which the median earnings for full-year workers were less than three-fourths of the national figure. By comparison, about 25 percent of the males were enrolled in programs related to these more poorly paid fields. Contributing a large supply of new entrants to these jobs each year facilitates the continuation of the low earnings characterizing them. For a large majority of women, high school is the time that formal career planning and training take place. These plans, and the related occupational preparation, have frequently been oriented to preparing women for a short period of employment in anticipation of an extended or permanent withdrawal from the labor market. This emphasis helps to explain the importance attached to training leading to clerical jobs. The problem with the short-term career planning and the occupational preparation geared to it is the built-in tendency to overlook the far-reaching changes that have been taking place in female participation in the labor force. These changes are described by the data on female labor-force participation in Table 5.6.

The most important change in labor-force participation since 1960 has been an upsurge in the proportion of young women in the work force, and especially women in the typical childrearing ages. For example, by 1973 over half of all women in the 20- to 44-year age group were either at work or looking for a job. By the early 1970s, mothers with school-age children were about as likely to be in the labor force as were unmarried young women in the 1950s.[9] In addition, later age at marriage and the greater frequency of divorce have made for a larger number of unmarried women who work. Of those who leave because of childrearing responsibilities, many seek to return to work soon after their children are born or after they are off to kindergarten, nursery school, or the first grade. Reentry into jobs held before is sometimes impossible, and often offers few long-term career prospects. For women who do not withdraw from the labor force because of family responsibilities, jobs entered into on the basis of short-term planning horizons frequently lead to dead ends. These problems are underscored by a recent survey of women in the 30-to-44 age group.

TABLE 5.6

Labor-Force Participation by Women—1960, 1973,
and Projected 1985
(in percent)

Age Group	Women in Labor Force		
	1960	1973	Projected 1985
All ages	37.8	44.7	46.0
20-24	46.2	61.1	65.0
25-34	36.0	50.1	51.0
35-44	43.5	53.3	54.5

Source: Manpower Report of the President, 1975, p. 57.

The survey reported that with the passage of time more of these women had retrogressed in their careers than had progressed. In other words, they were occupying a lesser job category at the time of the survey than the first job held for six months after leaving school.[10]

"Women's need for a wider range of occupational choices," according to the 1975 Manpower Report of the President, "remains acute."[11] A comparable need is present for blacks and for members of other disadvantaged groups. The scope of the problem points to a need for retraining and upgrading programs for adults to prepare them for employment in new careers. It also indicates the desirability of guidance programs that expand occupational aspirations, of second-career counseling, and of continued greater shifts in the distribution of enrollments in the vocational programs. The transition from school to work has dominated much of the planning in vocational-education and manpower programs. Allowing for the importance of this transition, it is only one turning-point for women or other persons with a disadvantaged labor-market status. For women who leave the labor force and then seek to return, the transition back into employment can pose equally difficult problems. For many who are already employed, the transition from a job with few prospects to a more promising career can represent a major problem. The vocational-education systems have not created the underlying problems that lend weight to these transitions, nor are they likely, by themselves, to provide the remedy. More essentially, they have tended to take the occupational choices of the recent past as givens and have accommodated to them. Programs more heavily oriented toward the needs of women and nonwhites can facilitate enrollment growth in a period of declining school-age population and contribute significantly to achieving equal employment goals in the coming decade.

PRESSURES FOR AND AGAINST CHANGE

A series of pressures influences the priorities in vocational education that affect the occupations trained for and influence who enrolls in the program. There is the interest of employers in obtaining a work force possessing the skills needed for their operations, or equipped with the basic knowledge to acquire specific skills with minimum training costs after they have been hired. There are the pressures for change in national legislation assigning a high priority to meeting the economy's anticipated manpower needs and expanding services for the disadvantaged and the handicapped. These are frequently reinforced by social pressures affecting legislation, national policy, and public opinion. Third, there are the influences tending toward a

IMPLICATIONS

maintenance of the existing priorities; these arise out of the presence of already established programs representing substantial investments in facilities and equipment and with a tenured faculty. Finally, student interests in the education and avocational, as well as the career, aspects of vocational education are often important in program planning.

Each of these influences carries with it a program orientation, which sometimes overlaps and sometimes differs from the orientation implied by other pressures. Emphasis on serving the manpower needs of industry leads to an emphasis on training skilled workers and technicians in the school programs. Considerations of efficiency in this kind of training would frequently encourage an investment in resources for educating the more capable with a lesser emphasis on the disadvantaged and the handicapped. The social goals of serving the disadvantaged stress the importance of enrolling more persons who are frequently hard to reach and teach, and who typically possess limited educational and occupational aspirations. The aim of placing a larger number of persons from disadvantaged backgrounds in jobs is more readily realized in occupations involving lesser skills for which there are many openings than in highly skilled positions with few openings and lengthy preparations. The presence of an existing faculty and facilities, or student interest, may encourage the continued existence of programs in areas that lead to few jobs.

Whatever accommodations are arrived at in reconciling differences in objectives, the choices of occupations to train for will loom heavily in program planning in vocational education in the next decade. In terms of the specific occupations considered in the study, a number stand out as offering sufficient potential for priority consideration in the high school and post-high school programs to warrant separate mention. They are fields in which the median earnings of full-year workers are expected to amount to 75 percent or more of the economy-wide median by 1985, or to nearly $11,500 or more in that year. In addition, they are large enough to account individually for an annual average of 10,000 or more job openings in the 1970-85 period. Their educational level is expected to be similar to that of the vocational students, since half or more of the work force in each occupation is projected to have completed between 12 and 15 years of schooling. The anticipated job openings and the representation of women and nonwhites in the 35 occupations meeting these conditions in the mid-1980s are described in Table 5.7.

All told, the 35 occupations listed are expected to generate an average of over a million job openings a year in the 1970 to 1985 period. The extent to which they offer realistic prospects for an expansion of vocational-training efforts will vary from one locality to another. A priority for training programs oriented toward these occupa-

TABLE 5.7

Projected Annual Average Job Openings, 1970-85; and Representation of Women and Nonwhites in 1970, Selected Study Occupations

Occupation	Annual Average Job Openings, 1970-85	Women and Nonwhites in Occupational Work Force, 1970 (in percent)	
		Women	Nonwhites
Drafters	17,000	8	4
Electrical and electronic-engineering technicians	13,300	6	5
Engineering and science technicians, n.e.c.	29,700	18	5
Personnel and labor-relations workers	29,100	31	6
Registered nurses	70,300	97	9
Buyers, wholesale and retail trade	11,800	29	2
Managers and administrators, n.e.c.	247,500	12	3
Managers and superintendents, building	13,000	41	6
Restaurant, cafeteria, and bar managers	22,300	34	3
Sales managers and department heads, retail trade	18,900	24	7
Real-estate agents and brokers	26,900	32	2
Sales representatives, manufacturing	16,800	8	2
Sales representatives, wholesale	31,200	6	2
Sales workers, retail trade	21,400	13	3
Computer and peripheral equipment operators	14,400	29	9
Miscellaneous clerical workers	50,200	65	9
Payroll and timekeeping clerks	14,300	69	6
Shipping and receiving clerks	15,100	14	13
Statistical clerks	22,200	65	8
Stock clerks and storekeepers	27,300	22	11
Air-conditioning, heating, and refrigeration mechanics	12,200	1	5
Auto mechanics	29,000	1	8
Carpenters	40,100	1	6
Electricians	23,100	2	4
Foremen	51,800	8	5
Heavy-equipment mechanics, including diesel	31,100	2	5
Machinists	15,200	3	6
Plumbers and pipefitters	18,300	1	6
Bus drivers	13,800	28	15
Checkers, examiners, and inspectors, manufacturing	35,300	48	9
Cutting operatives, n.e.c.	11,400	26	3
Delivery and route workers	27,100	3	11
Welders and flame cutters	26,000	6	10
Firefighters	11,700	1	3
Police and detectives	19,300	4	7

Sources: U.S. Bureau of the Census, *1970 Census of Population, Occupational Characteristics*, and Conference Board projections.

IMPLICATIONS

tions would foster a shift in vocational education toward a greater emphasis on the more skilled white-collar, craft, and service fields. Most, but not all, are fields in which women and nonwhites are already present in modest or sizable numbers. The major exceptions are in skilled crafts for women and specialized sales and managerial fields for nonwhites. Programs geared toward the occupations cited, therefore, can both contribute to meeting anticipated manpower needs and expand career prospects for persons from disadvantaged or other backgrounds.

In light of the multiplicity of objectives influencing vocational enrollments, it is reasonable to expect that the relation between vocational enrollments and the economy's manpower requirements will often be a loose one. But, since the availability of workers with the skills in demand is one of the underlying factors affecting the magnitude and direction of economic change, vocational education has a role in facilitating economic growth. In turn, the primary gainers from a dynamic economy are likely to be persons from disadvantaged and low-income backgrounds for whom barriers become less formidable in an expanding economy. These considerations suggest that manpower implications, such as those treated in this report, will continue to provide a critical dimension in planning vocational programs reflecting the needs of students and the goals of society.

NOTES

1. Harold L. Wilensky, "Careers, Counseling, and the Curriculum," The Journal of Human Resources, Winter 1967, p. 32.

2. Nils Kellgren, "An Active Labor Market Policy," Memorandum to the Secretary of Labor, 1963, p. 61.

3. Wellford W. Wilms, Public and Proprietory Vocational Training (Berkeley: University of California Press, 1974), p. 173 ff.

4. Manpower Report of the President, 1975, pp. 203, 314.

5. U.S. Department of Labor, Bureau of Labor Statistics, The U.S. Economy in 1985, Bulletin 1809, 1974, p. 36.

6. Manpower Report of the President, 1975, pp. 206, 207, 312, 313.

7. Career Thresholds: A Longitudinal Study of the Educational and Labor Market Experience of Male Youth, Vol. 3 (1968 data), Bureau of the Census and Center for Human Resources Research, Ohio State University. Published as Manpower Research Monograph No. 6, Department of Labor, 1971.

8. W. N. Grubb, and M. Lazerson, "Vocational Education in American Schooling: Historical Perspectives," Inequality in Education, March 1974, p. 6.

9. Manpower Report of the President, 1975, p. 57.

10. U.S. Department of Labor Manpower Administration, Dual Careers, Manpower Research Monograph, No. 21, 1970, Vol. 1.

11. Manpower Report of the President, 1975, p. 71.

APPENDIX A:
THE NATIONAL PROJECTIONS
Richard J. Rosen

INTRODUCTION

This appendix is concerned with the data and data sources, projection techniques, and benchmark checks utilized in the development of the projections analyzed in the study. The study represents an effort to project a series of occupational characteristics including the educational, racial, and sexual composition of the occupational work force and their earnings. While there are many projections of job openings, no other projections are currently available for these characteristics for large numbers of detailed occupations.

Two alternative approaches to occupational projections are generally available. The first is to use a mathematical model of each occupation in which the characteristics considered are stratified by age, sex and race, and education cohorts, and these cohorts are projected. While this approach clarifies the assumptions and interactions involved, interoccupational mobility over time, shifts in trends, and informed judgment become difficult to incorporate into the framework. The Bureau of Labor Statistics recently stated, "There is no reliable method to effectively project occupational age distribution . . . [because of] . . . insufficient data on occupational mobility."[1]

The approach taken in this study was to use recent historical data, especially Census data and judgments concerning the impact of current developments as a basis for projecting the proportion of women, nonwhites, college graduates, and so on, in each occupation. Special attention was given to trends indicated by a comparison of the 1960 and 1970 Census findings, especially where these could be confirmed by more recent information. While the specific findings presented have been derived by a series of projection techniques, they are consistent with the model of the economy used as the basis for the Department of Labor's manpower projections. At each step in the process, the data was examined for their "reasonableness." Data from the Current Population Survey (CPS) was used to help identify turning-points in the trend for sex and race (data on educational attainment are not available by detailed occupation from the CPS) or to provide an additional point in time, 1973, beyond the Decennial Census.

The technique used in the projections was that of examining the percentage point rather than the percent change in the characteristic.

This has a considerable "tapering effect" on the projections. For example, the proportion of bank officials and financial managers who were women went from 8.7 percent to 17.4 percent from 1960 to 1970, an increase of 8.7 percentage points. Projecting this change to 1980 would give a 26.1 percent figure for women. An alternative projection method would be to look at the percent change in a variable over time. In the example above there has been a 100 percent increase in the proportion of women bank officials. This trend continued to 1980 would yield a 34.8 percent figure. Such geometric projections tend to magnify large changes as they are carried forward into the future and often provide results that appear unrealistic.

The benchmark check for the projections of sex, race, and educational attainment was to compare the estimates for the study occupations with independent projections of the labor force by these characteristics prepared by the Bureau of Labor Statistics (BLS). The procedure used here was to sum employment in the study occupations for a characteristic, for example number of persons completing less than 12 years of education, in 1960 and 1970 and subtract this total from the BLS total for all occupations to yield a "residual" group. This residual group was then projected to 1980 and 1985 (as a group) using the same technique as for an individual occupation. The residual and study occupations were then totaled for the projected years and compared with the BLS labor-force projections for the same characteristic. An error of not more than 10 percent was set as a criterion of reasonableness for the aggregates. The differential in most instances was considerably less than 10 percent.

The technique used in projecting earnings was to relate changes in constant dollar earnings in the individual occupations to changes in productivity. Median earnings for persons who worked 50-52 weeks in each of the census years was taken as the earnings base. The productivity measure used was constant dollar Gross Product Originating (GPO) per employee by industry. The technique used in making these projections and the criteria for selecting the occupations considered in the study are discussed in greater detail later in this appendix.

THE ECONOMIC FRAMEWORK FOR THE STUDY

In order to interpret the results of a study of occupational characteristics, it is necessary to have a basic economic and social frame-behind the projections. Such a framework not only allows the analyst to better understand the results, but also provides indications of how alternative assumptions about the economic environment might affect the projections. In addition, the aggregates in the framework can

THE NATIONAL PROJECTIONS

serve as benchmarks for assessing the consistency and reasonableness of the occupational projections.

The overall economic and demographic framework for the study is that published by the Bureau of Labor Statistics in 1974.[2] This model assumes an average annual GNP growth rate of 4.2 percent during the 1970-85 period, a return to full employment by 1980 (that is, an unemployment rate of 4 percent), total civilian labor-force growth of 1.7 percent per year, and annual productivity growth measured in terms of GNP per worker of 2.5 percent between 1970 and 1985.

One of the limiting factors to growth in the 1980s will be a decline in the number of young workers in the 14-to-24 age group, a decline of 3.3 million between 1980 and 1985. This is a result of declining birth rates during the 1960s. The decline in the number of young people is offset by an expected increase in the labor-force participation of women and nonwhites over the coming decade. The major indicators summarizing the economic framework are shown in Appendix C, Table C.1.

Changes in these economic assumptions would affect the projections in several ways. If the 4.2 percent GNP growth rate were not attained, the prospects for providing jobs to an expanding labor force would decrease. For instance, if the rate of unemployment were 6 percent instead of 4 percent, there would be close to 2 million fewer persons at work. Women and nonwhites could be expected to have substantially higher unemployment rates in this event, and it would be more difficult for them to penetrate into new fields. The anticipated productivity growth and earnings levels would also probably be lower if the assured GNP growth rate were not attained.

Unforeseen shifts in industrial composition—often reflecting changes in national priorities—can also influence the demand for workers in various occupations and skill levels. A high priority assigned to energy research, development, and production would require a different mix of manpower than a high priority for, say, improving health care through national health insurance. The BLS is currently preparing projections based on alternative assumptions regarding unemployment and energy use in order to assess the economic and manpower impact of such changes more fully.

SELECTING THE OCCUPATIONS FOR STUDY

The study is concerned with the occupations that are either related to major vocational programs or are regarded as offering good prospects for future vocational programs. Occupations of a professional nature that generally require a four-year college degree or more were excluded as outside the sphere of the vocational-education system. Engineers, teachers, and physicians are examples. At the other end of the scale, occupations requiring little or no formal training, for which the majority of workers have less than a high school education, were also omitted. Janitors, maids, and ushers are illustrations.

This discussion suggests the need for a selection process for determining which occupations are within the scope of the vocational system. One of the selection criteria was that all occupations related to "major" vocational programs be included in the study. A projected enrollment level of 35,000 by 1977, according to U.S. Office of Education estimates, was used as the cutoff level of a major program. This resulted in the selection of about 50 vocational programs which are expected to account for over 80 percent of public vocational enrollments by 1977. These programs were related to 100 Census occupational titles. Nonprofessional occupations that did not meet the enrollment criterion were included if they appeared to be prospective candidates for vocational programs. These other occupations were selected on the basis of the current educational attainment of the workers in the occupation; their earnings level; and the projected number of job openings. Occupations not related to major vocational programs were included in the study if: (1) at least one-third of the work force in the occupation in 1970 had between 12 and 15 years of schooling; (2) the median earnings of full-year workers in 1970 were at least three-fourths of the national median for all occupations; and (3) an annual average of at least 10,000 job openings were expected in the occupation between 1970 and 1985. All three of these criteria had to be met for inclusion of occupations that did not meet the enrollment criterion.

The educational criterion implies that the current and future educational makeup of the occupation would be similar to that of the vocational graduates. The earnings cutoff suggests that the occupation should provide a reasonable prospect for decent earnings. The job openings standard assures that the number of jobs in the occupation over the next decade would be substantial enough to warrant attention by vocational educators. Twenty-three additional occupational titles were selected on the basis of meeting all three of these criteria.

Several vocational programs or census occupations were excluded although they met the standards discussed. These were programs or occupations that generally correspond to the "all other programs" designation in a vocational field or the "not elsewhere classified" occupations in a census group. In these cases, it is impossible to relate the vocational program to a specific occupation or family of

THE NATIONAL PROJECTIONS   101

related occupations, or the occupation to a particular program. All
told, the 123 occupations remaining after the exclusions accounted
for 55 percent of total civilian employment in 1970.

DATA AND DATA SOURCES

The basic data for the study relate to the characteristics of occupations and the people employed in them. Data on vocational enrollments and completions in programs related to the occupations also figure in the study. The data used come primarily from sources in the Bureau of Labor Statistics, the Bureau of the Census, and the U.S. Office of Education. Both published and unpublished materials were obtained from the agencies, including special counts from the 1 percent Public Use Samples from both the 1960 and 1970 Decennial Census.

Table A.1 identifies all of the various sources used for each data element and the information obtained. The Decennial Census provides historical data on the occupations and their characteristics. More recent data are available on an annual basis on the distribution of employment by race and sex from the Current Population Survey, but this information was often of limited value for individual occupations because of the small sample size. Projections of the educational attainment, race, and sex makeup of the aggregate labor force are available from Bureau of Labor Statistics published sources along with productivity data required to make earnings projections for the occupations.

Published data are generally sufficient for most of the occupational-characteristics information. Special tabulations from the 1970 Census were required to identify race and educational attainment by occupation for the under-35 group. A special tabulation from the 1960 Census was required to identify educational attainment for that year by detailed occupation. The published and unpublished data sources are summarized in Table A.1.

COMPARABILITY OF OCCUPATIONAL DATA
FROM VARIOUS SOURCES

As can be seen from the discussion of data and data sources, many sources were used to obtain the various types of occupational information needed for the study. It is therefore important to show where there is consistency among the sources and where adjustments were made to aid in maintaining consistency. Some data sources are deemed more reliable than others. Other series may have certain

TABLE A.1

Data Sources and Information Obtained for Occupational Characteristics Study

Data Sources	Information Obtained
Employment and job openings	
U.S. Dept. of Labor, Bureau of Labor Statistics, unpublished Occupation-by-Industry Matrix.	Nation-wide employment by occupation, 1970, 1980, and 1985.
U.S. Dept. of Labor, Bureau of Labor Statistics, Tomorrow's Manpower Needs, Supplement No. 4, 1974.	Separation rates by occupations, 1970, 1985.
U.S. Dept. of Commerce, Bureau of the Census, Census of Population, 1970, Detailed Characteristics: U.S. Summary, PC (1) - D1	Nation-wide employment by occupation, 1960, 1970.
Sex and race	
U.S. Dept. of Labor, Bureau of Labor Statistics	Unpublished data on employment by race and sex for detailed occupational titles from Current Population Survey 1960-73, selected years.
U.S. Dept. of Commerce, Bureau of the Census, Census of Population, 1970, Detailed Characteristics: U.S. Summary, PC (1) - D1; and Subject Report, Occupational Characteristics, PC (2) - 7A.	Employment by sex, 1960, 1970 and employment by race 1970 for detailed occupations.
U.S. Dept. of Commerce, Bureau of the Census, Census of Population, 1960, Subject Report, Occupational Characteristics, PC (2) - 7A.	Employment by race, 1960, for detailed occupations.
Unpublished tabulations from 1970 Census.	Employment by race, 1970, for detailed occupations.

Educational attainment

U.S. Dept. of Labor, Bureau of Labor Statistics, Educational Attainment of Workers, 1959, Special Labor Force Report No. 1; and Educational Attainment of Workers, March 1969, 1970, Special Labor Force Report No. 125.

Nation-wide employment by level of educational attainment, 1959, 1970.

U.S. Dept. of Labor, Manpower Report of the President, 1974.

Projected educational attainment for the labor force, 1980, 1990.

U.S. Dept. of Commerce, Bureau of the Census, Census of Population, 1970, Subject Report, Occupational Characteristics, PC (2) - 7A.

Educational attainment for all age groups by detailed occupation, 1970.

Unpublished tabulations from 1970 Census.

Educational attainment for under-35 age group by detailed occupation, 1960.

Unpublished tabulations from 1960 Census.

Educational attainment for all ages and under-35 age group by detailed occupation, 1960.

Earnings

U.S. Dept. of Commerce, Bureau of the Census, Census of Population, 1960, Subject Report, Occupational Characteristics, PC (2) - 7A; and Census of Population, 1970 Occupational Characteristics, PC (2) - 7A.

Median earnings by detailed occupation, persons working 50-52 weeks, 1960, 1970.

U.S. Dept. of Labor, Bureau of Labor Statistics, The U.S. Economy in 1985, Bulletin No. 1809, 1974.

Productivity data by industry; disposable personal income per worker, 1960, 1970, 1980, 1985.

Unpublished data, U.S. Dept. of Labor, Bureau of Labor Statistics.

Productivity data by industry, 1960, 1970, 1980, 1985.

Source: Compiled by author.

years or pieces missing. A final area of difficulty arises in moving from occupations and employment data to the vocational-program data related to the occupations.

The Decennial Census provides the bulk of the occupational characteristics detail required for the study. However, there are problems of comparability between the Census definitions for different years. The 1960 Census contained information on some 250 occupational titles, while in 1970 this number was expanded to almost 450. The new titles sometimes come from the splitting-off of an occupation into several occupations. For example, the occupation "linemen and servicemen, telegraph, telephone, and power" in 1960 became three occupations in 1970—"telephone installers and repairers," "electric power line and cable workers," and "telephone line and splicing workers." New titles also come about by breaking out occupations from the "not elsewhere classified" (n.e.c.) designations. "Computer programmers," for example, were not identified separately in 1960, but were included with "professional, technical, and kindred workers, n.e.c."; just as "precision machine operators," such as "drill press," "lathe and milling," and "punch and stamping press" were included in the "operatives and kindred workers, n.e.c." designation in 1960.

"Cross matching" of occupational titles between different Censuses is possible because a special retabulation of the 1960 Census according to 1970 occupational titles and definitions was undertaken by the Census Bureau.[3] This retabulation was done by sex so that complete comparability exists for this characteristic. For the other characteristics (race, education, and earnings), about two-thirds of the occupations studied (covering about 80 percent of employment) have directly comparable data for both years from the Census. For the other occupations, procedures were developed for making the projections adapted to the data requirements in each instance.

Data from the Current Population Survey (CPS), the monthly household survey conducted for the Bureau of Labor Statistics, proved to be of limited value in this study. While the occupational definitions used in the CPS are the same as for the Census, the small sample size often causes inconsistent changes in the proportion of women and nonwhites in individual occupations. For example, the proportion of practical nurses who were nonwhite jumped from 20 percent in 1962 to 27 percent by 1965, returned to 23 percent in the 1968 CPS, and was 25 in 1970 and 24 in 1973. The CPS data were consulted in particular instances where more information than the Decennial Census could provide was desirable. For example, if the 1960-70 change in the proportion of women was substantial, the CPS data were consulted for confirmation and any indication of change in that trend when comparing the 1960-65 period with the 1965-70 or the 1970-73 periods.

Also, for those occupations that did not appear in the 1960 Census, the CPS was consulted as it provided an additional point of reference, 1973, for the occupations. The CPS does not provide comprehensive earnings and educational attainment data by detailed occupations, and therefore was not consulted for these indicators.

The BLS national Occupation-by-Industry Matrix provides current and projected employment-by-occupation data, and this source is widely used in manpower planning. BLS uses the same occupational titles and definitions as Census and relies heavily on the Census data by occupation and industry. The BLS, however, incorporates special studies and surveys, information from professional associations, and the CPS data into the Matrix to obtain the "best estimate" of occupational employment. Because the BLS Matrix was used as the basis for the long-run employment projections, baseline demographic data from the Decennial Census must be adjusted to the BLS control totals for consistency. That is, the estimated number employed in an occupation in the 1970 Census may be slightly different than the corresponding figure in the BLS Matrix because other sources of data were used or because of other adjustments made by BLS. The demographic characteristics data for the occupation taken from the Census must, therefore, be scaled up or down to match the BLS Matrix total.

A critical link for this study relates the occupational indicators derived from a Census-BLS Matrix base to the vocational programs that prepare individuals for employment. This link has been made by the BLS and has been used in this study.[4] Any linkage between training and employment is likely to be imperfect. Some Office of Education vocational-program titles are related to what appear to be quite different occupations. For instance, the occupations listed as related to the advertising-services program include economists and decorators and window dressers. Another difficulty is that an occupation may be related to a number of different programs. For example, radio and TV mechanics and repairers are trained in the electronic technology program, as well as in the trades and industry area.

A final area of difficulty in the linkage is that the Office of Education data on enrollments are not always on the same level of detail as the BLS matching occupations. Where necessary, occupations and programs have been combined to fit the available data.

PROJECTION TECHNIQUES

Job Openings

Job openings in this report refer to average annual job openings in the 1970-85 period. There are two components in the average annual job openings—employment growth and attrition. An average annual concept is used because it would be misleading and probably inaccurate to estimate job openings in a single year, given the fluctuations in the business cycle. The employment data that provide the point of departure for the job-openings projections are the BLS estimates for the same year; no independent projections of employment by occupation have been undertaken.

Along with projections of occupational employment, the BLS has published rates of "separation" from the labor force for each occupation for 1970 and projected 1985. (See Table A.1.) These rates include separations owing to deaths and retirements for men; deaths, retirements, marriage, childbearing, and "other" reasons for women. The rates are "age-specific," with the rates for each age applied to the age distribution in the occupation in 1970 as reported in the Decennial Census to obtain an overall rate for the occupation. This figure is used to derive the attrition component in the job-openings figure.

These figures may be regarded as minimal figures for job openings because many of the elements of turnover are not included. This would include voluntary separations or "quits" as well as involuntary separations or layoffs. Job openings created by promotion are also not included. Job openings in the apprentice occupations may be understated because they do not include replacement of those persons who graduate to journeyman status.

Perhaps the greatest difficulty with the separation rate concept is that it treats, say, a 55-year-old male coal miner and a 55-year-old male teacher alike in estimating the chances of death or retirement. That is, the separation rates are derived from average working life statistics by age and sex and these rates are assumed to be the same for different occupations. They do not take into account the hazardousness of a job or the retirement practices in a particular industry. However, most occupations and industries do not differ greatly in separation rates, and research has indicated that the labor-force-wide separation rates are generally reliable.[5]

Sex and Race

The projections presented of the sex and race employment distribution by occupation are essentially surprise-free in that they are substantially influenced by recent trends. Underlying any trend is a series of often complex and conflicting forces. Why does the proportion of women in an occupation increase or decrease? Why are nonwhites increasing their representation more rapidly in some occupations than in others?

THE NATIONAL PROJECTIONS   107

For instance, is employment for women bus drivers growing more rapidly than for men because of the large demand for school bus drivers, a position unattractive to adult men because it is typically part-time and thus less lucrative? Are nonwhites making inroads into the health occupations because these occupations are growing rapidly, and therefore must take all qualified applicants to avert manpower bottlenecks, or have the low wages deterred white job-seekers who feel they can earn more in a different career? The underlying explanations cannot be projected, and the projections, unless otherwise stated, assume that the institutional or other factors that have caused a particular pattern of change in the past 15 years will continue.

The projection technique was to start with a straight-line trend extrapolation of the percentage-point change in employment based on the 1960 and 1970 Census. Stock and bond sales agents serve as an example of a projection that remained a straight-line projection. The proportion of women increased from 6 percent to 8.6 percent from 1960 to 1970 and is projected to increase to 11.2 percent by 1980 and to 12.5 percent by 1985.

Many factors were then considered in arriving at a final projection. Was the proportion of nonwhites increasing especially rapidly when overall employment in the occupation grew rapidly? If so, is the occupation expected to continue to grow rapidly? If its rate of growth is expected to taper off according to the BLS projections, should the rate of penetration of nonwhites also diminish? Job and die setters serves as such an instance. The representation of nonwhites in this occupation increased from 2.3 to 5.5 percent from 1960 to 1970. Total employment grew by 60 percent during the same period. A straight-line projection would place the proportion of nonwhites at almost 9 percent in 1980. However, total employment growth is expected to increase by only 35 percent during the 1970 to 1980 period, or by less than two-thirds of the historical rate. The proportion of nonwhites was, therefore, adjusted downward to 7.2 percent in 1980 and to 8.1 percent by 1985.

There are alternative approaches to the procedures outlined above. The method commonly used to project labor-force or population aggregates is to divide the population into age, race, and sex cohorts, and "age" the population over time. There are numerous technical problems associated with this approach when it is used for individual occupations. This procedure assumes a closed population for each occupation, where older workers die or retire and younger workers enter to replace them or to take new positions as the occupation grows in size. In reality, there is a constant flow among occupations. A 35-year-old machinist may be a foreman by age 45 and no longer be counted in the machinist occupation. A 25-year-old grinding-machine operator may be promoted to take his place. For these reasons, this technique is seldom used for individual occupational projections.

Special projections were prepared for the 16-to-34-year-old population in each occupation. Since this younger age group supplies the bulk of the new entrants into the labor force it should be a significant indicator of future changes in the representation of women and nonwhites in different occupations. The procedure utilized in projecting the under-35 age group was to relate the change in this group to movements in the "all-ages group" over time. The steps in preparing these projections are described in Table A.2.

TABLE A.2

Projecting the Distribution of Employment by Race in the 16-34 Age Group

Step	1960 White	1960 Non-White	1970 White	1970 Non-White	1980 White	1980 Non-White
1. Historical distribution of employment						
All ages (percent)	90	10	88	12	—	—
16-34 age group (percent)	85	15	80	20	—	—
2. Historical ratio of 16-34 age group to all ages	.94	1.50	.91	1.67		
3. Projected ratio of 16-34 age group to all ages	—	—	—	—	.88	1.84
4. Derived distribution of employment for 16-34 age group (percent)	—	—	—	—	76	26
5. Adjusted distribution of employment for 16-34 age group (percent)	—	—	—	—	75	25

Sources: U.S. Department of Labor, Bureau of Labor Statistics, Conference Board projections.

THE NATIONAL PROJECTIONS

Initially, the historical relationship between the 16-to-34 component and all ages for the occupation was computed (step 2, Table A.2). This relationship was extended to 1980 and 1985 on a straight-line basis (step 3). This ratio was applied to the projected proportion of whites and nonwhites (or men and women) to derive an initial distribution by race (or sex) for the 16-to-34-year-old group (step 4). The distribution was then "scaled" to equal 100 percent (step 5).

Using this procedure, it was found that there were few changes in the relationship between the all-ages group and the younger age group during the 1960 to 1970 period. The under-35 group did generally have a greater representation of nonwhites and women, however, suggesting progress toward more nearly equal representation in recent years. However, this comparison is limited since the "all-ages" group also includes the "under-35" group in proportions varying substantially from occupation to occupation.

As previously mentioned, the special retabulation of the 1960 Census provides complete comparability between the 1960 and 1970 Censuses for the occupational employment distribution by sex. However, gaps remain in the 1960 data indicating occupational representation by race. In such cases, projections were made based on the expected changes in similar occupations or groups of occupations, and on the most recent CPS data for the occupation. For occupations split off from 1960 titles, the 1970 data were recombined according to the 1960 definition. This occupation was then projected as a "regular" occupation, with the desired occupations "broken out" for the projected years. To cite an instance, salesclerks and salesworkers were combined to conform with the 1960 occupational title; or sales managers and department heads were used to project buyers, wholesale and retail trade; payroll and timekeeping clerks were used to project billing clerks. There are 31 occupations without any specific 1960 race data; however, they account for only 11 percent of the projected 1985 employment in the occupations studied.

The projections were tested for overall reasonableness by comparing projected employment by sex and by race with the BLS labor-force projections. The objective here was to determine whether the procedures utilized yielded results consistent with BLS projections for the entire economy. The steps were as follows:

1. Sum employment by sex and race for the occupations studied for 1960 and 1970.
2. Subtract this sum from the total employment by sex and race in all U.S. occupations in 1960 and 1970 to obtain the aggregate characteristics distribution of the residual occupations.

3. Project the proportion of men, women, whites, and nonwhites in the residual occupations to 1980 and 1985 using the same technique used for the individual occupations.
4. Apply the proportions obtained in step 3 to the BLS-projected total employment in the residual occupations for 1980 and 1985 to obtain estimated employment by sex and race for the residual occupations.
5. Sum projected employment by sex and by race for the occupations studied for 1980 and 1985.
6. Add the projections for the individual occupations and the residual group to obtain a derived estimate of total employment by sex and race.
7. Compare the estimate of total employment derived in this way with BLS-projected employment by sex and race.

The derived projections of employment by sex and race were well within 10 percent of the BLS projection, and the projections were therefore accepted as reasonable.

Table A.3 summarizes the benchmark check for sex and race. The 123 study occupations have a smaller representation of women than the entire economy. However, the proportion of women in these occupations was increasing during the 1960s and this percentage is projected to exceed slightly the overall representation figure by 1985. The reverse trend is evident in the residual, or nonstudy, occupations. By 1985, almost 60 percent of all employed women are expected to be at work in the occupations studied, up from 53 percent in 1970. The proportion of all men employed in the occupations is projected to decline slightly. Significantly, the derived total employment for males and for the overall economy is within 1 percent of the BLS total.

As mentioned earlier, consistent 1960 data on employment by race were not available for all of the occupations included in the study. Therefore, only 92 study occupations are utilized in the benchmark check. The remaining occupations appear in the residual group. The 92 occupations account for 90 percent of employment in the study occupations and should therefore serve as a valid benchmark comparison. Nonwhites were underrepresented in the occupations studied but were increasing their representation during the 1960-70 period. This trend is projected to continue. The residual group had proportionally more nonwhites than the overall labor force but is declining. This trend is expected to be reversed slightly by 1985, as the representation of nonwhites in the overall economy is projected by BLS to increase much more rapidly during the 1970-85 period than in the 1960s. As with the sex projections, the derived aggregate employment figures by race were within the 10 percent margin regarded as reasonable. The derived total for nonwhite employment was 6 percent less than the

TABLE A.3

Reconciliation of Employment Estimates by Sex and Race for Study Occupations with BLS Estimates of Total Employment—1960, 1970, and Projected 1985 (in thousands)

	Study[b] Occupations	Residual Occupations	Derived Total, All U.S. Occupations	BLS Total, All U.S. Occupations[a]	Derived Total All U.S. Occupations as a Percent of BLS Total	Study Occupations as a Percent of BLS Total
Sex						
1960						
Male	26,700	17,204	—	43,904	—	—
Female	9,912	11,962	—	21,874	—	—
1970						
Male	27,815	21,169	—	48,984	—	—
Female	15,585	14,057	—	29,642	—	—
1985						
Male	34,045	27,349	61,394	61,902	99.0	54.0
Female	23,191	16,905	40,096	39,588	101.0	34.0
Race						
1960						
White	31,749	27,101	—	58,850	—	—
Nonwhite	2,339	4,589	—	6,928	—	—
1970						
White	35,879	34,302	—	70,182	—	51.0
Nonwhite	3,125	5,320	—	8,445	—	37.0
1985						
White	45,630	44,047	89,677	88,869	101.0	51.0
Nonwhite	5,173	6,640	11,813	12,621	94.0	41.0

[a] BLS projections are for the labor force. They have been adjusted to reflect employment by sex and race based on the historical differential between their respective unemployment rates and the BLS overall unemployment rate of 4 percent in 1985.

[b] Refers to employment in 92 study occupations for which 1960 data were available.

Sources: U.S. Department of Labor, Bureau of Labor Statistics; Conference Board projections.

BLS projection, and for whites the independently derived total was 1 percent greater.

Tabulations from the 1973 and 1974 Current Population Survey by the BLS indicate that the projected representation of women and nonwhites in the occupations are not unrealistic in light of labor-market developments since the 1970 Census. A list of selected major occupations studied follows, showing the proportion of women and nonwhites in 1970 according to the Census, the 1973 and 1974 CPS, and Conference Board projections for 1980. While one or two years' CPS data based on small samples in individual occupations are far from conclusive, the CPS figures are generally consistent with the 1970 to 1980 projections. The comparison is presented in Table A.4.

Educational Attainment

Projections of educational attainment in the occupations were prepared in a similar manner to those for employment by sex and race. Projections are presented both for the all-ages group and for those in the 16-34 age group. The data for the projections come from both published and unpublished data from the 1960 and 1970 Census. There is no published educational attainment by detailed occupation data in the 1960 Census, and the data for the 16-34 age group in 1970 are published only for a limited number of specific occupations. Special tabulations from the Census Public Use Tapes were utilized to provide counts of educational attainment for these groups.

The breakdowns utilized for the study were: (1) those completing less than 12 years; (2) 12-15 years; and (3) 16 or more years of schooling. This classification makes it possible to identify the number of high school dropouts in an occupation and the potential competition from college graduates, and to focus on the prime target group for vocational education—those with between 12 and 15 years of schooling.

More than for the distribution of employment by race and sex, educational attainment is a function of the age distribution of the population. That is, younger workers, regardless of sex or race, tend to have higher levels of education than older workers. Accordingly, if an occupation has a large proportion of older workers who will die or retire over the next 15 years, the educational level can be expected to increase rapidly. This will be especially true if the occupation is expected to grow and many new and younger workers are attracted to it.

Other factors that will influence future changes in educational attainment levels will be the rate of technological change and anticipated demographic shifts in the labor force. Technological change

TABLE A.4

Distribution of Women and Nonwhites in Selected Occupations—1970 Census, 1973 and 1974 Current Population Survey, and 1980 Projections
(in percent)

Occupation	1970 Census		1973 Current Population Survey		1974 Current Population Survey		1980 Projections	
	Women	Nonwhites	Women	Nonwhites	Women	Nonwhites	Women	Nonwhites
Computer programmers	22.7	5.5	21.9	4.8	22.6	N.A.	20.0	6.8
Registered nurses	97.4	9.0	97.8	10.0	98.0	10.1	97.3	11.5
Draftsmen	8.0	4.4	7.8	5.8	7.7	6.7	10.5	6.5
Real-estate agents and brokers	32.3	2.2	36.4	1.5	38.3	N.A.	31.8	2.3
Bookkeepers	82.1	3.6	88.3	4.1	89.2	4.4	80.8	5.7
Secretaries	97.6	3.9	99.1	5.6	99.2	5.1	98.3	5.7
Carpenters	1.3	6.2	0.7	5.5	N.A.	6.1	2.2	7.1
Electricians	1.7	3.6	0.6	4.1	N.A.	4.5	2.7	5.1
Auto mechanics	1.4	8.5	0.5	8.9	N.A.	7.7	2.4	9.6
Assemblers	48.7	13.4	49.7	14.0	50.1	14.3	51.4	15.9
Welders	5.7	10.2	4.7	11.6	5.0	9.8	6.9	14.0
Bus drivers	28.3	15.3	36.2	19.6	37.4	20.4	43.0	19.4

Note: N.A. = Not Available.
Sources: U.S. Department of Labor, Bureau of Labor Statistics; The Conference Board estimates.

frequently displaces workers in less skilled occupations who have lower education levels (farm laborers, textile workers, and others), and generates new demands for workers with higher educational levels (computer programmers, aerospace engineers, health technologists, and others). The demographic shift is expected to result in a reduction in the number of young people in the population, particularly during the 1980-85 period. This shift, coupled with a tapering-off in the college-enrollment rate for young people, implies a slowing down in the rate of increase of educational levels in general and of college graduates in particular.*

While it would have been desirable to project the age distribution in each occupation by educational attainment group, in order to take account explicitly of the factors influencing changes in educational levels in an occupation, consideration of interoccupational mobility raise many questions about the relevance of this procedure.

First approximations for projections were developed by extending out the percentage point change in the three education groups to 1980 and 1985. The magnitudes of change in many cases are quite dramatic, especially declines in the percent completing less than 12 years. In some cases, continuing the trend would lead to a negative number. For example, the proportion of stock and bond sales agents with less than 12 years of education declined from 19 to 8 percent from 1960 to 1970. In this case, the rate of decline between 1960 and 1970 rather than the percentage point change was used as the first approximation for the group. Proportions were then scaled to 100 percent as needed.

The next step was to apply the percentages to the BLS-projected employment for 1980 and 1985 and compute percent changes for each group. These percent changes were then scrutinized for excesses. They were compared with the 1960-70 changes in the occupation and with anticipated changes in the entire labor-force educational levels between 1970 and 1985, as projected by the BLS.

A consistent pattern in the occupations emerges where the number completing less than 12 years of school declines, and the number completing 12-15 and 16 or more years rises. Fairly large changes can and do occur in the occupations. It should be remembered that more than half of those employed in a particular occupation by 1985 will often not have been in that occupation in 1970. Employment growth increases employment by between 1 and 2 percent a year in most oc-

---

*See Appendix C, Table C.1 for the population shift. See Richard B. Freeman, "Overinvestment in College Training," The Journal of Human Resources, Summer 1975, 287-311 for a discussion of the shift in college enrollment patterns.

THE NATIONAL PROJECTIONS   115

cupations, and the need to replace workers who die or retire each
year is of the order of magnitude of 3 percent a year. Compounded
over a 10-to 15-year period, the number of new workers in an occupation is obviously substantial. The educational attainment of this
new group is generally different than those already employed in the
occupation. Interoccupational shifts further reduce the number of
workers who remain in the same occupational classification over time.
    Projections for the 16-34 age group were then made using the
same method as was used for sex and race. That is, the ratio of the
16-34 group to the all-ages group for 1960 and 1970 was computed for
each educational attainment cohort and extended to 1980 and 1985.
The projected ratios were applied to the projections already prepared
for the all-ages group, and the derived proportions scaled to 100 percent. This younger age group may better reflect the characteristics
of new entrants into occupations, and, therefore, the type of competition faced by graduates of vocational programs. A benchmark check
of the educational attainment projections, using the BLS projections
for the labor force, was undertaken making use of the same methodology as described in the section on sex and race. Ninety-two of the
study occupations were used, since the remaining occupations did not
have 1960 educational attainment data.
    The historical data indicate that the occupations studied have
relatively fewer college graduates than the entire labor force and pro-
portionately more persons with less than a college degree. The residual occupations show the opposite trend. This is to be expected
since the residual group includes many more professional, technical,
and managerial occupations. The projection of the residual occupations to 1985 indicate the proportion without a high school diploma in
the group will approach that for the entire labor force. The gap between the proportion completing college in the occupations studied and
the residual occupations is expected to widen. Summing the residual
group projection and the study occupations for 1985 and comparing the
derived total with the total projected by BLS; the margins of difference
are well within the 10 percent range deemed as acceptable. The largest error, five percentage points, occurs in the smallest group—the
college graduates.
    Table A.5 provides the data for the benchmark check.

Earnings

    The projections of earnings are the most hypothetical of the in-
dicators presented. Future earnings in occupations depend on a variety of factors. Shifts in the supply and demand for workers with the

TABLE A.5

Reconciliation of Estimates of Employment by Level of Educational Attainment for Occupations Studied with BLS Estimates—1960, 1970, and Projected 1985

	1960			1970			1985		
	Less than 12 Years	12-15 Years	16 Years or More	Less than 12 Years	12-15 Years	16 Years or More	Less than 12 Years	12-15 Years	16 Years or More
BLS total, all U.S. occupations*									
Number	33,086	26,246	6,446	29,249	39,628	9,750	23,952	58,255	19,283
Percent Distribution	50.3	39.9	9.8	37.2	50.4	12.4	23.6	57.4	19.0
Study occupations									
Number	17,851	14,317	1,918	14,996	21,390	2,619	11,536	34,810	4,458
Percent Distribution	52.4	42.0	5.6	38.5	54.8	6.7	22.7	68.5	8.8
Residual occupations									
Number	15,235	11,919	4,528	14,253	19,235	7,131	11,658	25,242	13,786
Percent Distribution	48.1	37.6	14.3	35.1	47.3	17.6	23.0	49.8	27.2
Derived total, all U.S. occupations									
Number	—	—	—	—	—	—	23,194	60,052	18,244
Percent Distribution	—	—	—	—	—	—	22.8	59.2	18.0
Derived total, all U.S. occupations as a percent of BLS total	—	—	—	—	—	—	97.0	103.0	95.0
Study occupations as a percent of BLS total	54	55	30	51	54	27	48	60	23

*1960 figures for all occupations are interpolated from 1959 and 1962 BLS data as 1960 data are not available. Both 1960 and 1970 figures were adjusted to include 16- and 17-year-olds who were not included in the BLS data base until 1972 and are included in their projections. Of this group, 96 percent were assigned to the under-12-years-of-schooling category and 4 percent to the 12-15-years category based on the 1972 BLS data. In 1970 the distribution without the 16- and 17-year-olds was 34.8%, 52.3%, and 12.9% for those completing less than 12, 12-15, and 16 years or more of schooling, respectively.

Sources: 1975 Manpower Report of the President; 1960 and 1970 Census of Population; The Conference Board.

requisite skills, the presence or absence of unions, and the rate of growth in productivity in industries employing persons in different occupations are prime factors influencing earnings. Allowing for all of these factors, over time, productivity increases may be regarded as the means by which industry is able to pay increased wages. As workers produce more per unit of labor input, resources are generated that allow for increased compensation. Productivity changes may be reflected in market-determined wages, and, also, in gains from collective bargaining. It is this latter concept, therefore, that should serve as the basis for long-term projections of real earnings.

An important factor affecting wages is the rate of inflation. Since money-wage rates in some industries are more closely indexed to inflation than others through such means as automatic cost-of-living adjustments, "constant-dollar" projections, as in the present study, provide an imperfect approximation of changes in real wages.

The procedure utilized in making the projections is as follows:

1. Each occupation was linked to an industry where the majority of workers were employed.
2. Historical and projected productivity data for the industries were compiled from BLS published and unpublished sources; constant-dollar Gross Product Originating (GPO) per employee was used for this purpose.
3. The ratio of median earnings for workers working 50 to 52 weeks in the occupation to GPO per employee was computed for 1960 and 1970, and projected to 1985.
4. The projected ratio was then applied to the BLS projections of GPO for the industry to derive projected median earnings.

The ratio of median earnings to GPO per employee was projected to 1980 and 1985 by using a logarithmic function; assigning a value of 1 for 1960, 11 for 1970, and projecting the ratio for year 21 (1980) and year 26 (1985). The equation took the form of:

$$RJ\ 85 = RJ\ 60 + B\ (\log 26)$$

where RJ is the ratio of earnings to GOP for occupation J, and B is the difference in the 1960 and 1970 ratios for occupation J.

The use of a logarithmic formulation is particularly suitable to time-trend analysis, especially since only two points in time were available. This could result in inaccurate measurement of trend if either year is an aberrant one, either on the earnings or productivity side. Since log functions tend to "taper off" geometric trends, such aberrant measurements would be moderated.

Table A.6 outlines the industries and related occupations used in the projection procedure.

TABLE A.6

Industrial Sectors Supplying Productivity Benchmarks for Earnings Projections in Related Occupations

Industrial Sector	Related Occupations
Agriculture	Farm owners, managers, foremen, and laborers; farm implement mechanics
Manufacturing	All nonmedical technician occupations included in study; All craft workers and operatives, except transportation, included in study (except as specified individually); sales representatives, manufacturing
Durable manufacturing	Stock clerks and storekeepers; painters, manufactured articles
Printing	All printing occupations included in study
Aircraft parts	Aircraft mechanics and repairers
Nondurable manufacturing	Sewers and stitchers
Transportation	Bus drivers; truck drivers
Communications	Telephone line and splicing workers; telephone installers and repairers
Electric utilities	Electric power line and cable workers
Wholesale and retail trade	Buyers and shippers, farm products; managers and administrators, n.e.c.; delivery and route workers

Wholesale trade	Sales representatives, wholesale
Retail trade	Sales managers and department heads; restaurant, cafeteria, and bar managers; salesclerks; salesworkers
Finance, insurance, and real estate	Bank officials; stock and bond sales agents; managers and superintendents of buildings; real-estate agents, brokers, and appraisers
Services	Gardeners and groundskeepers; salespeople, service and construction; recreation workers; childcare workers; dressmakers; auto mechanics; auto-body repairers; designers; decorators; cooks; food-service workers; bartenders; hairdressers and cosmetologists
Hospitals	All health occupations in study
Educational services	School monitors
Hotel and lodging places	Housekeepers, except private households
Other personal services	Radio and TV repairers; air-conditioning and heating mechanics; miscellaneous mechanics and repairers
Total, nonagricultural industries	All clerical occupations included in study (except as specified individually); graders and sorters; personnel and labor-relations workers; all construction crafts included in study; firefighters; police and related occupations

Source: Conference Board listing.

With few exceptions, the industries related to particular occupations are self-explanatory. Health occupations are related to hospitals, farm occupations to agriculture, banking and real-estate occupations to the finance, insurance, and real-estate industry. Clerical occupations were related to productivity in all nonagricultural industries, as virtually all industries require these types of workers. Public service occupations, firefighters, police, and so on were also related to all nonagricultural industries because of the difficulties in measuring productivity in the public sector.

A special problem arose for construction workers (carpenters, electricians, painters, bulldozer operators, and so on) were productivity in all nonmanufacturing industries was used rather than productivity in the construction industry itself. This was because of difficulty interpreting the significance of the productivity data for the construction industry. For example, while GPO per employee declined in construction by 5 percent from 1960-70, real earnings of carpenters and electricians rose by 23 percent, painters by 21 percent, and plumbers by 26 percent. These changes are quite comparable with the 24 percent increase in GPO per worker recorded for all nonagricultural industries during the period. Whatever the reason (influential national unions, data inadequacies, supply/demand imbalance) productivity changes in all nonagricultural industries appeared to be a better measure of wage changes for the construction-related occupations than productivity data for the industry alone. If alternate terminal or base years were used to determine productivity in the construction industry (for example, 1958, 1959, 1971, or 1972), the decline would still occur.

The methodology utilized can be assessed by projecting median earnings for all U.S. occupations based on GPO per worker data for the entire economy from BLS. The median earnings projection can then be compared with the average personal income per worker projection from the BLS model for the same year. It would be reasonable to expect that the changes in median earnings would approximate the change in personal income per worker. This comparison is shown in Table A.7.

While the median earnings and personal-income estimates pertain to economy-wide aggregates, the relatively close similarity in the rates of change of the two independently derived measures suggests that changes in the earnings projections are consistent with the projected changes in GPO per worker.

TABLE A.7

Median Earnings and Personal Income per Worker,
United States, 1970, and Projected 1985
(in 1973 dollars)

	1960	1970	1985	Average Annual Rate of Growth	
				1960-70	1970-85
Median earnings in all occupations	7,260	9,945	15,260	3.2	2.9
Personal income per worker	8,320	11,310	16,510	3.1	2.6

Sources: U.S. Department of Labor, Bureau of Labor Statistics; Conference Board projections.

NEXT STEPS IN RESEARCH

All of the projections for this study, with the exception of the job-openings indicator, represent attempts by The Conference Board to extend the range of occupational projections. The research in this study indicates that such projections are feasible, even with present data limitations. The projections can and should be updated periodically, and can serve as the basis for more effective vocational-education planning, counseling, and placement. They can help assess priorities for vocational education based on labor-market information which can serve as an input into the planning process and the setting of program targets.

The research also indicates a need for improvement in the data base, both on the Census-BLS side and the vocational-education reporting side. Most of the gaps in the Census-BLS data occurred in relating the 1960 data to the 1970 occupational definitions. Data on race, education, and earnings were not available for 1960 based on the 1970 definitions. If substantial changes are made in the 1980 Census occupational titles, the Census Bureau should consider a more extensive recount of 1970 data by the new definitions than was done for 1960. BLS data from the Current Population Survey were found to be of somewhat limited value because of the small sample size. Although it was not initially designed to provide occupational detail, but rather to measure unemployment, it is nonetheless the only comprehensive occupational series generated between Census years. Expanding the sample size, as BLS plans, would increase the statistical reliability and scope of the manpower information and increase its usefulness for planning in vocational education. Another difficulty in the CPS is that it did not adopt the 1970 occupational definitions until its 1972 survey. There is, therefore, no common point of time for the two series to be linked for some occupations. BLS should adopt the 1980 titles in the CPS as soon as these titles have become available.

The Bureau of Labor Statistics should consider initiating, as one of its ongoing activities, occupational projections similar to those prepared in this project. If the projections developed are useful for vocational planning, BLS with its specialized staff and technical skills would be the logical place to undertake this work. While BLS does acknowledge the technical difficulties in making projections similar to those contained here, difficulties often due to interoccupational shifts, the agency is already conducting research in this area. Once national projections of the indicators are made, state-by-state estimates could be developed using techniques similar to those used in the National/State Occupation-by-Industry Matrix System.

The Office of Education vocational-education reporting system can also facilitate the continued development of indicators similar to those presented in this report. More detailed and more standardized reporting of enrollments would facilitate comparison with the occupations. For example, under reporting requirements in effect from 1970 to 1974, enrollments for all metalworking occupations were reported together to the Office of Education. This cluster included several large and diverse programs: machine shop, machine tool, tool and die, sheetmetal, various welding programs, and brazing and soldering. While there is some overlap in the occupations related to these programs, there are 16 different Census occupational titles associated with the "metalworking occupations" designation. Prior to 1970, data were collected for the individual programs within the metalworking group, and it is understood that the Office of Education has returned to this earlier classification.

Another area where more detailed reporting would aid in analysis of occupational indicators would be in the "business data-processing systems occupations" group. Occupations falling in this group include computer programmers (who are also trained in the scientific data technology program), keypunch operators, and computer and peripheral equipment operators. These occupations clearly encompass a wide range of skills within the data-processing field.

A considerable margin of uncertainty surrounds the vocational-education data because of the nonstandardized interpretation of such terms as "enrollment," "program," and the like. Experience in working with the states of New Jersey and Kentucky in this project indicate that differences exist in the application of these terms. For example, is typing a "program" by itself, or a course within a secretarial program? While New Jersey reported almost 50,000 persons in the typing program, Kentucky reports none since they do not consider it a program. The Office of Education should establish standard definitions of programs to be used in all reports submitted to it.

It is difficult to assess the progress made in the vocational programs in expanding opportunities for women or nonwhites because of the absence of adequate data on the makeup of enrollments. Reporting on the representation by sex in the different program areas was discontinued after 1972, while the reporting by race has referred only to total enrollments. It is understood that the Office of Education plans to resume this reporting.

Although the present study has utilized the linkages between occupations and vocational programs developed by the Bureau of Labor Statistics, those familiar with the linkages generally regard them as inadequate. A careful reading of the "cross-over" developed by BLS reveals that there are no Census occupational titles associated with two large technical programs—police science technology and civil technology. These two programs have projected enrollments of 107,000 and 40,000 respectively in 1977. Still other programs are related to occupational titles that clearly go beyond the program but for which graduates would be qualified for a "piece" of the occupation. Still other programs are related to such a wide variety of occupational titles that meaningful comparisons become impossible. For example, the supervisory, administration, and management program is related to the following occupations: clerical supervisors, n.e.c.; office managers, n.e.c.; assessors, controllers, and treasurers; and credit and collection agents.

Work is currently under way at the Bureau of Labor Statistics, the Office of Management and Budget, and the Office of Education to design a new "standard occupational classification system." It is hoped that this new system will eliminate many of the problems described above; however, the system is several years away from being complete, and it will likely take several more years until it is accepted and used in the field.

In conclusion, the range of occupational indicators available in the past has been too limited to provide an effective basis for planning in vocational education. The present study represents a first step in extending this range. While the techniques utilized are often imperfect, they indicate potentials for improvements in the information base for planning, potentials that can be realized with more research.

NOTES

1. U.S. Department of Labor, Bureau of Labor Statistics, Tomorrow's Manpower Needs, Supplement No. 4, 1974, p. 6.

2. U.S. Department of Labor, Bureau of Labor Statistics, The U.S. Economy in 1985, Bulletin 1809, 1974.

3. U.S. Department of Commerce, Bureau of the Census, 1970 Occupation and Industry Classification Systems in Terms of Their 1960 Occupation and Industry Elements, Technical Paper, No. 26, 1972.

4. U.S. Department of Labor, Bureau of Labor Statistics, "Matching 1970 Census Based BLS National-State Matrix Occupational Categories to Office of Education Instruction Programs" (unpublished memo), May 31, 1974.

5. U.S. Department of Labor, Bureau of Labor Statistics, Tomorrow's Manpower Needs, Vol. 1, Bulletin No. 1606, 1969, pp. 47-55.

APPENDIX B:
REPLICABILITY OF THE NATIONAL PROJECTIONS FOR INDIVIDUAL STATES
Richard J. Rosen

INTRODUCTION

To test the replicability of the national indicators at the state level, two states, Kentucky and New Jersey, were selected. These states were chosen in part because they represent diverse economic and industrial bases, regional locations, occupational patterns, and educational systems. The availability of employment projections and the relevant educational data also figured in the selection.

In determining whether the national projections of occupational characteristics could also be prepared for states, many issues had to be addressed. These issues include whether: (1) consistent economic framework data existed for the states; (2) sufficient occupational data were available from published sources; (3) the data were sufficiently reliable to make projections; and (4) benchmark checks could be developed to test the reasonableness of the projections.

Based on currently available data, projections of the sex and race indicators for occupations appear feasible but with limitations noted in this appendix. Projections of the earnings indicator are probably less feasible because of technical problems related to measuring productivity and because of the limited statistical reliability of the data in some cases. Projections of educational attainment, at least for the larger occupations and states, are possible if special tabulations from the Census are obtained.

THE ECONOMIC FRAMEWORK FOR STATE PROJECTIONS

Both states participating in the study have adopted the national economic framework assumptions in the Bureau of Labor Statistics projections in preparing their own estimates. There is, therefore, consistency between the national and state projections for such important variables as labor-force growth, employment, level of unemployment, productivity, aggregate federal expenditures, and so on. The historic relationship between the magnitudes and changes in magnitudes for a given state variable and the same variable in the overall economy figure for 1980 developed by the BLS. For example, the national model assumes a 4 percent unemployment rate for 1980. The states have not adopted this rate, but have determined what a 4 percent unemployment rate nationally will mean for their state based on the historical movement of the state rate compared with the comparable national rate. This may mean a higher or lower rate than the national figure in 1980 in many states. The fact that the states have "linked" into the national projections is a decided advantage in preparing the indicators for individual states. Historical and projected growth rates for occupations can be more readily compared among the states or nationally, since the economic assumptions are generally similar in most states.

DATA, DATA SOURCES, AND COMPARABILITY

The available data for state occupational indicators are less extensive than for the entire United States. The Current Population Survey does not provide reliable estimates of employment by detailed occupations for the states because of the small size of the sample drawn from many states. The Census Bureau did not publish data on educational attainment by occupation for 1960 for states, and educational data for 1970 are limited to a list of about 50 major occupations and groups. A similar situation obtains for earnings data, with a limited list of occupations for both 1960 and 1970.

The most consistent data are available for the sex and race indicators. The special Census retabulation of 1960 employment, according to the 1970 occupational definitions, provides comprehensive comparability for the sex indicator for the states. Race is comparable for about half the occupations covering the majority of employment included in the study. Complete 1970 data on race are available for the states, but only about half of the published 1960 titles are comparable because of changes in occupational definitions and because the 1960 race data are reported only at the "intermediate" level of detail.

Occupational employment and job-openings projections to 1980 were prepared by both states participating in the study and served as the take-off point for the other occupational indicators. Kentucky is one of about 30 states cooperating with the Occupational Employment Statistics (OES) Program of the Bureau of Labor Statistics. This is a cooperative effort on the part of the state Employment Service and the BLS to develop state and metropolitan occupational-employment projections. While not participating in the OES program, New Jersey followed the BLS methodology in deriving their employment and job-openings estimates.[1]

The data for the occupational indicators come from several sources. The state employment-security agencies provided the data on employment and job openings. The 1960 and 1970 Decennial Censuses provided the needed occupational data for the sex and race indicators as well as for earnings and educational attainment. Vocational enrollments or completions by program came from the state education agency or the U.S. Office of Education. Data from the U.S. Department of Labor and the National Planning Association were used for the benchmark checks of the projections.

The specific sources of data for each of the states are presented in Table B.1.

STATISTICAL RELIABILITY OF THE DATA

Apart from the availability of data, there is the question of statistical reliability. Data from the Census relating to the indicators considered are based on a sample of the population, and as such are subject to statistical error as well as to the usual reporting, coding, and classifying errors which occur in a complete enumeration. Published data for 1960 for states are based on a 25 percent sample, while data from the 1970 Census are from a 20 percent sample for the characteristics used in this study.

The Census Bureau has published tables indicating the range of statistical error given the number of persons in the population under investigation. When looking at state data, it is important to recognize that the error associated with percentages based on relatively small numbers can be substantial. For example, in the estimate that half of the workers in an occupation completed 12-15 years of education, the standard error at the 90 percent confidence level would be ± 2 percentage points if there were 10,000 employed in the occupation in 1970. Of the occupations studied, only about 40 occupations in New Jersey and half that number in Kentucky had 10,000 persons employed in 1970. The standard error if total employment was 5,000 is ± 3.5 percentage points. Therefore, the chances are 9 out of 10 that an estimate of 50 percent with 5,000 employed would fall between 46.5 and 53.5 percent.

Similar degrees of variation are present in the 1960 data. Therefore, in examining the change in representation of women or nonwhites in an occupation, it should be remembered that the reported increase in representation may, in fact, be larger or smaller than the true increase in the underlying population, depending on the estimating errors arising from sampling fluctuations associated with the 1960 and 1970 data. Therefore, small changes in the representation of women or blacks should be regarded as having questionable statistical significance in general, and in particular when associated with the smaller occupations, that is, those with fewer than 5,000 persons employed.

TABLE B.1

Data Sources and Information Obtained for Kentucky and New Jersey Projections

Data Source	Information Obtained
Kentucky	
Total employment and job openings	
Kentucky Department of Human Resources, <u>Annual Manpower Planning Report</u>, FY 1975.	Total state employment by occupation, 1970, 1980; average annual job openings by occupation, 1970-80.
Sex and race	
U.S. Department of Commerce, Bureau of the Census, Census of Population, 1970, <u>Detailed Characteristics: Kentucky</u>, PC (1) - D19.	Employment by sex 1960, 1970, and employment by race, 1970, for detailed occupations.
U.S. Department of Commerce, Bureau of the Census, Census of Population, 1960, <u>Detailed Characteristics: Kentucky</u>, PC (1) - D19.	Employment by race, 1960, for detailed occupations.
U.S. Department of Labor, <u>1975 Manpower Report of the President</u>.	U.S. labor force by race 1960, 1970, and 1980.
National Planning Association, <u>Regional Demographic Projections 1960-85</u>, 1972.	Kentucky labor force by sex 1960, 1970, and 1980.
Educational attainment	
See Sex and Race sources above.	Employment by level of education for selected occupations, 1970.
Earnings	
See Sex and Race sources above.	Median earnings for selected occupations and groups, 1960, 1970.
Vocational education data	
Kentucky Department of Education, <u>Kentucky State Plan for the Administration of Vocational Education</u>, 1975.	Completions from vocational programs, 1975 and 1980.
U.S. Department of Health, Education, and Welfare, Office of Education, "Enrollments in Vocational Education Programs," Kentucky, O.E. Form 3138, 1971.	Enrollment by sex in vocational programs, 1971.

New Jersey

Total employment and job openings

New Jersey Department of Labor and Industry, *New Jersey's Manpower Challenge of the Eighties*, 1975. — Total state employment by occupation, 1970, 1980; average annual job openings, 1970-80.

Sex and race

U.S. Department of Commerce, Bureau of the Census, Census of Population, 1970, *Detailed Characteristics: New Jersey*, PC (1) - D32. — Employment by sex, 1960, 1970, and employment by race, 1970.

U.S. Department of Commerce, Bureau of the Census, Census of Population, 1960, *Detailed Characteristics: New Jersey*, PC (1) - D32. — Employment by race, 1960, for detailed occupations.

U.S. Department of Labor, *Manpower Report of the President*, 1975. — U.S. labor force by race, 1960, 1970, and 1980.

National Planning Association, *Regional Demographic Projections 1960-85*, 1972. — New Jersey labor force by sex, 1960, 1970, and 1980.

Educational attainment

See Sex and Race sources above. — Employment by level of education for selected occupations, 1970.

Earnings

See Sex and Race sources above. — Median earnings for selected occupations and groups, 1960, 1970.

Vocational education data

New Jersey Department of Education, Division of Vocational Education, unpublished enrollment data, 1975. — Projected enrollment in vocational programs, 1976.

U.S. Department of Health, Education, and Welfare, Office of Education, "Enrollment in Vocational Education Programs," New Jersey, O.E. Form 3138, 1972. — Enrolled by sex in vocational programs, 1972.

Source: Conference Board compilation.

USE OF NATIONAL TREND DATA OR OTHER SURROGATE MEASURES FOR THE STATE

There are two reasons why national trend data or other surrogate measures were used in making projections for the states. First, published data are not available for all occupations included in the study. Second, even if the data were available, their statistical reliability may be such that they would provide an inaccurate statement of trend. For example, data on educational attainment and earnings for detailed occupational titles are not published for the states. Special tabulations can be obtained to provide the data for the majority of occupations; however, the question of accuracy must be considered. Census data at the national level are both more complete and statistically more reliable. In such cases, the more reliable trends shown in national data may be preferable to those reported in the state data.

Examination of the 1970 Census data for major occupations and groups indicates that, in terms of educational attainment, states can vary substantially from the national pattern. For example, Kentucky generally lags behind the United States in educational attainment, while New Jersey generally has somewhat higher levels. Even in states where there is currently a divergence from the national pattern, national data and projections may still be relevant, as there has been a narrowing of the "education gap" among the states. This is in part due to the migration of the population over time. In those areas in which the states are becoming more like the national norm over time, the trends in the national projections can supply useful benchmarks for state projections, and, in some instances, the need for special state projections diminishes. Table B.2 compares the educational levels for selected occupations in Kentucky, New Jersey, and the United States for 1970. The data in the table underscore the fact that substantial differences as well as similarities exist between the state and national patterns.

Differences in occupational earnings among the states appear to be the result of differences in the overall level of earnings in the state rather than reflecting differentials in the relative earnings of different occupations within the state. That is, while the level of earnings may differ, the ratio of earnings in the occupation to earnings in the state or nation often vary within a fairly narrow range. Cost of living disparities are obviously an important factor in explaining the differences, as are differences in industrial makeup and union strength. Table B.3 compares median earnings in the two states and nationally for selected occupations. For purposes of comparison, the data showing ratio of median earnings in the occupation to median earnings in the state (or nation) are important. Although the data in the table are

TABLE B.2

Educational Attainment of Workers in Kentucky, New Jersey, and the United States—Major Occupational Groups and Selected Occupations, 1970
(in percent)

Distribution of Educational Attainment

Major Occupational Group or Occupation	Kentucky			New Jersey			United States		
	Less than 12 Years	12-15 Years	16 Years or More	Less than 12 Years	12-15 Years	16 Years or More	Less than 12 Years	12-15 Years	16 Years or More
Professional, technical, and kindred workers	7.0	35.4	57.6	6.3	37.2	56.5	6.2	38.0	55.8
Registered nurses	11.8	74.3	13.9	6.4	78.7	14.9	8.8	74.6	16.6
Managers and administrators, except farm	29.9	50.6	19.5	20.7	49.8	29.5	22.6	54.1	23.3
Salesworkers	37.8	53.1	9.1	32.6	52.8	14.6	31.0	57.1	11.8
Salesworkers, retail trade	46.2	50.5	3.3	44.5	51.2	4.3	39.5	56.3	4.2
Clerical and kindred workers	21.4	74.0	4.5	25.3	70.4	4.3	21.1	73.8	5.1
Office machine operators	14.4	85.3	0.3	20.9	78.0	1.1	15.8	82.8	1.4
Secretaries, stenographers, and typists	8.6	88.0	3.4	12.4	85.1	2.5	9.8	86.1	4.1
Craftsmen	59.0	39.3	1.7	51.5	46.1	2.4	49.2	48.6	2.1
Carpenters	76.1	23.4	0.5	57.7	41.3	1.0	60.1	38.8	1.1
Construction craftsmen, except carpenters	65.3	34.1	0.6	57.6	41.5	0.9	55.3	43.7	1.0
Auto mechanics, including body repairmen	70.9	28.7	0.4	58.6	40.8	0.6	57.4	41.9	0.7
Mechanics and repairmen, except auto	56.7	42.3	1.0	47.7	51.1	1.2	45.3	53.3	1.4
Machinists	48.7	51.1	0.2	52.7	46.2	1.1	45.5	53.7	0.8
Metal craftsmen, except mechanics and machinists	51.0	48.1	0.9	52.7	46.4	0.9	48.5	50.6	0.9
Foremen	44.5	49.1	6.4	41.5	50.5	8.0	39.4	53.9	6.7

(continued)

(Table B.2 continued)

Major Occupational Group or Occupation	Kentucky			New Jersey			United States		
	Less than 12 Years	12-15 Years	16 Years or More	Less than 12 Years	12-15 Years	16 Years or More	Less than 12 Years	12-15 Years	16 Years or More
Operatives, except transportation	64.7	34.8	0.5	67.8	31.4	0.8	60.8	38.4	0.8
Assemblers	49.1	50.6	0.3	58.9	40.1	1.0	51.5	47.7	0.8
Precision machine operatives	61.1	38.4	0.5	59.8	39.4	0.8	52.6	46.7	0.7
Sewers and stitchers	67.5	32.5	0.0	82.6	16.9	0.5	69.7	29.9	0.4
Transportation equipment operatives	70.0	29.5	0.5	64.1	35.0	0.9	60.3	38.8	0.9
Truck drivers	76.0	23.7	0.3	69.2	30.2	0.6	65.8	33.7	0.5
Laborers, except farm	72.0	27.4	0.6	69.3	29.6	1.1	66.2	32.8	1.0
Farmers and farm managers	75.1	23.0	1.9	53.6	40.9	5.5	56.5	39.7	3.8
Farm laborers and farm foremen	84.0	15.2	0.8	70.2	27.9	1.9	74.8	23.8	1.5
Service workers, except private household	64.7	34.2	1.1	59.3	39.0	1.7	55.7	42.7	1.7
Food-service workers	73.2	26.3	0.5	64.9	34.1	0.9	61.6	37.4	1.0
Practical nurses	35.1	63.8	1.1	29.1	69.9	1.0	29.1	69.9	1.0
Other health-service workers	55.0	43.4	1.6	47.6	50.4	1.9	45.4	52.7	1.9
Protective-service workers	51.9	45.9	2.2	40.4	56.2	3.4	35.2	61.3	3.5
All occupations	48.2	41.8	10.0	39.5	46.2	14.4	37.2	50.4	12.4

Note: Details may not add to totals because of rounding.
Source: 1970 Census of Population, see Table B.1.

TABLE B.3

Median Earnings of Full-Year Workers, New Jersey, Kentucky, and United States—Selected Occupations, 1970

Occupation	New Jersey		Kentucky		United States	
	Earnings (dollars)	Ratio to State Median	Earnings (dollars)	Ratio to State Median	Earnings (dollars)	Ratio to U.S. Median
Buyers, purchasing agents, sales managers	12,524	1.59	9,634	1.55	11,011	1.55
Managers and administrators	13,815	1.75	10,484	1.69	11,846	1.67
Insurance agents, brokers, and underwriters[a]	11,994	1.52	9,781	1.58	10,688	1.50
Sales representatives, manufacturing[a]	13,434	1.70	10,670	1.72	11,933	1.68
Salesclerks, retail trade	4,986	0.63	4,286	0.69	4,678	0.66
Bookkeepers[b]	5,520	0.70	4,635	0.75	5,053	0.71
Secretaries[b]	5,775	0.73	4,750	0.77	5,486	0.77
Typists[b]	4,875	0.62	4,509	0.73	4,936	0.69
Carpenters[a]	8,978	1.14	6,540	1.05	7,850	1.10
Electricians[a]	9,967	1.26	9,294	1.50	9,663	1.36
Painters and paperhangers[a]	7,784	0.99	6,332	1.02	7,388	1.04
Plumbers and pipefitters[a]	9,869	1.25	9,073	1.46	9,386	1.32
Foremen	10,898	1.38	9,153	1.47	9,968	1.40
Air-conditioning, heating, and refrigerator mechanics and repairmen[a]	9,315	1.18	8,030	1.29	8,535	1.20
Radio and TV mechanics and repairmen[a]	8,512	1.08	7,150	1.15	7,937	1.12
Sheetmetal workers and tinsmiths[a]	9,749	1.24	8,774	1.41	9,020	1.27
Tool and die makers[a]	10,391	1.32	9,192	1.48	10,503	1.48
Welders and flame cutters[a]	8,777	1.11	7,508	1.21	8,021	1.13
Firefighters[a]	9,699	1.23	7,598	1.22	9,543	1.34
Police and detectives[a]	9,357	1.19	7,189	1.16	9,155	1.29
All occupations	7,889	—	6,207	—	7,114	—

[a]Median earnings for male workers only.
[b]Median earnings for female workers only.
Source: 1970 Census of Population.

far from conclusive, they suggest strong elements making for similarity in the structure of earnings-by-occupation between individual states and the entire nation.

National trend data, along with other surrogates, were also used in projecting the race indicator for some occupations. Consistent race data were only available for half the occupational titles because of redefinition of titles between the 1960 and 1970 Censuses and because 1960 race data were published for fewer than 100 occupations and groups. In some cases, the occupation was projected based on the projected movement of a similar occupation for which 1960 data were available. The use of the real-estate agent and broker occupation to project real-estate appraisers is an instance. In a number of occupations, the state projections were made based on the national trend for the occupation: 17 occupations in Kentucky and 32 in New Jersey were projected based on national trends.

National data, therefore, have varied uses in preparing occupational indicators for states. They can be used to compare the state's position for a particular characteristic relative to the United States; they can act as a surrogate measure of future trends in the state, or be used to make state projections for individual occupations. The uses depend on the degree of similarity between the state and the United States, the degree to which the state is expected to follow the national pattern in the future, and the statistical reliability of the state data in comparison with the national.

DERIVING BENCHMARK CHECKS FOR THE PROJECTIONS

Undertaking comprehensive benchmark checks of the state projections does not appear feasible because of the lack of consistent state labor-force projections and data gaps. The National Planning Association (NPA) has prepared projections of state labor forces by sex; however, there are currently no systematic projections of state labor forces by race. The economic assumptions and the base-year data in the projections are slightly different from those used by the BLS; their use must therefore be limited.

In general, the shift in representation of women as projected by the NPA is mirrored in the study occupations. This is more true in New Jersey than in Kentucky. The proportion of women in Kentucky is projected to increase more rapidly than the labor force as a whole, but it also did so in the 1960-70 period. It appears that the occupations with the most rapid growth are those in which women predominate in Kentucky. Women are projected to account for just over one-

TABLE B.4

Employment by Sex, Occupations Studied and All State Occupations for Kentucky and New Jersey—1960, 1970, and Projected 1980

	1960		1970		1980	
	Male	Female	Male	Female	Male	Female
Kentucky						
Employment in occupations studied						
Number	377,976	101,284	378,554	157,944	442,717	224,783
Percent distribution	78.9	21.1	70.6	29.4	66.3	33.7
Employment in all state occupations						
Number	660,728	275,216	690,216	386,564	841,110	498,240
Percent distribution	70.6	29.4	64.1	35.9	62.8	37.2
Employment in occupations studied as percent of all state occupations	57.2	36.8	54.8	40.9	52.6	45.1
New Jersey						
Employment in occupations studied						
Number	N.A.	N.A.	954,796	606,779	1,117,794	797,241
Percent distribution	N.A.	N.A.	61.1	38.9	58.4	41.6
Employment in all state occupations						
Number	N.A.	N.A.	1,665,987	999,592	1,923,834	1,298,672
Percent distribution	N.A.	N.A.	62.5	37.5	59.7	40.3
Employment in occupations studied as percent of all state occupations	N.A.	N.A.	57.3	60.7	58.1	61.4

Note: N.A. = Not Available.
Sources: U.S. Bureau of the Census, Department of Commerce, Census of the Population, 1960 and 1970; N.J. Department of Labor and Industry; Kentucky Department of Human Resources.

TABLE B.5

Employment by Race, Occupations Studied and All State Occupations for Kentucky and New Jersey—1970 and Projected 1980

	1970		1980	
	White	Black	White	Black
Kentucky				
Employment in occupations studied				
Number	514,705	21,793	663,830	33,670
Percent distribution	95.9	4.1	95.2	4.8
Employment in all state occupations				
Number	1,004,635	72,145	1,238,900	100,450
Percent distribution	93.3	6.7	92.5	7.5
Employment in occupations studied as percent of all state occupations	51.2	30.2	53.6	33.5
New Jersey				
Employment in occupations studied				
Number	1,448,389	115,186	1,742,197	172,838
Percent distribution	92.6	7.4	91.0	9.0
Employment in all state occupations				
Number	2,412,349	253,230	2,858,367	364,143
Percent distribution	90.5	9.5	88.7	11.3
Employment in occupations studied as percent of all state occupations	60.0	45.5	61.0	47.5

Sources: Same as Table B.4.

half of the employment increase in the occupations studied; however, only 14 percent of this increase is expected to occur as a result of increased penetration of women into the occupations. Table B.4 compares the representation of women in the study occupations with the entire state based on the historical data from the Censuses, and projections by the NPA and The Conference Board. Employment by sex is not available for 1960 for New Jersey because the projected employment data were based on "place of work," and the New Jersey Department of Labor and Industry, which prepared the 1970 and projected 1980 employment estimates by occupation, did not recompute the 1960 Census data from its reported "place of residence" basis.

A preliminary guide to the anticipated changes in the racial composition of the state labor force can be derived by comparing the proportion of blacks and whites in the state in 1960 and 1970 with the comparable national distribution, and estimating 1980 for the state based on this relationship and projections of the national labor force prepared by the Bureau of Labor Statistics. State estimates obtained in this manner cannot be used to verify occupational projections as they are derived from secondary sources and are only rough benchmarks themselves. Table B.5 compares employment by race in the occupations studied with 1970 and projected 1980 employment for the two states. Data for 1960 are not shown, since they are available for only half the occupations.

Projected movements by sex and race in the occupations studied appear to be reasonable when compared with anticipated movements in the state labor forces of Kentucky and New Jersey. More information is needed, however, to improve the benchmark check procedure for states. Information on the recent patterns of geographic and occupational mobility be race and sex, in particular, would improve the empirical basis for the projections.

CONCLUSIONS REGARDING FEASIBILITY OF PREPARING STATE INDICATORS

Both states included in this study had existing projections of employment and job openings for occupations. The projections were based on techniques developed by the Bureau of Labor Statistics and were consistent with the BLS national model of the economy. These projections could be used without alteration or adjustment as a point of departure for developing demographic indicators for the occupations included in the study.

Less information on occupational characteristics of workers is currently available for states than is available at the national level.

Existing data are sufficient to prepare projections for sex and race; however, special tabulations from the 1960 Census by race would decrease the number of occupations for which national trend or surrogate data need be used. Published data are not sufficient to prepare projections of educational attainment and earnings. Comparison of the two states and national data reveals that the relative rank of occupations in terms of earnings is fairly close, indicating that national projections (which can be expected to be more reliable statistically) may be a good surrogate for state projections.

Educational-attainment projections could be prepared, at least for the larger occupations, if special tabulations from the Censuses were obtained. States with educational-attainment distributions similar to the entire labor force might consider using national projections as a surrogate. States with dissimilar patterns should examine the historical data to determine to what extent, if any, the state is becoming like the nation over time. If such a trend exists, national education projections could also be considered as benchmarks or possible surrogates. This would allow projections to be prepared for many occupations for which the state data were not sufficiently reliable.

A combination of state and national data on occupational characteristics can be used to develop occupational indicators for states that are comparable with the projections at the national level. While comparable, it is reasonable to expect that the state projections will generally be less reliable. This will be especially true for small occupations and in those instances in which surrogates are employed with only limited benchmarks based on original state data. However, the state projections can be improved by making use of special Census tabulations and by surveys. These indicators are useful because they can extend the range of manpower information currently available to state vocational planners beyond the traditional measures of employment and job openings by providing information on the sexual, racial, educational attainment, and earnings levels of occupations. Allowing for their imperfections, the indicators can serve as substitutes for subjective hunches about future labor-force developments relevant for planning in vocational education.

NOTE

1. For a full discussion of these methodologies use: U.S. Department of Labor, Bureau of Labor Statistics, Tomorrow's Manpower Needs, Vol. 1, Developing Area Manpower Projections, BLS Bulletin No. 1606, 1969; Ibid., Supplement No. 4, Estimating Occupational

Separations From the Labor Force for States; New Jersey Department of Labor and Industry, New Jersey's Manpower Challenge of the Eighties, 1975; Kentucky Department for Human Resources, Annual Manpower Report, FY 1975.

APPENDIX C:
STATISTICAL TABLES

TABLE C.1

Selected National Economic Framework Indicators—1960, 1970, and Projected 1980 and 1985

	1960	1970	1980	1985	Average Annual Growth Rate			
					1960–70	1970–80	1980–85	1970–85
Population 14 years and over (in thousands)	127,334	151,067	174,734	182,932	1.7	1.5	0.9	1.3
14–24 years	27,334	40,539	44,858	41,615	4.0	1.0	-1.5	0.3
25–44 years	47,134	48,413	62,334	71,991	0.3	2.6	2.9	2.7
45 years and over	52,866	62,115	67,542	69,326	1.6	0.8	0.5	0.7
Total labor force (in thousands)	72,142	85,903	101,809	107,716	1.8	1.7	1.1	1.5
Civilian labor force (in thousands)	69,578	82,715	99,809	105,716	1.7	1.9	1.2	1.7
Civilian employment (in thousands)	65,778	78,627	95,817	101,487	1.8	2.0	1.2	1.7
Unemployment (in thousands)	3,852	4,088	3,992	4,229	0.6	-0.2	1.2	0.2
Unemployment rate	5.5	4.9	4.0	4.0	N.A.	N.A.	N.A.	N.A.
Gross National Product (in billions of 1973 dollars)	757.4	1,114.9	1,750.8	2,051.4	3.9	4.6	3.2	4.2
Gross National Product per worker (in 1973 dollars)	11,080	13,625	17,900	19,820	2.1	2.8	2.1	2.5
Personal income* (in billions of 1973 dollars)	568.6	925.1	1,431.7	1,708.6	5.0	4.5	3.6	4.2
Personal income per worker (in 1973 dollars)	8,320	11,310	14,635	16,510	3.1	2.6	2.4	2.5
Average annual man-hours per worker, private economy	2,067	1,968	1,920	1,888	-0.5	-0.3	-0.3	-0.3

Note: N.A. = Not Available.
* Published figures were deflated using personal consumption expenditures deflator from Department of Commerce.

Sources: U.S. Department of Labor, Bureau of Labor Statistics; U.S. Department of Commerce, Bureau of the Census. Population projections based on Census Series E fertility projections.

TABLE C.2

Study Occupations and All Civilian Occupations, 1970 and Projected 1985

Indicator	1970			1985		
	Study Occupations	All Occupations	Occupations Studied as Percent of All Occupations	Study Occupations	All Occupations	Occupations Studied as Percent of All Occupations
Employment (in thousands)	43,399	78,627	55	57,235	101,490	56
Male	27,815	48,960	57	34,045	61,902	55
Female	15,585	29,667	53	23,191	39,588	59
White	39,888	70,182	57	51,356	88,869	58
Nonwhite	3,511	8,445	42	5,879	12,621	47
Years of school completed (in thousands)						
Less than 12	16,741	29,249	57	13,033	23,952	54
12-15	23,697	39,628	60	39,003	58,255	67
16 or more	2,961	9,750	30	5,199	19,283	27
Median earnings* (in 1973 dollars)	8,725	9,945	88	13,870	15,260	91

Note: Details may not add to totals because of rounding.
*Refers to workers who worked 50 weeks or more during the year.
Sources: U.S. Department of Labor, Bureau of Labor Statistics; The Conference Board.

TABLE C.3

Median Earnings of Full-Year Workers in Study Occupations and Ratio of
Occupational Median to Economy-wide Median—1970 and Projected 1980 and 1985
(in 1973 dollars)

Occupation	Median Earnings			Ratio of Occupational Median to Economy-wide Median		
	1970	1980	1985	1970	1980	1985
Professional, technical, and kindred workers						
Computer programmers	13,600	18,240	20,490	1.37	1.34	1.34
Designers	14,260	19,320	21,550	1.43	1.42	1.41
Drafters	11,200	16,210	18,100	1.13	1.19	1.19
Electrical and electronic-engineering technicians	11,200	15,470	17,410	1.13	1.14	1.14
Engineering and science technicians, n.e.c.	10,650	14,670	16,460	1.07	1.08	1.08
Mechanical-engineering technicians	13,430	18,500	20,760	1.35	1.36	1.36
Other technicians, except health	10,810	14,930	16,800	1.09	1.10	1.10
Personnel and labor-relations workers	13,820	18,870	21,300	1.40	1.39	1.40
Recreation workers	9,330	12,490	13,880	0.94	0.92	0.91
Registered nurses	8,090	10,330	11,970	0.81	0.76	0.78
Therapists	9,630	12,020	13,820	0.97	0.88	0.91
Tool programmers, numerical control	12,620	17,390	19,520	1.27	1.28	1.28
Managers and administrators, except farm						
Bank officials and financial managers	15,990	22,600	25,480	1.61	1.66	1.67
Buyers and shippers, farm products	12,370	17,640	19,760	1.24	1.30	1.29
Buyers, wholesale and retail trade	12,780	16,720	18,490	1.28	1.23	1.21

Managers and administrators, n.e.c.	16,770	23,200	26,040	1.69	1.70	1.71
Managers and superintendents, building	9,500	13,500	15,280	0.96	0.99	1.00
Restaurant, cafeteria, and bar managers	11,230	15,220	17,040	1.13	1.12	1.12
Sales managers and department heads, retail	12,780	16,720	18,490	1.28	1.23	1.21
Salesworkers						
Insurance agents, brokers, and underwriters	11,010	14,910	16,630	1.11	1.10	1.09
Real-estate agents and brokers	12,820	18,290	20,720	1.29	1.34	1.37
Sales representatives, manufacturing	15,540	22,760	26,110	1.56	1.67	1.71
Sales representatives, wholesale	13,690	18,950	21,030	1.38	1.39	1.38
Salesclerks, retail trade	6,470	8,380	9,480	0.65	0.62	0.62
Salesworkers, retail trade	11,090	14,350	16,230	1.11	1.05	1.06
Salespeople, service and construction	11,852	16,330	18,310	1.19	1.20	1.20
Stock and bond sales agents	23,070	32,600	36,840	2.32	2.40	2.41
Clerical and kindred workers						
Billing clerks	7,500	9,850	10,990	0.75	0.72	0.72
Bookkeepers	6,530	8,600	9,600	0.66	0.63	0.63
Bookkeeping and billing-machine operators	6,440	8,450	9,400	0.65	0.62	0.62
Calculating-machine operators	6,730	8,830	9,850	0.68	0.65	0.65
Computer and peripheral equipment operators	9,170	12,170	13,430	0.92	0.89	0.88
Insurance adjustors, examiners, and investigators	10,920	14,780	16,490	1.10	1.09	1.08
Keypunch operators	6,800	9,020	10,100	0.68	0.66	0.66
Miscellaneous clerical workers	8,120	10,660	11,890	0.82	0.78	0.78
Office machine operators, n.e.c.	6,600	8,670	9,670	0.66	0.64	0.63
Payroll and timekeeping clerks	7,870	10,340	11,530	0.79	0.76	0.76
Real-estate appraisers	15,450	22,040	24,970	1.55	1.62	1.64

(continued)

(Table C.3 continued)

Occupation	Median Earnings			Ratio of Occupational Median to Economy-wide Median		
	1970	1980	1985	1970	1980	1985
Secretaries, legal, medical and other	6,860	9,040	10,100	0.69	0.66	0.66
Shipping and receiving clerks	8,080	10,750	12,040	0.81	0.79	0.79
Statistical clerks	8,230	10,805	12,053	0.83	0.79	0.79
Stenographers	7,520	10,190	11,490	0.76	0.75	0.75
Stock clerks and storekeepers	9,813	14,230	16,050	0.99	1.05	1.05
Tabulating-machine operators	7,590	9,960	11,110	0.76	0.73	0.73
Typists	6,070	7,970	8,890	0.61	0.59	0.58
Craftsmen and kindred workers						
Air-conditioning, heating, and refrigeration mechanics	10,760	14,240	15,800	1.08	1.05	1.04
Aircraft mechanics and repairers	11,440	19,680	22,310	1.15	1.45	1.46
Auto-body repairers	9,740	12,850	14,250	0.98	0.95	0.93
Auto mechanics	9,070	11,970	13,270	0.91	0.88	0.87
Brickmasons and stonemasons	10,610	14,130	15,690	1.07	1.04	1.03
Bulldozer operators	9,240	12,360	13,780	0.93	0.91	0.90
Cabinetmakers	8,230	10,650	11,720	0.83	0.78	0.77
Carpenters	9,720	12,940	14,390	0.98	0.95	0.94
Carpenter apprentices	7,560	10,040	11,150	0.76	0.74	0.73
Crane, derrick, and hoist operators	10,720	14,340	15,970	1.08	1.05	1.05
Data-processing machine repairers	12,410	17,140	19,290	1.25	1.26	1.26
Decorators and window dressers	7,780	10,280	11,380	0.78	0.76	0.75

Electricians	11,780	15,690	17,450	1.18	1.15	1.14
Electric power line and cable workers	11,390	15,550	18,740	1.15	1.15	1.23
Excavating, grading, and road-machine operators	9,770	13,070	14,580	0.98	0.96	0.96
Farm-implement mechanics and repairers	8,050	10,620	11,780	0.81	0.78	0.77
Foremen	12,320	17,020	19,160	1.24	1.25	1.26
Heavy-equipment mechanics, including diesel	10,300	13,590	15,070	1.04	1.00	0.99
Job and die setters, metal	10,660	15,330	17,090	1.07	1.13	1.12
Machinists	10,400	14,930	16,640	1.05	1.10	1.09
Machinist apprentices	8,240	11,850	13,200	0.83	0.87	0.87
Miscellaneous mechanics and repairers	9,680	13,840	15,370	0.97	1.02	1.01
Painter apprentices	7,580	10,290	11,520	0.76	0.76	0.75
Painters, construction and maintenance	9,040	11,990	13,310	0.91	0.88	0.87
Paperhangers	10,380	14,580	16,500	1.04	1.07	1.08
Pattern and model makers, except paper	12,580	18,260	20,420	1.27	1.34	1.34
Photoengravers and lithographers	12,500	16,090	18,000	1.26	1.18	1.18
Plumbers and pipefitters	11,570	15,490	17,260	1.16	1.14	1.13
Printing-press apprentices	9,400	12,080	13,510	0.95	0.89	0.89
Printing-press operators	10,580	13,600	15,200	1.06	1.00	1.00
Printing-trades apprentices, except print pressmen	7,380	9,490	10,610	0.74	0.70	0.70
Radio and TV repairers	9,520	12,630	14,030	0.96	0.93	0.92
Sheetmetal apprentices	8,270	11,960	13,360	0.83	0.88	0.88
Sheetmetal workers and tinsmiths	10,920	15,890	17,780	1.10	1.17	1.17
Structural-metal craftsmen	9,190	11,990	12,890	0.92	0.88	0.84
Telephone installers and repairers	11,150	15,270	18,350	1.12	1.12	1.20
Telephone linemen and splicers	10,230	14,010	16,830	1.03	1.03	1.10

(continued)

(Table C.3 continued)

	Median Earnings			Ratio of Occupational Median to Economy-wide Median		
Occupation	1970	1980	1985	1970	1980	1985
Tilesetters	10,090	13,430	14,910	1.01	0.99	0.98
Upholsterers	7,820	10,310	11,400	0.79	0.76	0.75
Operatives						
Assemblers	7,590	10,140	11,280	0.76	0.75	0.74
Bus drivers	8,950	12,590	14,310	0.90	0.93	0.94
Checkers, examiners, and inspectors, manufacturing	8,370	11,370	12,720	0.84	0.84	0.83
Cutting operatives, n.e.c.	7,980	11,540	12,890	0.80	0.85	0.84
Delivery and route workers	9,060	11,610	12,720	0.91	0.85	0.83
Dressmakers and seamstresses, except factory	4,390	5,960	6,650	0.44	0.44	0.44
Drill-press operatives	8,670	12,540	14,010	0.87	0.92	0.92
Graders and sorters, manufacturing	6,450	8,560	9,590	0.65	0.63	0.63
Grinding-machine operatives	10,130	14,650	16,370	1.02	1.08	1.07
Lathe and milling-machine operatives	9,950	14,400	16,080	1.00	1.06	1.05
Painters, manufactured articles	8,440	12,140	13,530	0.85	0.89	0.89
Other precision machine operatives	10,070	14,460	16,110	1.01	1.06	1.06
Punch and stamping-press operatives	8,490	12,290	13,720	0.85	0.90	0.90
Sawyers	7,030	10,120	11,290	0.71	0.75	0.74
Sewers and stitchers	4,880	6,160	6,970	0.49	0.45	0.46
Solderers	6,560	9,370	10,410	0.66	0.69	0.68
Truck drivers	9,640	14,050	16,160	0.97	1.03	1.06

Welders and flame cutters	9,640	13,760	15,290	0.97	1.01	1.00
Service workers						
Bartenders	7,700	9,840	10,810	0.77	0.72	0.71
Cooks, except private household	5,470	7,620	8,570	0.55	0.56	0.56
Childcare workers, except private household	3,840	5,000	5,500	0.37	0.37	0.36
Crossing guards and bridge tenders	6,750	8,420	9,230	0.68	0.62	0.60
Firefighters	11,610	16,000	18,130	1.17	1.18	1.19
Food-service workers, n.e.c., except private household	4,430	6,170	6,930	0.45	0.45	0.45
Hairdressers and cosmetologists	5,770	7,770	8,650	0.58	0.57	0.57
Health aides, except nursing	5,440	6,730	7,720	0.55	0.50	0.51
Housekeepers, except private household	6,470	8,210	9,000	0.65	0.60	0.59
Marshals and constables	9,260	12,730	14,420	0.93	0.94	0.95
Nursing aides, orderlies, and attendants	4,890	6,050	6,940	0.49	0.44	0.45
Police and detectives	11,100	15,270	17,300	1.12	1.12	1.13
Practical nurses	5,870	7,650	8,910	0.59	0.56	0.58
School monitors	3,870	5,170	5,640	0.39	0.38	0.37
Sheriffs and bailiffs	9,520	12,880	14,500	0.96	0.95	0.95
Laborers, except farm						
Carpenter helpers	6,410	8,880	10,000	0.64	0.65	0.66
Gardeners and groundskeepers, except farm	6,830	9,290	10,380	0.69	0.68	0.68
Farm occupations						
Farm foremen	8,360	11,790	14,620	0.84	0.87	0.96
Farm managers	10,210	15,200	19,210	1.03	1.12	1.26
Farm laborers, wage workers	4,750	7,080	8,950	0.48	0.52	0.59
Farmers, owners and tenants	7,780	12,340	15,910	0.78	0.91	1.04

(continued)

(Table C.3 continued)

Occupation	Median Earnings			Ratio of Occupational Median to Economy-wide Median		
	1970	1980	1985	1970	1980	1985
All U.S. occupations	9,945	13,600	15,260	N.A.	N.A.	N.A.

Note: Earnings refer to persons who worked 50 weeks or more. Figures adjusted to 1973 dollars using personal consumption expenditures deflator from Department of Commerce.
N.A. = Not Available.
Sources: 1970 Census of Population; The Conference Board.

TABLE C.4

Employment in 1960 and 1970 and Projected 1980 and 1985, Study Occupations
(in thousands)

Occupation	Employment				Average Annual Growth Rate			
	1960	1970	1980	1985	1960-70	1970-80	1970-85	1980-85
Professional, technical, and kindred workers	1,209	2,117	3,224	3,745	5.8	4.3	3.9	3.0
Computer programmers	9	177	250	290	†	3.5	3.4	3.0
Designers	74	120	164	178	4.9	3.2	2.7	1.7
Drafters	231	316	425	485	3.2	3.0	2.9	2.7
Electrical and electronic-engineering technicians	103	154	237	317	4.1	4.4	4.9	6.0
Engineering and science technicians, n.e.c.	109	190	355	525	5.7	6.5	7.0	8.1
Mechanical-engineering technicians	12	12	15	18	0.0	0.2	2.7	4.4
Other technicians, except health	4	37	77	95	†	7.6	6.5	4.3
Personnel and labor-relations workers	100	286	478	550	11.0	5.3	4.5	2.8
Recreation workers	33	60	92	105	6.2	4.4	3.8	2.7
Registered nurses	503	680	980	1,000	3.1	3.7	2.6	0.4
Therapists	27	82	147	178	11.8	6.1	5.3	3.9
Tool programmers, numerical control	4	3	4	4	-2.8	2.9	2.3	1.0
Managers and administrators, except farm	6,186	5,760	7,830	7,917	-0.7	3.1	2.1	0.2
Bank officials and financial managers	200	398	600	646	7.1	4.2	3.3	1.5
Buyers and shippers, farm products	37	25	20	20	-3.8	-2.1	-1.5	-0.1

(continued)

149

(Table C.4 continued)

Occupation	Employment				Average Annual Growth Rate			
	1960	1970	1980	1985	1960-70	1970-80	1970-85	1980-85
Buyers, wholesale and retail trade	82	155	210	226	6.6	3.1	2.6	1.5
Managers and administrators, n.e.c.	5,256	4,344	5,906	5,879	-1.9	3.1	2.0	-0.1
Managers and superintendents, building	53	100	150	173	6.7	4.2	3.7	2.8
Restaurant, cafeteria, and bar managers	412	463	553	545	1.2	1.8	1.1	-0.3
Sales managers and department heads, retail	146	275	391	428	6.6	3.6	3.0	1.8
Salesworkers	4,112	4,608	5,862	6,107	1.1	2.4	1.9	0.8
Insurance agents, brokers, and under-writers	328	412	523	576	2.3	2.4	2.3	1.9
Real-estate agents and brokers	234	316	414	450	3.1	2.7	2.4	1.7
Sales representatives, manufacturing	443	394	476	493	1.7	1.9	1.5	0.7
Sales representatives, wholesale	493	635	810	837	2.6	2.5	1.9	0.6
Salesclerks, retail trade	2,031	2,190	2,782	2,825	0.8	2.4	1.7	0.3
Salesworkers, retail trade	408	407	497	523	*	2.0	1.7	1.0
Salespeople, service and construction	140	151	219	250	0.8	3.8	3.4	2.7
Stock and bond sales agents	35	103	141	153	11.4	3.2	2.7	1.7
Clerical and kindred workers	4,975	8,139	10,743	11,861	5.0	2.8	2.5	2.0
Billing clerks	51	123	193	220	9.2	4.6	3.9	2.6
Bookkeepers	921	1,540	1,850	1,900	5.3	1.8	1.4	0.5
Bookkeepers and billing-machine operators	55	69	85	93	2.3	2.2	2.1	1.7
Calculating-machine operators	35	34	37	37	-0.3	0.7	0.6	0.2
Computer and peripheral equipment operators	2	150	246	289	†	5.1	4.5	3.3

150

Insurance adjustors, examiners, and investigators	61	105	136	152	5.6	2.6	2.5	2.3
Keypunch operators	174	300	265	242	5.6	-1.2	-1.4	-1.8
Miscellaneous clerical workers	292	447	715	748	4.3	4.8	3.5	0.9
Office machine operators, n.e.c.	29	52	77	88	5.9	4.0	3.6	2.6
Payroll and timekeeping clerks	121	175	223	238	3.8	2.4	2.1	1.4
Real-estate appraisers	16	24	34	38	4.1	3.4	3.1	2.5
Secretaries, legal, medical and other	1,511	2,785	4,042	4,786	6.3	3.8	3.7	3.4
Shipping and receiving clerks	329	438	500	504	2.9	1.3	0.9	0.8
Statistical clerks	163	291	350	375	6.0	1.9	1.7	1.4
Stenographers	269	128	96	78	-7.2	-2.8	-3.2	-4.1
Stock clerks and storekeepers	401	496	626	670	2.2	2.3	2.0	1.4
Tabulating-machine operators	26	9	4	3	-10.0	-6.9	-7.1	-7.4
Typists	519	973	1,264	1,400	6.5	2.7	2.5	2.1
Craftsmen and kindred workers	6,463	8,232	9,796	10,637	2.4	1.7	1.7	1.7
Air-conditioning, heating, and refrigeration mechanics	71	130	215	265	6.2	5.2	4.9	4.3
Aircraft mechanics and repairers	93	120	160	190	2.6	2.9	3.1	3.5
Auto-body repairers	111	159	175	187	3.6	1.0	1.1	1.3
Auto mechanics	604	837	975	1,050	3.3	1.5	1.5	1.5
Brickmasons and stonemasons	167	172	205	235	0.3	1.8	2.1	2.8
Bulldozer operators	98	100	121	150	0.2	1.9	2.7	4.4
Cabinetmakers	76	75	83	83	-0.1	1.0	0.7	*
Carpenters	832	985	1,125	1,200	1.7	1.3	1.3	1.3
Carpenter apprentices	7	9	11	12	2.6	2.1	2.0	1.7
Crane, derrick, and hoist operators	137	170	194	199	2.2	1.3	1.1	0.6

(continued)

(Table C.4 continued)

	Employment				Average Annual Growth Rate		
	1960	1970	1980	1985	1960-70	1970-80	1970-85	1980-85
Data-processing machine repairers	-0-	36	73	93	†	7.3	6.5	5.1
Decorators and window dressers	51	70	96	101	3.3	3.3	2.5	1.0
Electricians	339	450	581	650	2.9	2.6	2.5	2.3
Electric power line and cable workers	75	100	113	120	2.9	1.3	1.2	1.1
Excavating, grading, and road-machine operators	203	280	346	420	3.3	2.1	2.7	3.9
Farm-implement mechanics and repairers	57	46	50	52	-2.0	0.8	0.8	0.8
Foremen	1,017	1,375	1,562	1,675	3.1	1.3	1.3	1.4
Heavy-equipment mechanics, including diesel	322	687	875	934	7.9	2.5	2.1	1.3
Job and die setters, metal	63	100	135	146	4.8	3.1	2.6	1.6
Machinists	448	361	400	465	-2.1	1.0	1.0	3.0
Machinist apprentices	12	10	11	12	-2.1	1.1	0.9	0.5
Miscellaneous mechanics and repairers	151	158	189	197	0.5	1.8	1.5	0.8
Painter apprentices	2	2	2	2	-0.6	0.6	1.5	3.3
Painters, construction and maintenance	415	400	436	445	-4.0	0.9	0.7	0.4
Paperhangers	23	10	14	15	-8.1	3.2	2.7	1.8
Pattern and model makers, except paper	44	42	41	39	-0.4	-0.3	-0.5	-0.9
Photoengravers and lithographers	27	36	46	50	2.2	3.2	2.7	1.8
Plumbers and pipefitters	300	355	460	500	1.7	2.6	2.3	1.7
Printing-press apprentices	1	3	4	4	†	3.9	2.4	-0.5
Printing-press operators	73	139	165	170	6.7	1.7	1.4	0.7

152

Printing-trades apprentices, except pressmen	10	6	4	3	-4.5	-4.0	-4.5	-5.6
Radio and TV repairers	100	137	150	167	3.3	0.9	1.3	2.2
Sheetmetal apprentices	4	6	8	8	3.4	3.2	2.5	1.2
Sheetmetal workers and tinsmiths	139	155	162	163	1.1	0.5	0.3	0.1
Structural-metal craftsmen	63	79	100	112	2.3	2.4	2.4	2.3
Telephone installers and repairers	177	280	339	348	4.7	1.9	1.3	0.5
Telephone linemen and splicers	41	52	53	54	2.3	0.2	0.3	0.4
Tilesetters	43	32	36	38	-2.9	1.2	1.2	1.1
Upholsterers	67	68	81	83	0.1	1.8	1.3	0.4
Operatives	5,785	6,889	8,029	8,319	1.8	1.5	1.3	0.7
Assemblers	707	944	1,068	1,100	2.9	1.2	1.0	0.6
Bus drivers	174	229	297	315	2.8	2.6	2.1	1.2
Checkers, examiners, and inspectors, manufacturing	516	690	811	830	3.0	1.6	1.2	0.5
Cutting operatives, n.e.c.	197	239	288	297	2.0	1.9	1.5	0.6
Delivery and route workers	591	817	965	1,008	3.3	1.7	1.4	0.9
Dressmakers and seamstresses, except factory	138	110	107	104	-2.2	-0.3	-0.4	-0.5
Drill-press operatives	61	76	88	91	2.3	1.5	1.2	0.7
Graders and sorters, manufacturing	43	45	51	51	0.6	1.2	0.8	*
Grinding-machine operatives	83	145	180	192	5.7	2.2	1.9	1.3
Lathe and milling-machine operatives	100	155	182	189	4.5	1.6	1.3	0.8
Painters, manufactured articles	174	178	190	197	0.3	0.6	0.7	0.7
Other precision-machine operatives	47	77	100	109	5.1	2.7	2.4	1.7
Punch and stamping-press operatives	166	180	214	222	0.8	1.8	1.4	0.7

(continued)

(Table C.4 continued)

Occupation	Employment				Average Annual Growth Rate			
	1960	1970	1980	1985	1960-70	1970-80	1970-85	1980-85
Sawyers	113	120	144	145	0.6	1.8	1.3	0.2
Sewers and stitchers	813	926	1,045	1,048	1.3	1.2	0.8	0.1
Solderers	66	42	29	24	-4.3	-3.6	-3.7	-4.0
Truck drivers	1,438	1,378	1,581	1,627	-0.4	1.4	1.1	0.6
Welders and flame cutters	358	538	689	770	4.2	2.5	2.4	2.3
Service workers	2,683	4,354	5,924	6,686	5.0	3.0	2.9	2.5
Bartenders	172	189	222	235	0.9	1.6	1.5	1.2
Cooks, except private household	562	821	950	1,000	3.9	1.5	1.3	1.0
Childcare workers, except private household	96	339	483	546	13.5	3.6	3.2	2.5
Crossing guards and bridge tenders	31	46	52	54	4.1	1.2	1.1	0.8
Firefighters	140	181	258	315	2.6	3.6	3.8	4.0
Food-service workers, n.e.c., except private household	244	389	483	512	4.8	2.2	1.8	1.2
Hairdressers and cosmetologists	301	480	600	662	4.8	2.3	2.2	2.0
Health aides, except nursing	35	133	249	280	14.3	6.5	5.1	2.3
Housekeepers, except private household	72	111	161	179	4.4	3.8	3.2	2.2
Marshals and constables	6	6	8	9	-0.6	3.1	2.9	2.4
Nursing aides, orderlies, and attendants	465	834	1,203	1,360	6.0	3.7	3.3	2.5
Police and detectives	269	388	520	588	3.8	2.9	2.8	2.5
Practical nurses	260	370	641	835	3.6	5.6	5.6	5.4
School monitors	2	27	40	50	†	4.2	4.3	4.6
Sheriffs and bailiffs	28	40	54	61	3.7	3.1	2.9	2.5

Laborers, except farm	515	654	631	625	2.4	-0.4	-0.3	-0.2
Carpenter helpers	99	117	81	70	1.7	-3.7	-3.4	-2.8
Gardeners and groundskeepers, except farm	416	537	550	555	2.6	0.3	0.2	0.2
Farm occupations	4,686	2,651	1,681	1,339	-5.5	-4.5	-4.5	-4.5
Farm foremen	24	31	27	25	2.6	-1.6	-1.4	-1.1
Farm managers	13	33	45	46	9.8	3.1	2.3	0.5
Farm laborers, wage workers	1,404	897	536	401	-4.4	-5.0	-5.2	-5.6
Farmers, owners and tenants	3,245	1,690	1,073	867	-6.3	-4.4	-4.4	-3.7
Total, all occupations studied	36,612	43,399	53,720	57,235	1.7	2.2	1.9	1.3
Total, all U.S. occupations	65,778	78,627	95,817	101,490	1.8	2.0	1.7	1.2

Note: Details may not add to total because of rounding.
*Less than 0.1 percent growth rate.
†Calculation of growth rate not meaningful because of low base-year figure.
Source: U.S. Department of Labor, Bureau of Labor Statistics.

TABLE C.5

Projected Average Annual Job Openings, 1970–85, Study Occupations

Occupation	Average Annual Job Openings, 1970–85		
	Total	Growth	Openings due to Attrition
Professional, technical, and kindred workers	204,000	108,700	95,300
Computer programmers	12,300	7,600	4,700
Designers	7,700	3,900	3,800
Drafters	17,000	11,300	5,700
Electrical and electronic-engineering technicians	13,300	10,900	2,400
Engineering and science technicians, n.e.c.	29,700	22,300	7,400
Mechanical-engineering technicians	600	400	200
Other technicians, except health	5,300	3,900	1,400
Personnel and labor-relations workers	29,100	17,600	11,500
Recreation workers	6,000	3,000	3,000
Registered nurses	70,300	21,300	49,000
Therapists	12,600	6,400	6,200
Tool programmers, numerical control	100	100	0
Managers and administrators, except farm	344,200	143,300	200,900
Bank officials and financial managers	30,300	13,700	16,600
Buyers and shippers, farm products	400	-300	700
Buyers, wholesale and retail trade	11,800	7,100	4,700
Managers and administrators, n.e.c.	247,500	102,300	145,200
Managers and superintendents, building	13,000	4,900	8,100

Restaurant, cafeteria, and bar managers	22,300	5,500	16,800
Sales managers and department heads, retail	18,900	10,200	8,700
Salesworkers	316,500	100,000	216,500
Insurance agents, brokers, and underwriters	23,700	10,900	12,800
Real-estate agents and brokers	26,900	8,900	17,900
Sales representatives, manufacturing	16,800	6,600	10,200
Sales representatives, wholesale	31,200	13,500	17,700
Salesclerks, retail trade	175,500	42,300	133,200
Salesworkers, retail trade	21,400	7,700	13,700
Salespeople, service and construction	14,000	6,600	7,400
Stock and bond sales agents	7,000	3,300	3,600
Clerical and kindred workers	794,700	228,200	566,500
Billing clerks	16,500	6,500	10,000
Bookkeepers	117,000	24,000	93,000
Bookkeeping and billing-machine operators	6,700	1,600	5,100
Calculating-machine operators	2,400	200	2,200
Computer and peripheral equipment operators	14,400	9,300	5,100
Insurance adjustors, examiners, and investigators	6,800	3,100	3,700
Keypunch operators	13,900	-3,900	17,700
Miscellaneous clerical workers	50,200	20,100	30,100
Office machine operators, n.e.c.	6,000	2,400	3,600
Payroll and timekeeping clerks	14,300	4,200	10,100
Real-estate appraisers	2,000	900	1,100
Secretaries, legal, medical and other	364,800	113,400	251,400
Shipping and receiving clerks	15,100	4,400	10,700
Statistical clerks	22,200	5,600	16,600

(continued)

(Table C.5 continued)

	Average Annual Job Openings, 1970-85		
		Openings due to	
Occupation	Total	Growth	Attrition
Stenographers	3,700	-3,300	7,100
Stock clerks and storekeepers	27,300	11,600	15,700
Tabulating-machine operators	*	-400	200
Typists	111,600	28,500	83,100
Craftsmen and kindred workers	342,100	161,500	180,600
Air-conditioning, heating, and refrigeration mechanics	12,200	9,000	3,200
Aircraft mechanics and repairers	6,700	4,700	2,100
Auto-body repairers	3,900	1,900	2,000
Auto mechanics	29,000	14,200	14,800
Brickmasons and stonemasons	7,400	4,200	3,200
Bulldozer operators	5,400	3,300	2,000
Cabinetmakers	2,800	500	2,300
Carpenters	40,100	14,300	25,700
Carpenter apprentices	500	200	300
Crane, derrick, and hoist operators	5,100	1,900	3,200
Data-processing machine repairers	4,200	3,800	400
Decorators and window dressers	5,900	2,100	3,800
Electricians	23,100	13,300	9,800
Electric power line and cable workers	2,400	1,300	1,100
Excavating, grading, and road-machine operators	15,300	9,300	6,000
Farm-implement mechanics and repairers	1,400	400	1,100

158

Foremen	51,800	20,000	31,800
Heavy-equipment mechanics, including diesel	31,100	16,500	14,600
Job and die setters, metal	5,100	3,100	2,000
Machinists	15,200	6,900	8,300
Machinist apprentices	300	100	200
Miscellaneous mechanics and repairers	8,800	3,700	5,200
Painter apprentices	100	0	100
Painters, construction and maintenance	14,200	3,000	11,200
Paperhangers	800	300	500
Pattern and model makers, except paper	700	−200	900
Photoengravers and lithographers	2,000	1,100	900
Plumbers and pipefitters	18,300	9,700	8,700
Printing-press apprentices	100	100	0
Printing-press operators	4,900	2,100	2,800
Printing-trades apprentices, except print pressmen	*	−200	100
Radio and TV repairers	4,400	2,000	2,400
Sheetmetal apprentices	300	200	100
Sheetmetal workers and tinsmiths	3,100	500	2,600
Structural-metal craftsmen	3,600	2,200	1,400
Telephone installers and repairers	7,400	4,500	2,900
Telephone linemen and splicers	500	100	400
Tilesetters	900	400	500
Upholsterers	3,200	1,000	2,200
Operatives	307,500	95,300	212,200
Assemblers	44,500	10,400	34,100
Bus drivers	13,800	5,700	8,100

(continued)

(Table C.5 continued)

	Average Annual Job Openings, 1970–85		
		Openings due to	
Occupation	Total	Growth	Attrition
Checkers, examiners, and inspectors, manufacturing	35,300	9,300	26,000
Cutting operatives, n.e.c.	11,400	3,900	7,500
Delivery and route workers	27,100	12,700	14,400
Dressmakers and seamstresses, except factory	7,500	-400	7,900
Drill-press operatives	3,000	1,000	2,000
Graders and sorters, manufacturing	2,400	400	2,000
Grinding-machine operatives	6,400	3,100	3,300
Lathe and milling-machine operatives	5,400	2,300	3,200
Painters, manufactured articles	5,000	1,300	3,800
Other precision machine operatives	4,000	2,200	1,800
Punch and stamping-press operatives	7,900	2,800	5,100
Sawyers	4,800	1,700	3,100
Sewers and stitchers	64,700	8,100	56,600
Solderers	300	-1,200	1,500
Truck drivers	38,000	16,600	21,400
Welders and flame cutters	26,000	15,500	10,500
Service workers	428,800	155,500	273,300
Bartenders	10,200	3,100	7,100
Cooks, except private household	52,300	11,900	40,300
Childcare workers, except private household	43,500	13,800	29,700
Crossing guards and bridge tenders	3,800	500	3,300

Firefighters	11,700	8,900	2,800
Food-service workers, n.e.c., except private household	31,300	8,200	23,100
Hairdressers and cosmetologists	49,100	12,100	37,000
Health aides, except nursing	22,000	9,800	12,200
Housekeepers, except private household	12,700	4,500	8,100
Marshals and constables	500	200	300
Nursing aides, orderlies, and attendants	97,200	35,100	62,100
Police and detectives	19,300	13,300	6,000
Practical nurses	69,300	31,000	38,300
School monitors	3,000	1,600	1,400
Sheriffs and bailiffs	2,900	1,400	1,500
Laborers, except farm	20,300	-1,900	22,200
Carpenter helpers	*	-3,100	1,500
Gardeners and groundskeepers, except farm	21,900	1,200	20,700
Farm occupations	*	-87,500	80,700
Farm foremen	400	-400	800
Farm managers	2,100	900	1,200
Farm laborers, wage workers	*	-33,100	19,200
Farmers, owners and tenants	4,600	-54,900	59,500
Total, all occupations studied	2,753,000	905,000	1,848,000
Total, all U.S. occupations	4,946,000	1,524,000	3,422,000
Occupations studied as a percent of all U.S. occupations	56	59	54

<u>Note</u>: Details may not add to totals because of rounding.
*Job openings resulting from attrition are exceeded by projected decline in employment.
<u>Sources</u>: U.S. Department of Labor; The Conference Board.

TABLE C.6

Employment by Sex, 1970 and Projected 1980 and 1985, Study Occupations
(in thousands)

Occupation	1970		Employment 1980		1985	
	Male	Female	Male	Female	Male	Female
Professional, technical, and kindred workers	1,148	968	1,763	1,461	2,152	1,595
Computer programmers	136	40	200	50	236	54
Designers	92	28	118	46	124	54
Drafters	291	25	380	45	428	57
Electrical and electronic-engineering technicians	145	9	221	16	294	23
Engineering and science technicians, n.e.c.	156	34	283	72	411	115
Mechanical-engineering technicians	12	*	14	1	17	1
Other technicians, except health	33	4	67	10	82	13
Personnel and labor-relations workers	197	89	337	141	392	158
Recreation workers	36	24	61	31	73	32
Registered nurses	18	662	27	954	28	972
Therapists	30	52	53	94	64	114
Tool programmers, numerical control	2	1	3	1	3	2
Managers and administrators, except farm	4,879	881	6,745	1,084	6,765	1,152
Bank officials and financial managers	329	69	472	128	495	151
Buyers and shippers, farm products	24	1	19	1	19	1
Buyers, wholesale and retail trade	118	37	158	52	180	46
Managers and administrators, n.e.c.	3,840	504	5,286	620	5,291	588

Managers and superintendents, building	59	41	93	57	110	63
Restaurant, cafeteria, and bar managers	327	136	424	129	350	195
Sales managers and department heads, retail	182	93	294	97	320	108
Salesworkers	2,848	1,759	3,479	2,382	3,577	2,530
Insurance agents, brokers, and underwriters	361	51	442	81	479	97
Real-estate agents and brokers	214	102	245	168	248	202
Sales representatives, manufacturing	361	33	445	31	465	28
Sales representatives, wholesale	594	41	740	71	754	83
Salesclerks, retail trade	771	1,419	938	1,845	929	1,896
Salesworkers, retail trade	335	52	423	74	439	84
Salespeople, service and construction	100	52	122	97	129	121
Stock and bond sales agents	93	9	125	16	134	19
Clerical and kindred workers	1,775	6,363	2,094	8,644	2,128	9,733
Billing clerks	23	100	35	158	40	180
Bookkeepers	276	1,264	355	1,495	378	1,522
Bookkeeping and billing-machine operators	7	61	9	77	9	84
Calculating-machine operators	3	31	6	31	7	30
Computer and peripheral equipment operators	106	44	160	86	180	109
Insurance adjustors, examiners, and investigators	78	30	93	43	99	53
Keypunch operators	32	268	11	254	5	237
Miscellaneous clerical workers	159	288	190	526	173	575
Office machine operators, n.e.c.	17	35	30	42	41	47
Payroll and timekeeping clerks	54	121	57	166	54	184
Real-estate appraisers	23	1	32	2	35	3
Secretaries, legal, medical and other	65	2,720	70	3,971	67	4,719
Shipping and receiving clerks	375	63	397	103	384	120

(continued)

(Table C.6 continued)

Occupation	1970 Male	1970 Female	1980 Male	1980 Female	1985 Male	1985 Female
Statistical clerks	103	188	117	233	105	270
Stenographers	8	120	8	88	8	70
Stock clerks and storekeepers	385	111	441	185	448	222
Tabulating-machine operators	4	5	1	3	1	2
Typists	56	917	82	1,182	95	1,305
Craftsmen and kindred workers	7,923	306	9,326	471	10,069	568
Air-conditioning, heating, and refrigeration mechanics	129	1	212	3	260	5
Aircraft mechanics and repairers	116	4	153	7	180	10
Auto-body repairers	157	2	172	4	182	5
Auto mechanics	825	12	952	23	1,020	30
Brickmasons and stonemasons	170	2	201	4	230	5
Bulldozer operators	99	1	118	3	146	4
Cabinetmakers	71	4	77	6	76	7
Carpenters	972	13	1,100	25	1,168	32
Carpenter apprentices	8	*	11	*	12	*
Crane, derrick, and hoist operators	168	2	189	4	194	5
Data-processing machine repairers	35	1	71	2	91	2
Decorators and window dressers	29	41	31	65	28	74
Electricians	442	8	566	16	629	21
Electric power line and cable workers	99	1	112	1	119	1
Excavating, grading, and road-machine operators	277	3	340	6	412	8

Farm-implement mechanics and repairers	46	*	49	1	51	1
Foremen	1,265	110	1,417	145	1,508	167
Heavy-equipment mechanics, including diesel	674	13	853	23	906	28
Job and die setters, metal	98	2	130	5	140	6
Machinists	350	11	381	19	439	26
Machinist apprentices	10	*	11	*	11	*
Miscellaneous mechanics and repairers	152	7	183	7	191	6
Painter apprentices	2	0	2	*	2	*
Painters, construction and maintenance	385	15	413	22	420	25
Paperhangers	9	1	12	2	13	2
Pattern and model makers, except paper	40	2	38	3	35	4
Photoengravers and lithographers	29	4	39	7	42	8
Plumbers and pipefitters	351	4	452	8	490	10
Printing-press apprentices	3	*	4	*	4	*
Printing-press operators	128	11	152	13	151	19
Printing-trades apprentices, except print pressmen	6	*	4	*	3	*
Radio and TV repairers	132	5	143	7	159	9
Sheetmetal apprentices	6	0	8	*	9	*
Sheetmetal workers and tinsmiths	152	3	157	5	157	6
Structural-metal craftsmen	78	1	99	1	111	1
Telephone installers and repairers	270	10	323	16	329	19
Telephone linemen and splicers	51	1	53	*	54	0
Tilesetters	32	*	35	1	37	1
Upholsterers	57	11	65	16	65	18
Operatives	4,726	2,163	5,429	2,600	5,593	2,725
Assemblers	484	460	519	549	520	580

(continued)

(Table C.6 continued)

Occupation	1970 Male	1970 Female	1980 Male	1980 Female	1985 Male	1985 Female
Bus drivers	164	65	169	188	156	159
Checkers, examiners, and inspectors, manufacturing	359	331	407	404	409	421
Cutting operatives, n.e.c.	177	62	201	87	200	97
Delivery and route workers	792	25	936	29	978	30
Dressmakers and seamstresses, except factory	5	105	6	101	6	98
Drill-press operatives	60	16	68	19	69	22
Graders and sorters, manufacturing	16	29	20	31	21	30
Grinding-machine operatives	136	9	168	13	177	15
Lathe and milling-machine operatives	147	8	170	12	176	13
Painters, manufactured articles	152	26	159	31	163	34
Other precision machine operatives	68	8	88	12	94	14
Punch and stamping-press operatives	126	54	147	67	151	71
Sawyers	110	10	127	17	125	20
Sewers and stitchers	57	869	67	979	68	980
Solderers	7	35	3	27	1	23
Truck drivers	1,357	21	1,534	47	1,565	62
Welders and flame cutters	507	31	641	48	712	58
Service workers	1,430	2,924	1,787	4,137	1,941	4,745
Bartenders	149	40	152	69	150	85
Cooks, except private household	305	516	369	581	396	604
Childcare workers, except private household	23	316	48	435	63	485

Occupation						
Crossing guards and bridge tenders	19	27	12	40	9	45
Firefighters	179	2	253	5	308	7
Food-service workers, n.e.c., except private household	94	295	87	396	62	450
Hairdressers and cosmetologists	48	432	50	550	50	611
Health aides, except nursing	21	112	48	202	58	222
Housekeepers, except private household	30	81	46	115	52	127
Marshals and constables	6	*	8	*	9	*
Nursing aides, orderlies, and attendants	128	706	150	1,053	151	1,209
Police and detectives	374	14	495	25	556	32
Practical nurses	14	356	17	624	18	817
School monitors	2	24	2	38	2	48
Sheriffs and bailiffs	38	2	50	4	57	4
Laborers, except farm	635	18	605	25	597	28
Carpenter helpers	114	2	78	3	67	3
Gardeners and groundskeepers, except farm	521	16	528	22	530	25
Farm occupations	2,451	200	1,540	141	1,223	116
Farm foremen	29	2	24	2	23	2
Farm managers	32	1	43	2	43	3
Farm laborers, wage workers	779	118	450	86	331	70
Farmers, owners and tenants	1,611	79	1,023	51	826	41
Total, all occupations studied	27,815	15,585	32,767	20,946	34,045	23,191
Total, all U.S. occupations	48,984	29,642	58,594	37,223	61,902	39,588
Occupations studied as a percent of all U.S. occupations	57	53	56	56	55	59

Note: Details may not add to totals because of rounding.
*Fewer than 500 persons employed.
Sources: U.S. Department of Labor; 1970 Census of Population; The Conference Board.

TABLE C.7

Distribution of Employment by Sex, 1970 and Projected 1980 and 1985, Study Occupations
(in percent)

Occupation	1970 Male	1970 Female	1980 Male	1980 Female	1985 Male	1985 Female
Professional, technical, and kindred workers	54.3	45.7	54.7	45.3	57.4	42.6
Computer programmers	77.3	22.7	80.0	20.0	81.3	18.7
Designers	76.5	23.5	72.0	28.0	69.7	30.3
Drafters	92.0	8.0	89.5	10.5	88.2	11.8
Electrical and electronic-engineering technicians	94.3	5.7	93.3	6.7	92.8	7.2
Engineering and science technicians, n.e.c.	82.3	17.7	79.6	20.4	78.2	21.8
Mechanical-engineering technicians	97.1	2.9	94.2	5.8	92.7	7.3
Other technicians, except health	89.2	10.8	87.0	13.0	85.9	14.1
Personnel and labor-relations workers	68.8	31.2	70.5	29.5	71.3	28.7
Recreation workers	59.6	40.4	66.5	33.5	69.0	31.0
Registered nurses	2.6	97.4	2.7	97.3	2.8	97.2
Therapists	36.4	63.6	36.0	64.0	35.8	64.2
Tool programmers, numerical control	84.9	15.1	69.8	30.2	62.3	37.7
Managers and administrators, except farm	84.7	15.3	86.2	13.8	85.4	14.6
Bank officials and financial managers	82.6	17.4	78.6	21.4	76.5	23.5
Buyers and shippers, farm products	97.9	2.1	96.9	3.1	96.4	3.6
Buyers, wholesale and retail trade	70.6	29.4	76.7	23.3	79.7	20.3
Managers and administrators, n.e.c.	88.4	11.6	89.5	10.5	89.0	11.0
Managers and superintendents, building	59.3	40.7	62.2	37.8	63.7	36.3
Restaurant, cafeteria, and bar managers	66.2	33.8	64.9	35.1	64.2	35.8

Sales managers and department heads, retail	75.9	24.1	75.2	24.8	74.8	25.2
Salesworkers	61.8	38.2	59.4	40.6	58.6	41.4
Insurance agents, brokers, and underwriters	87.5	12.5	84.6	15.4	83.1	16.9
Real-estate agents and brokers	67.7	32.3	68.2	31.8	55.1	44.9
Sales representatives, manufacturing	91.5	8.5	93.4	6.6	94.3	5.7
Sales representatives, wholesale	93.6	6.4	91.3	8.7	90.1	9.9
Salesclerks, retail trade	35.2	64.8	33.7	66.3	32.9	67.1
Salesworkers, retail trade	87.2	12.8	85.1	14.9	84.0	16.0
Salespeople, service and construction	65.9	34.1	55.7	44.3	51.4	48.6
Stock and bond sales agents	91.4	8.6	88.8	11.2	87.5	12.5
Clerical and kindred workers	21.8	78.2	19.5	80.5	17.9	82.1
Billing clerks	18.4	81.6	18.1	81.9	18.0	82.0
Bookkeepers	17.9	82.1	19.2	80.8	19.9	80.1
Bookkeeping and billing-machine operators	10.4	89.6	10.2	89.8	10.1	89.9
Calculating-machine operators	9.2	90.8	16.4	83.6	19.7	80.3
Computer and peripheral equipment operators	70.8	29.2	65.0	35.0	62.1	37.9
Insurance adjustors, examiners, and investigators	74.4	25.6	68.2	31.8	65.1	34.9
Keypunch operators	10.6	89.4	4.1	95.9	2.0	98.0
Miscellaneous clerical workers	35.5	64.5	26.5	73.5	23.1	76.9
Office machine operators, n.e.c.	32.5	67.5	42.0	58.0	46.7	53.3
Payroll and timekeeping clerks	31.0	69.0	25.6	74.4	22.9	77.1
Real-estate appraisers	95.9	4.1	94.8	5.2	91.3	8.7
Secretaries, legal, medical and other	2.4	97.6	1.7	98.3	1.4	98.6
Shipping and receiving clerks	85.7	14.3	79.4	20.6	76.2	23.8
Statistical clerks	35.5	64.5	30.5	69.5	28.0	72.0
Stenographers	6.6	93.4	8.8	91.2	9.9	90.1

(continued)

(Table C.7 continued)

Occupation	1970 Male	1970 Female	1980 Male	1980 Female	1985 Male	1985 Female
Stock clerks and storekeepers	77.6	22.4	70.4	29.6	66.8	33.2
Tabulating-machine operators	48.1	51.9	31.8	68.2	26.7	73.3
Typists	5.8	94.2	6.5	93.5	6.8	93.2
Craftsmen and kindred workers	96.3	3.7	95.2	4.8	94.7	5.3
Air-conditioning, heating, and refrigeration mechanics	99.1	0.9	98.5	1.5	98.2	1.8
Aircraft mechanics and repairers	97.0	3.0	95.5	4.5	94.7	5.3
Auto-body repairers	99.0	1.0	98.0	2.0	97.5	2.5
Auto mechanics	98.6	1.4	97.6	2.4	97.1	2.9
Brickmasons and stonemasons	98.8	1.2	98.1	1.9	97.8	2.2
Bulldozer operators	98.6	1.4	97.7	2.3	97.2	2.8
Cabinetmakers	95.1	4.9	92.6	7.4	91.5	8.5
Carpenters	98.7	1.3	97.8	2.2	97.3	2.7
Carpenter apprentices	98.6	1.4	98.2	1.8	97.5	2.5
Crane, derrick, and hoist operators	98.7	1.3	97.9	2.1	97.5	2.5
Data-processing machine repairers	97.7	2.3	97.7	2.3	97.7	2.3
Decorators and window dressers	41.6	58.4	32.2	67.8	27.5	72.5
Electricians	98.3	1.7	97.3	2.7	96.8	3.2
Electric power line and cable workers	98.8	1.2	99.3	0.7	99.5	0.5
Excavating, grading, and road-machine operators	99.0	1.0	98.4	1.6	98.1	1.9
Farm-implement mechanics and repairers	98.9	1.1	97.8	2.2	97.3	2.7
Foremen	92.0	8.0	90.7	9.3	90.0	10.0
Heavy-equipment mechanics, including diesel	98.1	1.9	97.4	2.6	97.0	3.0

170

Job and die setters, metal	97.5	2.5	96.5	3.5	96.0	4.0
Machinists	97.0	3.0	95.3	4.7	94.4	5.6
Machinist apprentices	97.4	2.6	96.4	3.6	96.5	3.5
Miscellaneous mechanics and repairers	95.8	4.2	96.5	3.5	96.8	3.2
Painter apprentices	98.9	1.1	98.3	1.7	98.0	2.0
Painters, construction and maintenance	96.2	3.8	94.9	5.1	94.3	5.7
Paperhangers	89.6	10.4	87.6	12.4	86.0	14.0
Pattern and model makers, except paper	95.3	4.7	92.2	7.8	90.6	9.4
Photoengravers and lithographers	87.4	12.6	85.2	14.8	84.1	15.9
Plumbers and pipefitters	99.0	1.0	98.3	1.7	97.9	2.1
Printing-press apprentices	98.0	2.0	97.4	2.6	97.1	2.9
Printing-press operators	92.0	8.0	89.8	10.2	88.7	11.3
Printing-trades apprentices, except print pressmen	95.1	4.9	93.7	6.3	93.0	7.0
Radio and TV repairers	96.2	3.8	95.3	4.7	94.9	5.1
Sheetmetal apprentices	99.2	0.8	99.1	0.9	99.0	1.0
Sheetmetal workers and tinsmiths	97.9	2.1	96.9	3.1	96.4	3.6
Structural-metal craftsmen	98.8	1.2	99.1	0.9	99.2	0.8
Telephone installers and repairers	96.6	3.4	95.2	4.8	94.5	5.5
Telephone linemen and splicers	98.7	1.3	99.2	0.8	99.4	0.6
Tilesetters	98.7	1.3	97.4	2.6	96.8	3.2
Upholsterers	83.7	16.3	80.2	19.8	78.4	21.6
Operatives	68.6	31.4	67.6	32.4	67.3	32.7
Assemblers	51.3	48.7	48.6	51.4	47.3	52.7
Bus drivers	71.7	28.3	57.0	43.0	49.6	50.4
Checkers, examiners, and inspectors, manufacturing	52.0	48.0	50.2	49.8	49.3	50.7
Cutting operatives, n.e.c.	74.2	25.8	69.8	30.2	67.4	32.6

(continued)

(Table C.7 continued)

Occupation	1970 Male	1970 Female	1980 Male	1980 Female	1985 Male	1985 Female
Delivery and route workers	96.9	3.1	97.0	3.0	97.0	3.0
Dressmakers and seamstresses, except factory	4.3	95.7	5.3	94.7	5.8	94.2
Drill-press operatives	78.5	21.5	77.8	22.2	76.0	24.0
Graders and sorters, manufacturing	35.6	64.4	39.0	61.0	40.7	59.3
Grinding-machine operatives	94.0	6.0	92.9	7.1	92.3	7.7
Lathe and milling-machine operatives	94.7	5.3	93.6	6.4	93.0	7.0
Painters, manufactured articles	85.5	14.5	83.8	16.2	82.9	17.1
Other precision machine operatives	89.4	10.6	87.6	12.4	86.7	13.3
Punch and stamping-press operatives	70.0	30.0	68.7	31.3	68.0	32.0
Sawyers	92.1	7.9	88.4	11.6	86.5	13.5
Sewers and stitchers	6.2	93.8	6.4	93.6	6.5	93.5
Solderers	17.2	82.8	8.8	91.2	4.6	95.4
Truck drivers	98.5	1.5	97.0	3.0	96.2	3.8
Welders and flame cutters	94.3	5.7	93.1	6.9	92.5	7.5
Service workers	32.8	67.2	30.2	69.8	29.0	71.0
Bartenders	78.7	21.3	68.7	31.3	63.7	36.3
Cooks, except private household	37.2	62.8	38.8	61.2	39.6	60.4
Childcare workers, except private household	6.8	93.2	10.0	90.0	11.6	88.4
Crossing guards and bridge tenders	40.6	59.4	24.1	75.9	15.9	84.1
Firefighters	98.8	1.2	98.1	1.9	97.8	2.2
Food-service workers, n.e.c., except private household	24.1	75.9	18.1	81.9	12.1	87.9

Occupation						
Hairdressers and cosmetologists	10.0	90.0	8.4	91.6	7.6	92.4
Health aides, except nursing	16.1	83.9	19.2	80.8	20.8	79.2
Housekeepers, except private household	27.3	72.7	28.6	71.4	29.3	70.7
Marshals and constables	95.9	4.1	95.6	4.4	95.5	4.5
Nursing aides, orderlies, and attendants	15.4	84.6	12.5	87.5	11.1	88.9
Police and detectives	96.3	3.7	95.2	5.2	94.5	5.4
Practical nurses	3.7	96.3	2.7	97.3	2.2	97.8
School monitors	8.8	91.2	5.5	94.5	4.2	95.8
Sheriffs and bailiffs	94.1	5.9	93.2	6.8	92.7	7.3
Laborers, except farm	97.2	2.8	96.0	4.0	95.5	4.5
Carpenter helpers	97.9	2.1	97.8	2.2	96.1	3.9
Gardeners and groundskeepers, except farm	97.0	3.0	96.0	4.0	95.5	4.5
Farm occupations	92.5	7.5	91.6	8.4	91.3	8.7
Farm foremen	93.8	6.2	91.7	8.3	90.6	9.4
Farm managers	96.0	4.0	94.9	5.1	94.3	5.7
Farm laborers, wage workers	86.8	13.2	84.0	16.0	82.6	17.4
Farmers, owners and tenants	95.3	4.7	95.3	4.7	95.3	4.7
Total, all occupations studied	64.1	35.9	61.0	39.0	59.5	40.5
Total, all U.S. occupations	62.3	37.7	62.1	38.8	61.0	39.0

Note: Details may not add to totals because of rounding.
Sources: U.S. Department of Labor; 1960 and 1970 Census of Population; The Conference Board.

TABLE C.8

Employment by Race, 1970 and Projected 1980 and 1985, Study Occupations
(in thousands)

Occupation	1970		1980		1985	
	White	Nonwhite	White	Nonwhite	White	Nonwhite
Professional, technical, and kindred workers	1,972	145	2,929	295	3,365	380
Computer programmers	168	9	233	17	268	22
Designers	115	5	153	11	164	14
Drafters	302	14	397	28	448	37
Electrical and electronic-engineering technicians	146	8	220	17	291	26
Engineering and science technicians, n.e.c.	180	10	327	28	477	48
Mechanical-engineering technicians	12	*	14	1	17	1
Other technicians, except health	34	3	70	7	85	10
Personnel and labor-relations workers	268	18	440	38	502	48
Recreation workers	50	10	71	21	78	27
Registered nurses	619	61	867	113	872	128
Therapists	75	7	133	14	159	19
Tool programmers, numerical control	3	*	4	*	4	*
Managers and administrators, except farm	5,584	176	7,527	302	7,579	338
Bank officials and financial managers	388	10	578	22	619	27
Buyers and shippers, farm products	25	*	20	*	20	*
Buyers, wholesale and retail trade	151	4	205	5	220	6
Managers and administrators, n.e.c.	4,222	122	5,693	213	5,644	235
Managers and superintendents, building	94	6	145	5	170	3

Occupation							
Restaurant, cafeteria, and bar managers	449	14	524	28	511	34
Sales managers and department heads, retail	255	20	362	29	395	33
Salesworkers	4,444	164	5,572	289	5,764	342
Insurance agents, brokers, and underwriters	397	15	497	26	544	32
Real-estate agents and brokers	309	7	404	10	439	11
Sales representatives, manufacturing	387	7	463	13	477	16
Sales representatives, wholesale	622	13	787	23	809	28
Salesclerks, retail trade	2,087	103	2,601	181	2,616	209
Salesworkers, retail trade	396	11	479	18	501	22
Salespeople, service and construction	145	6	205	14	232	19
Stock and bond sales agents	101	2	136	4	147	6
Clerical and kindred workers	7,585	553	9,784	954	10,681	1,180
Billing clerks	116	7	178	15	200	20
Bookkeepers	1,485	55	1,745	105	1,771	129
Bookkeeping and billing-machine operators	62	6	75	11	80	13
Calculating-machine operators	31	3	33	4	32	5
Computer and peripheral equipment operators	136	14	215	32	247	42
Insurance adjustors, examiners, and investigators	101	4	126	7	143	9
Keypunch operators	259	41	216	49	191	51
Miscellaneous clerical workers	407	39	629	86	646	102
Office machine operators, n.e.c.	47	5	63	9	75	13
Payroll and timekeeping clerks	164	11	203	20	214	24
Real-estate appraisers	24	*	33	1	37	1
Secretaries, legal, medical and other	2,672	113	3,811	230	4,473	314
Shipping and receiving clerks	380	58	423	76	421	83
Statistical clerks	267	24	310	40	326	49

(continued)

(Table C.8 continued)

Occupation	1970 White	1970 Nonwhite	1980 White	1980 Nonwhite	1985 White	1985 Nonwhite
Stenographers	120	8	87	9	69	9
Stock clerks and storekeepers	439	57	551	74	588	82
Tabulating-machine operators	8	1	4	1	2	1
Typists	868	105	1,079	185	1,169	231
Craftsmen and kindred workers	7,708	522	8,993	804	9,657	980
Air-conditioning, heating, and refrigeration mechanics	124	6	201	14	245	20
Aircraft mechanics and repairers	112	8	146	14	171	19
Auto-body repairers	148	11	162	13	172	15
Auto mechanics	766	71	881	94	943	107
Brickmasons and stonemasons	140	32	158	47	176	59
Bulldozer operators	87	13	98	23	118	32
Cabinetmakers	71	4	82	1	82	1
Carpenters	924	61	1,045	80	1,109	91
Carpenter apprentices	8	1	10	1	11	1
Crane, derrick, and hoist operators	148	22	163	30	165	34
Data-processing machine repairers	35	1	68	5	90	3
Decorators and window dressers	66	4	90	6	95	7
Electricians	434	16	552	30	612	38
Electric power line and cable workers	96	4	105	8	109	11
Excavating, grading, and road-machine operators	262	18	314	32	375	45
Farm-implement mechanics and repairers	45	2	48	2	50	2

Foremen	1,312	63	1,448	114	1,529	146
Heavy-equipment mechanics, including diesel	651	36	816	60	863	71
Job and die setters, metal	94	5	125	10	134	12
Machinists	341	20	367	33	419	45
Machinist apprentices	9	1	10	1	10	2
Miscellaneous mechanics and repairers	151	7	175	15	179	18
Painter apprentices	1	*	1	*	2	*
Painters, construction and maintenance	359	41	380	56	382	63
Paperhangers	9	1	13	1	14	1
Pattern and model makers, except paper	41	1	39	2	37	2
Photoengravers and lithographers	33	1	45	1	49	1
Plumbers and pipefitters	335	20	427	33	461	40
Printing-press apprentices	3	*	4	*	4	*
Printing-press operators	130	9	153	12	157	13
Printing-trades apprentices, except print pressmen	6	*	4	*	3	*
Radio and TV repairers	129	8	140	10	155	12
Sheetmetal apprentices	6	*	8	*	8	*
Sheetmetal workers and tinsmiths	149	6	154	8	153	9
Structural-metal craftsmen	76	3	96	3	108	4
Telephone installers and repairers	267	13	314	25	317	31
Telephone linemen and splicers	49	3	48	5	48	6
Tilesetters	29	3	31	5	32	6
Upholsterers	62	6	72	9	70	13
Operatives	6,097	792	6,931	1,103	7,086	1,232
Assemblers	817	126	898	170	912	188
Bus drivers	194	35	240	58	247	68

(continued)

(Table C.8 continued)

Occupation	1970 White	1970 Nonwhite	1980 White	1980 Nonwhite	1985 White	1985 Nonwhite
Checkers, examiners, and inspectors, manufacturing	631	59	727	84	735	95
Cutting operatives, n.e.c.	231	8	275	14	281	16
Delivery and route workers	730	87	840	125	865	143
Dressmakers and seamstresses, except factory	97	13	90	16	86	18
Drill-press operatives	70	6	80	8	82	9
Graders and sorters, manufacturing	39	6	43	8	42	9
Grinding-machine operatives	132	13	161	19	170	22
Lathe and milling-machine operatives	148	7	172	10	177	12
Painters, manufactured articles	151	27	155	40	157	40
Other precision machine operatives	72	5	92	8	100	9
Punch and stamping-press operatives	162	18	189	25	194	28
Sawyers	99	21	120	24	121	24
Sewers and stitchers	814	112	855	190	825	223
Solderers	38	5	25	4	24	4
Truck drivers	1,189	189	1,377	204	1,423	203
Welders and flame cutters	483	55	592	96	648	122
Service workers	3,591	761	4,846	1,078	5,441	1,245
Bartenders	178	11	208	13	221	14
Cooks, except private household	638	183	762	188	814	186
Childcare workers, except private household	283	56	396	86	444	102
Crossing guards and bridge tenders	42	4	46	6	48	6

Firefighters	176	5	251	7	306		9
Food-service workers, n.e.c., except private household	307	82	393	90	423		89
Hairdressers and cosmetologists	440	40	561	39	625		37
Health aides, except nursing	105	28	195	55	217		63
Housekeepers, except private household	95	16	136	25	151		28
Marshals and constables	6	*	8	*	9		*
Nursing aides, orderlies, and attendants	613	221	869	335	972		388
Police and detectives	362	26	473	47	528		60
Practical nurses	283	87	461	180	581		254
School monitors	24	2	36	4	45		5
Sheriffs and bailiffs	38	2	51	3	57		4
Laborers, except farm	513	141	504	126	503		122
Carpenter helpers	90	27	66	14	59		11
Gardeners and groundskeepers, except farm	423	114	438	112	444		111
Farm occupations	2,394	257	1,573	108	1,275		64
Farm foremen	28	3	23	3	22		3
Farm managers	31	2	43	2	44		2
Farm laborers, wage workers	694	203	445	91	344		57
Farmers, owners and tenants	1,641	49	1,062	12	865		2
Total, all occupations studied	39,888	3,511	48,659	5,059	51,356		5,879
Total, all U.S. occupations	70,182	8,445	84,439	11,378	88,869		12,621
Occupations studied as a percent of all U.S. occupations	57	42	58	45	58		47

Note: Details may not add to totals because of rounding.

*Fewer than 500 persons employed.

Sources: U.S. Department of Labor; 1970 Census of Population; The Conference Board.

TABLE C.9

Distribution of Employment by Race, 1970 and Projected 1980 and 1985, Study Occupations
(in percent)

Occupation	1970 White	1970 Nonwhite	1980 White	1980 Nonwhite	1985 White	1985 Nonwhite
Professional, technical, and kindred workers	93.2	6.8	90.8	9.2	89.9	10.1
Computer programmers	94.5	5.5	93.2	6.8	92.5	7.5
Designers	95.6	4.4	93.4	6.6	92.3	7.7
Drafters	95.6	4.4	93.5	6.5	92.4	7.6
Electrical and electronic-engineering technicians	94.8	5.2	92.8	7.2	91.8	8.2
Engineering and science technicians, n.e.c.	94.8	5.2	92.2	7.8	90.9	9.1
Mechanical-engineering technicians	97.0	3.0	95.5	4.5	94.4	5.6
Other technicians, except health	92.5	7.5	90.5	9.5	89.5	10.5
Personnel and labor-relations workers	93.6	6.4	92.0	8.0	91.2	8.8
Recreation workers	83.6	16.4	77.6	22.4	74.6	25.4
Registered nurses	91.0	9.0	88.5	11.5	87.2	12.8
Therapists	91.6	8.4	90.3	9.7	89.6	10.4
Tool programmers, numerical control	96.0	4.0	92.8	7.2	93.0	7.0
Managers and administrators, except farm	96.9	3.1	96.1	3.9	95.7	4.3
Bank officials and financial managers	97.5	2.5	96.4	3.6	95.8	4.2
Buyers and shippers, farm products	98.8	1.2	99.0	1.0	99.1	0.9
Buyers, wholesale and retail trade	97.5	2.5	97.4	2.6	97.3	2.7
Managers and administrators, n.e.c.	97.2	2.8	96.4	3.6	96.0	4.0
Managers and superintendents, building	94.2	5.8	96.8	3.2	98.1	1.9

Restaurant, cafeteria, and bar managers	97.0	3.0	94.9	5.1	93.8	6.2
Sales managers and department heads, retail	92.8	7.2	92.5	7.5	92.3	7.7
Salesworkers	96.4	3.6	95.1	4.9	94.4	5.6
Insurance agents, brokers, and underwriters	96.4	3.6	95.1	4.9	94.4	5.6
Real-estate agents and brokers	97.8	2.2	97.7	2.3	97.6	2.4
Sales representatives, manufacturing	98.2	1.8	97.3	2.7	96.8	3.2
Sales representatives, wholesale	98.0	2.0	97.1	2.9	96.6	3.4
Salesclerks, retail trade	95.3	4.7	93.5	6.5	92.6	7.4
Salesworkers, retail trade	97.3	2.7	96.3	3.7	95.8	4.2
Salespeople, service and construction	95.9	4.1	93.7	6.3	92.6	7.4
Stock and bond sales agents	97.8	2.2	96.8	3.2	96.3	3.7
Clerical and kindred workers	93.2	6.8	91.1	8.9	90.1	9.9
Billing clerks	94.1	5.9	92.0	8.0	90.9	9.1
Bookkeepers	96.4	3.6	94.3	5.7	93.2	6.8
Bookkeeping and billing-machine operators	90.9	9.1	87.6	12.4	86.0	14.0
Calculating-machine operators	92.0	8.0	89.2	10.8	87.6	12.4
Computer and peripheral equipment operators	90.6	9.4	87.2	12.8	85.5	14.5
Insurance adjustors, examiners, and investigators	96.0	4.0	94.5	5.5	93.8	6.2
Keypunch operators	86.4	13.6	81.5	18.5	79.0	21.0
Miscellaneous clerical workers	91.2	8.8	88.0	12.0	86.4	13.6
Office machine operators, n.e.c.	90.6	9.4	87.2	12.8	85.5	14.5
Payroll and timekeeping clerks	93.8	6.2	91.1	8.9	89.8	10.2
Real-estate appraisers	98.0	2.0	97.9	2.1	97.8	2.2
Secretaries, legal, medical and other	96.1	3.9	94.3	5.7	93.5	6.5
Shipping and receiving clerks	86.8	13.2	84.7	15.3	83.6	16.4
Statistical clerks	91.6	8.4	88.5	11.5	87.0	13.0

(continued)

(Table C.9 continued)

Occupation	1970 White	1970 Nonwhite	1980 White	1980 Nonwhite	1985 White	1985 Nonwhite
Stenographers	93.7	6.3	90.3	9.7	88.6	11.4
Stock clerks and storekeepers	88.6	11.4	88.1	11.9	87.8	12.2
Tabulating-machine operators	86.5	13.5	81.6	18.4	79.2	20.8
Typists	89.2	10.8	85.4	14.6	83.5	16.5
Craftsmen and kindred workers	93.7	6.3	91.7	8.3	90.8	9.2
Air-conditioning, heating, and refrigeration mechanics	95.3	4.7	93.4	6.6	92.4	7.6
Aircraft mechanics and repairers	93.5	6.5	91.3	8.7	90.2	9.8
Auto-body repairers	93.3	6.7	92.4	7.6	91.9	8.1
Auto mechanics	91.5	8.5	90.4	9.6	89.8	10.2
Brickmasons and stonemasons	81.6	18.4	77.2	22.8	75.0	25.0
Bulldozer operators	87.0	13.0	81.4	18.6	78.6	21.4
Cabinetmakers	95.0	5.0	98.8	1.2	98.8	1.2
Carpenters	93.8	6.2	92.9	7.1	92.4	7.6
Carpenter apprentices	94.2	5.8	92.8	7.2	92.1	7.9
Crane, derrick, and hoist operators	87.1	12.9	84.4	15.6	83.0	17.0
Data-processing machine repairers	96.9	3.1	93.6	6.4	96.3	3.7
Decorators and window dressers	93.9	6.1	93.6	6.4	93.4	6.6
Electricians	96.4	3.6	94.9	5.1	94.1	5.9
Electric power line and cable workers	95.6	4.4	92.6	7.4	91.1	8.9
Excavating, grading, and road-machine operators	93.7	6.3	90.7	9.3	89.2	10.8
Farm-implement mechanics and repairers	96.2	3.8	95.8	4.2	95.6	4.4

Foremen	95.4	4.6	92.7	7.3	91.3	8.7
Heavy-equipment mechanics, including diesel	94.7	5.3	93.2	6.8	92.4	7.6
Job and die setters, metal	94.5	5.5	92.8	7.2	91.9	8.1
Machinists	94.4	5.6	91.7	8.3	90.3	9.7
Machinist apprentices	91.5	8.5	87.6	12.4	85.6	14.4
Miscellaneous mechanics and repairers	95.3	4.7	92.3	7.7	90.8	9.2
Painter apprentices	85.2	14.8	81.6	18.4	79.8	20.2
Painters, construction and maintenance	89.8	10.2	87.2	12.8	85.9	14.1
Paperhangers	94.5	5.5	93.0	7.0	92.2	7.8
Pattern and model makers, except paper	97.6	2.4	96.1	3.9	95.3	4.7
Photoengravers and lithographers	98.0	2.0	98.0	2.0	98.0	2.0
Plumbers and pipefitters	94.5	5.5	92.9	7.1	92.1	7.9
Printing-press apprentices	95.8	4.2	94.3	5.7	93.6	6.4
Printing-press operators	93.7	6.3	92.9	7.1	92.5	7.5
Printing-trades apprentices, except print pressmen	95.1	4.9	93.2	6.8	92.2	7.8
Radio and TV repairers	93.8	6.2	93.1	6.9	92.7	7.3
Sheetmetal apprentices	95.6	4.4	95.3	4.7	95.2	4.8
Sheetmetal workers and tinsmiths	96.3	3.7	94.9	5.1	94.2	5.8
Structural-metal craftsmen	95.7	4.3	96.4	3.6	96.7	3.3
Telephone installers and repairers	95.5	4.5	92.5	7.5	91.0	9.0
Telephone linemen and splicers	94.5	5.5	90.9	9.1	89.1	10.9
Tilesetters	89.3	10.7	86.4	13.6	84.9	15.1
Upholsterers	90.8	9.2	88.8	11.2	84.8	15.2
Operatives	88.5	11.5	86.3	13.7	85.1	14.8
Assemblers	86.6	13.4	84.1	15.9	82.9	17.1
Bus drivers	84.7	15.3	80.6	19.4	78.5	21.5

(continued)

(Table C.9 continued)

	Distribution of Employment					
	1970		1980		1985	
Occupation	White	Nonwhite	White	Nonwhite	White	Nonwhite
Checkers, examiners, and inspectors, manufacturing	91.5	8.5	89.6	10.4	88.6	11.4
Cutting operatives, n.e.c.	96.6	3.4	95.3	4.7	94.6	5.4
Delivery and route workers	89.3	10.7	87.0	13.0	85.8	14.2
Dressmakers and seamstresses, except factory	87.8	12.2	84.6	15.4	83.0	17.0
Drill-press operatives	92.0	8.0	90.7	9.3	90.0	10.0
Graders and sorters, manufacturing	86.2	13.8	84.1	15.9	83.0	17.0
Grinding-machine operatives	91.0	9.0	89.5	10.5	88.7	11.3
Lathe and milling-machine operatives	95.7	4.3	94.4	5.6	93.7	6.3
Painters, manufactured articles	85.1	14.9	81.6	18.4	79.8	20.2
Other precision machine operatives	93.7	6.3	92.2	7.8	91.4	8.6
Punch and stamping-press operatives	90.0	10.0	88.3	11.7	87.4	12.6
Sawyers	82.6	17.4	83.3	16.7	83.6	16.4
Sewers and stitchers	87.9	12.1	81.8	18.2	78.7	21.3
Solderers	89.2	10.8	85.2	14.8	83.2	16.8
Truck drivers	86.3	13.7	87.1	12.9	87.5	12.5
Welders and flame cutters	89.8	10.2	86.0	14.0	84.1	15.9
Service workers	82.5	17.5	81.8	18.2	81.4	18.6
Bartenders	94.2	5.8	94.0	6.0	93.9	6.1
Cooks, except private household	77.7	22.3	80.2	19.8	81.4	18.6
Childcare workers, except private household	83.4	16.6	79.3	20.7	80.0	20.0
Crossing guards and bridge tenders	90.3	9.7	89.3	10.7	88.8	11.2

Firefighters	97.3	2.7	97.1	2.9	97.0	3.0
Food-service workers, n.e.c., except private household	79.0	21.0	81.4	18.6	82.6	17.4
Hairdressers and cosmetologists	91.7	8.3	93.5	6.5	94.4	5.6
Health aides, except nursing	79.2	20.8	78.1	21.9	77.5	22.5
Housekeepers, except private household	85.3	14.7	84.7	15.3	84.4	15.6
Marshals and constables	97.5	2.5	97.5	2.5	97.5	2.5
Nursing aides, orderlies, and attendants	73.5	26.5	72.2	27.8	71.5	28.5
Police and detectives	93.4	6.6	91.0	9.0	89.8	10.2
Practical nurses	76.5	23.5	71.9	28.1	69.6	30.4
School monitors	92.0	8.0	90.7	9.3	90.0	10.0
Sheriffs and bailiffs	95.7	4.3	94.4	5.6	93.7	6.3
Laborers, except farm	78.4	21.6	80.0	20.0	80.5	19.5
Carpenter helpers	77.2	22.8	82.2	17.8	84.7	15.3
Gardeners and groundskeepers, except farm	78.8	21.2	79.6	20.4	80.0	20.0
Farm occupations	90.3	9.7	93.6	6.4	95.2	4.8
Farm foremen	90.0	10.0	87.7	12.3	86.5	13.5
Farm managers	95.4	4.6	95.6	4.4	95.7	4.3
Farm laborers, wage workers	77.4	22.6	83.0	17.0	85.8	14.3
Farmers, owners and tenants	97.1	2.9	98.9	1.1	99.8	0.2
Total, all occupations studied	91.9	8.1	90.6	9.4	89.7	10.3
Total, all U.S. occupations	89.3	10.7	88.1	11.9	87.6	12.4

Note: Details may not add to totals because of rounding.
Source: U.S. Bureau of the Census, Department of Commerce, Census of the Population, 1970.

TABLE C.10

Distribution of Employment by Level of Educational Attainment, 1970 and Projected 1980 and 1985, Study Occupations

(in percent)

Occupation	1970 Less than 12 Years	1970 12-15 Years	1970 16 Years or More	1980 Less than 12 Years	1980 12-15 Years	1980 16 Years or More	1985 Less than 12 Years	1985 12-15 Years	1985 16 Years or More
Professional, technical, and kindred workers	9.9	68.7	21.4	7.1	70.1	22.8	5.8	71.3	22.9
Computer programmers	1.6	56.7	41.7	1.4	49.2	49.4	1.3	45.4	53.3
Designers	11.2	58.6	30.2	7.4	59.3	33.3	5.5	59.6	34.9
Electrical and electronic-engineering technicians	11.5	83.0	5.5	6.7	87.2	6.1	4.3	89.3	6.4
Engineering and science technicians, n.e.c.	14.3	72.7	13.0	8.4	77.1	14.5	5.5	79.2	15.3
Mechanical-engineering technicians	17.2	68.1	14.7	10.2	73.1	16.7	6.7	75.6	17.7
Other technicians, except health	12.1	72.3	15.6	7.0	75.8	17.2	4.5	77.5	18.0
Personnel and labor-relations workers	8.9	52.0	39.1	8.8	54.6	36.6	8.8	55.9	35.3
Recreation workers	15.2	52.8	32.0	17.4	57.0	25.6	18.5	59.1	22.4
Registered nurses	9.6	74.5	15.9	5.4	76.4	18.2	3.3	77.3	19.4
Therapists	6.3	38.3	55.4	2.4	41.9	55.6	1.7	42.6	55.7
Tool programmers, numerical control	6.0	70.4	23.6	3.4	71.3	25.3	2.1	71.7	26.2
Managers and administrators, except farm	25.4	54.5	20.1	15.3	59.8	24.8	10.9	62.0	27.1
Bank officials and financial managers	6.1	58.2	35.7	2.5	50.6	46.9	2.1	45.4	52.5
Buyers and shippers, farm products	40.3	51.4	8.3	24.9	64.7	10.4	17.2	71.4	11.4
Buyers, wholesale and retail trade	21.6	61.2	17.2	15.5	67.1	17.4	12.5	70.0	17.5
Managers and administrators, n.e.c.	25.6	53.6	20.8	15.9	58.8	25.3	11.1	61.4	27.5
Managers and superintendents, building	36.8	50.7	12.5	19.7	62.9	17.4	11.2	69.0	19.7
Restaurant, cafeteria, and bar managers	39.8	53.5	6.7	20.7	70.1	9.2	15.7	73.8	10.5
Sales managers and department heads, retail	23.0	63.5	13.5	16.5	69.8	13.7	13.3	72.9	13.8
Salesworkers	29.5	58.2	12.2	21.4	64.7	13.9	16.1	68.7	15.2
Insurance agents, brokers, and underwriters	12.5	62.9	24.6	4.1	68.2	27.7	2.6	68.2	29.2
Sales representatives, manufacturing	15.7	57.2	27.1	8.3	59.4	32.3	4.6	60.5	34.9
Sales representatives, wholesale	21.5	61.8	16.7	12.6	68.7	18.7	8.2	72.1	19.7
Salesclerks, retail trade	40.3	56.0	3.7	31.2	64.3	4.5	26.7	68.4	4.9
Salesworkers, retail trade	31.9	61.6	6.5	20.4	71.7	7.9	14.6	76.8	8.6
Salespeople, service and construction	26.3	59.7	14.0	15.1	68.6	16.3	4.5	78.0	17.5
Stock and bond sales agents	7.5	39.3	53.2	2.8	31.9	65.3	0.5	28.2	71.3
Clerical and kindred workers	16.4	78.6	5.0	10.5	83.9	5.6	8.1	86.2	5.7
Billing clerks	17.5	80.1	2.4	6.5	90.7	2.8	4.5	92.4	3.1
Bookkeepers	16.3	78.4	5.3	11.5	81.7	6.8	9.1	83.3	7.6
Bookkeeping and billing-machine operators	15.6	82.4	2.0	5.8	92.0	2.2	44.0	93.7	2.3

Calculating-machine operators	20.8	77.4	1.8	8.0	89.9	2.1	5.5	92.2	2.3
Computer and peripheral equipment operators	8.6	86.5	4.9	3.0	91.8	5.2	2.0	92.6	5.4
Insurance adjustors, examiners, and investigators	6.5	58.4	35.1	2.7	61.7	35.6	2.2	61.9	35.9
Keypunch operators	13.8	84.6	1.6	6.2	92.0	1.8	2.8	95.3	1.9
Miscellaneous clerical workers	20.7	70.4	8.9	8.0	81.5	10.5	5.5	83.2	11.3
Office machine operators, n.e.c.	30.7	66.8	2.5	12.8	84.0	3.2	9.1	87.3	3.6
Payroll and timekeeping clerks	18.0	78.7	3.3	9.9	87.0	3.1	7.7	89.3	3.0
Real-estate appraisers	8.0	53.2	38.8	4.1	59.2	36.7	1.0	63.0	36.0
Secretaries, legal, medical and other	8.4	86.3	5.3	6.0	89.2	4.8	5.1	90.5	4.4
Shipping and receiving clerks	47.0	51.3	1.7	38.0	59.7	2.3	33.5	63.9	2.6
Statistical clerks	18.4	74.5	7.1	6.9	84.9	8.2	4.7	86.5	8.8
Stenographers	7.4	89.3	3.3	4.1	92.5	3.5	2.5	93.9	3.6
Stock clerks and storekeepers	39.7	57.5	2.8	29.2	67.0	3.8	24.0	71.7	4.3
Tabulating-machine operators	17.8	79.8	2.4	6.7	90.5	2.8	4.6	92.4	3.0
Typists	14.4	83.0	2.6	9.4	87.4	3.2	6.9	89.6	3.5
Craftsmen and kindred workers	49.6	48.5	1.9	37.6	60.1	2.3	32.3	65.2	2.5
Air-conditioning, heating, and refrigeration mechanics	47.9	50.8	1.3	36.2	62.1	1.7	30.4	67.7	1.9
Aircraft mechanics and repairers	30.9	67.5	1.6	20.1	78.2	1.7	14.7	83.5	1.8
Auto-body repairers	59.1	40.4	0.5	47.9	51.7	0.4	42.3	57.3	0.4
Auto mechanics	57.1	42.2	0.7	43.4	55.6	1.0	36.6	62.3	1.1
Brickmasons and stonemasons	62.6	36.5	0.9	52.0	46.8	1.2	46.7	52.0	1.3
Bulldozer operators	69.7	29.8	0.5	58.3	41.3	0.4	52.6	47.1	0.3
Cabinetmakers	59.7	38.6	1.7	52.7	44.9	2.4	49.2	48.1	2.7
Carpenters	60.4	38.5	1.1	48.0	50.6	1.4	41.8	56.6	1.6
Carpenter apprentices	24.2	75.8	0.0	11.8	88.1	0.1	8.8	91.0	0.2
Crane, derrick, and hoist operators	66.3	33.3	0.4	53.8	45.7	0.5	47.4	51.9	0.6
Data-processing machine repairers	6.1	88.5	5.4	7.0	75.8	17.2	4.5	77.5	18.0
Decorators and window dressers	29.0	63.0	8.0	22.5	69.5	8.0	19.3	72.7	8.0
Electricians	36.5	62.1	1.4	26.0	72.3	1.7	20.8	77.4	1.8
Electric power line and cable workers	11.5	83.0	5.5	6.7	87.2	6.1	4.3	89.3	6.4
Excavating, grading, and road machine operators	67.5	32.0	0.5	62.5	37.0	0.5	60.0	39.5	0.5
Farm-implement mechanics and repairers	53.6	45.4	1.0	39.9	58.7	1.4	33.1	65.3	1.6
Foremen	40.7	53.2	6.1	26.5	65.9	7.6	21.9	69.7	8.4
Heavy-equipment mechanics, including diesel	54.0	45.3	0.7	40.3	58.7	1.0	33.5	65.4	1.1
Job and die setters, metal	59.7	39.7	0.6	47.3	51.9	0.8	41.1	58.0	0.9

(continued)

187

	Distribution of Employment								
	1970			1980			1985		
Occupation	Less than 12 Years	12-15 Years	16 Years or More	Less than 12 Years	12-15 Years	16 Years or More	Less than 12 Years	12-15 Years	16 Years or More
Machinists	46.3	52.9	0.8	36.0	63.1	0.9	30.9	68.2	0.9
Machinist apprentices	23.1	76.5	0.4	17.4	81.9	0.7	14.6	84.6	0.8
Miscellaneous mechanics and repairers	43.0	55.3	1.7	32.0	66.3	1.7	26.5	71.8	1.7
Painter apprentices	45.2	54.8	0.0	37.2	62.8	0.0	33.6	66.4	0.0
Painters, construction and maintenance	66.7	32.1	1.2	57.3	41.4	1.3	52.6	46.0	1.4
Paperhangers	62.3	35.0	2.7	52.7	44.4	2.9	47.9	49.1	3.0
Pattern and model makers, except paper	36.9	61.6	1.5	24.7	73.7	1.6	18.6	79.7	1.7
Photoengravers and lithographers	29.2	67.9	2.9	20.3	77.0	2.7	17.2	80.2	2.6
Plumbers and pipefitters	50.8	48.1	1.1	34.7	63.6	1.7	29.2	68.8	2.0
Printing-press apprentices	25.6	73.7	0.7	18.1	81.0	0.9	14.3	84.7	1.0
Printing-press operators	39.2	59.7	1.1	27.8	70.6	1.6	23.7	74.5	1.8
Printing-trades apprentices, except print pressmen pressmen	25.6	74.0	0.4	17.2	82.6	0.2	14.4	85.4	0.2
Radio and TV repairers	32.4	65.3	2.3	23.1	74.8	2.1	18.5	79.5	2.0
Sheetmetal apprentices	17.3	82.7	0.0	7.1	92.9	0.0	5.0	95.0	0.0
Sheetmetal workers and tinsmiths	46.9	52.3	0.8	35.8	63.3	0.9	31.5	67.6	0.9
Structural-metal craftsmen	54.0	45.1	0.9	38.8	59.9	1.2	31.2	67.3	1.4
Telephone installers and repairers	18.2	81.4	0.4	10.9	88.9	0.2	7.2	92.6	0.2
Telephone linemen and splicers	14.7	84.2	1.1	8.7	90.4	0.9	5.7	93.5	0.8
Tilesetters	59.7	39.5	0.8	47.1	51.7	1.2	40.9	57.8	1.3
Upholsterers	64.7	34.6	0.7	55.4	43.8	0.8	50.8	48.4	0.8
Operatives	59.5	39.8	0.7	49.1	50.0	0.9	44.0	55.0	1.0
Assemblers	53.0	46.4	0.6	43.0	56.3	0.7	38.0	61.2	0.8
Bus drivers	53.0	45.8	1.2	40.0	58.4	1.6	33.5	64.7	1.8
Checkers, examiners, and inspectors, manufacturing	48.9	49.6	1.5	39.2	59.1	1.7	35.3	62.9	1.8
Cutting operatives, n.e.c.	64.3	35.1	0.6	50.2	49.0	0.8	43.1	56.0	0.9
Delivery and route workers	51.4	47.6	1.0	41.4	57.6	1.0	36.4	62.6	1.0
Dressmakers and seamstresses, except factory	60.2	37.9	1.9	50.3	47.3	2.4	45.3	52.0	2.7
Drill-press operatives	58.4	41.2	0.4	45.5	53.9	0.6	39.1	60.3	0.6
Graders and sorters, manufacturing	67.3	32.1	0.6	53.8	45.3	0.9	47.1	51.9	1.0
Grinding-machine operatives	57.0	42.4	0.6	43.4	55.8	0.8	38.2	60.9	0.9

Occupation									
Lathe and milling-machine operatives	49.2	50.1	0.7	38.4	60.7	0.9	33.0	66.0	1.0
Painters, manufactured articles	65.2	34.2	0.6	60.7	38.7	0.6	58.6	40.8	0.6
Other precision machine operatives	53.1	46.4	0.5	37.1	62.3	0.6	29.1	70.2	0.7
Punch and stamping-press operatives	61.8	37.8	0.4	49.5	50.0	0.5	43.4	56.1	0.5
Sawyers	73.3	26.2	0.5	62.2	37.1	0.7	56.6	42.6	0.8
Sewers and stitchers	70.3	29.3	0.4	61.4	38.1	0.5	57.0	42.5	0.5
Solderers	58.8	40.6	0.6	45.5	53.8	0.7	38.9	60.4	0.8
Truck drivers	66.3	33.1	0.6	56.5	42.6	0.9	51.6	47.3	1.1
Welders and flame cutters	59.6	40.0	0.4	48.7	50.8	0.5	43.3	56.2	0.5
Service workers	46.5	51.5	2.0	34.7	63.0	2.3	29.5	68.1	2.4
Bartenders	50.5	46.3	3.2	34.4	60.9	4.7	28.9	65.6	5.5
Cooks, except private household	66.1	33.1	0.8	59.8	39.3	0.9	56.7	42.4	0.9
Childcare workers, except private household	48.4	47.7	3.9	39.0	56.4	4.6	34.3	60.8	4.9
Crossing guards and bridge tenders	59.6	39.5	0.9	47.6	51.6	0.8	41.6	57.6	0.8
Firefighters	26.8	71.8	1.4	15.5	82.9	1.6	9.9	88.4	1.7
Food-service workers, n.e.c., except private household	64.0	35.1	0.9	57.6	41.4	1.0	54.4	44.5	1.1
Hairdressers and cosmetologists	33.6	65.8	0.6	24.0	75.4	0.6	19.2	80.2	0.6
Health aides, except nursing	38.0	57.7	4.3	27.2	69.1	3.7	22.3	74.1	3.6
Housekeepers, except private household	43.4	50.9	5.8	23.2	68.6	8.2	17.0	74.9	8.1
Marshals and constables	42.3	52.7	5.0	24.5	67.6	7.9	19.3	71.3	9.4
Nursing aides, orderlies, and attendants	51.0	47.8	1.2	38.6	60.3	1.1	32.4	66.5	1.1
Police and detectives	20.1	73.8	6.1	9.3	83.4	7.3	6.8	85.3	7.9
Practical nurses	29.9	69.1	1.0	15.3	84.0	0.7	11.6	87.8	0.6
School monitors	29.6	66.4	3.9	22.5	72.9	4.6	18.9	76.2	4.9
Sheriffs and bailiffs	32.0	63.8	4.2	17.6	78.3	4.1	10.4	85.5	4.1
Laborers, except farm	71.2	27.4	1.5	62.2	35.8	2.0	57.9	39.9	2.2
Carpenter helpers	71.1	28.0	0.9	57.8	41.1	1.1	51.2	47.5	1.3
Gardeners and groundskeepers, except farm	71.2	27.2	1.6	62.9	35.0	2.1	58.8	38.9	2.3
Farm occupations	64.1	33.1	2.8	51.0	44.9	4.1	44.1	51.1	4.8
Farm foremen	58.5	35.3	6.2	46.2	46.1	7.7	40.1	51.5	8.4
Farm managers	44.7	43.9	11.4	36.6	53.3	10.1	32.6	58.0	9.4
Farm laborers, wage workers	78.3	20.6	1.1	70.7	27.7	1.6	66.9	31.2	1.9
Farmers, owners and tenants	57.0	39.5	3.5	41.9	53.1	5.0	34.3	59.9	5.8
Total, all occupations studied	38.5	54.8	6.7	27.5	63.9	8.6	22.7	68.5	8.8
Total, all U.S. occupations	37.2	50.4	12.4	27.3	56.3	16.4	22.8	59.2	18.0

Note: Details may not add to totals because of rounding.
Sources: U.S. Department of Labor; 1970 Census of Population; The Conference Board.

TABLE C.11

Vocational Programs Related to Occupations Included in Conference Board Study

Occupation—BLS Title	Related Vocational Programs
Buyers and shippers, farm products Farmers, owners and tenants Farm managers Farm foremen Farm laborers, wage workers	Agricultural production
Gardeners, except farm and groundskeepers	Landscaping
Bank officials and financial managers Stock and bond sales agents	Finance and credit
Delivery and route workers	Food distribution
Sales managers and department heads, retail	General merchandise
Buyers, wholesale, and retail trade Restaurant, cafeteria, and bar managers Salesclerks, retail trade Salesworkers, retail trade Salespeople, service and construction Managers and administrators, n.e.c.	Apparel and accessories
Sales representatives, manufacturing Sales representatives, wholesale	Industrial marketing Hardware, building materials, farm and garden supplies and equipment
Insurance agents, brokers, and underwriters Insurance adjustors, examiners, and investigators	Insurance
Managers and superintendents, building	Real estate

Occupation—BLS Title	Related Vocational Programs
Real-estate agents and brokers	
Real-estate appraisers	
Recreation workers	Recreation and tourism
Bus drivers	Transportation
Registered nurses	Nursing (associate degree)
Practical nurses	Practical (vocational) nurses
Nursing aides, orderlies, and attendants	Nursing assistance (aide)
Therapists	Occupational therapy Inhalation therapy Physical therapy Psychiatric aide
Health aides, except nursing	Medical assistant (physician's office)
Childcare workers, except private household	Care and guidance of children
School monitors	
Dressmakers and seamstresses, except factory	Dressmaking
Sewers and stitchers	Clothing management, production, and service Home furnishing, equipment, and service
Restaurant, cafeteria, and bar managers	Food management, production, and service
Housekeepers, except private household	

(continued)

(Table C.11 continued)

Occupation—BLS Title	Related Vocational Programs
Bookkeepers Bookkeeping and billing-machine operators Calculating-machine operators Tabulating-machine operators Payroll and timekeeping clerks	Bookkeepers Machine operators (billing, bookkeeping, and computing)
Computer and peripheral equipment operators	Computer and console operators
Computer programmers	Programmers Scientific data processors
Keypunch operators	Keypunch and coding-equipment operators
Billing clerks Office machine operators, n.e.c. Miscellaneous clerical workers Payroll and timekeeping clerks Statistical clerks Bookkeeping and billing-machine operators	General office clerks Filing, office machine, and general office clerks, other
Shipping and receiving clerks Graders and sorters, manufacturing	Shipping and receiving clerks
Stock clerks and storekeepers	Stock and inventory clerks
Personnel and labor-relations workers workers	Interview and test technicians Personnel assistants
Secretaries, legal, medical and other	Secretary
Stenographers Typists	Stenographer Clerk typist Typist

Occupation—BLS Title	Related Vocational Programs
Electrical and electronic-engineering technicians	Electrical technology
Other technicians, except health	Electronic technology
Data-processing machine repairers	
Radio and TV repairers	
Mechanical-engineering technicians	Mechanical technology
Engineering and science technicians, n.e.c.	
Tool programmers, numerical control	
Air-conditioning, heating, and refrigeration mechanics	Air conditioning Cooling Heating
Auto-body repairers	Body and fender
Painters, manufactured articles	
Foremen	Foremanship, supervision, and management development
Printing-trades apprentices, except printing press	Printing-press occupations
Printing-press operators	
Printing-press apprentices	
Photoengravers and lithographers	Photoengraving Lithography, photography, and platemaking
Job and die setters, metal	Machine shop
Machinists	
Machinist apprentices	
Pattern and model makers, except paper	
Other precision machine operatives	

(continued)

(Table C.11 continued)

Occupation—BLS Title	Related Vocational Programs
Cutting operatives, n.e.c. Drill-press operatives Grinding-machine operatives Lathe and milling-machine operatives Other precision machine operatives Punch and stamping-press operatives Sawyers	Machine tool operation
Job and die setters, metal Structural-metal crafts workers Punch and stamping-press operatives	Metal trades combined
Sheetmetal workers and tinsmiths Sheetmetal apprentices	Sheetmetal
Welders and flame cutters	Electric welding Combination welding
Solderers	Brazing and soldering
Hairdressers and cosmetologists	Cosmetology
Auto mechanics Farm-implement mechanics and repairers Heavy-equipment mechanics, including diesel Aircraft mechanics and repairers	Mechanics Agricultural power and machinery Aircraft maintenance
Designers Decorators and window dressers	Interior decorating
Carpenters Carpenter helpers Carpenter apprentices	Carpentry

Occupation—BLS Title	Related Vocational Programs
Electricians	Electricity Electrical occupations
Bulldozer operators Excavating, grading, and road-machine operators Crane, derrick, and hoist operators	Operation, heavy equipment
Brickmasons and stonemasons Tilesetters	Masonry
Painters, construction and maintenance Paperhangers Painter apprentices	Painting and decorating
Plumbers and pipefitters	Plumbers and pipefitters
Drafters	Drafting
Telephone line and splicing workers Electric power line and cable workers	Industrial electrician Linemen
Telephone installers and repairers	Communications
Radio and TV repairers	Radio and TV
Firefighters	Fireman training
Crossing guards and bridge tenders Marshals and constables Police and detectives Sheriffs and bailiffs	Law-enforcement training Police science technology

(continued)

(Table C.11 continued)

Occupation—BLS Title	Related Vocational Programs
Cooks, except private household	Cook/chef
Food-service workers, n.e.c., except private household	
Miscellaneous mechanics and repairers	Small engine repair
Upholsterers	Upholstering
Cabinetmakers	Woodworking
Sawyers	
Assemblers	No related program
Checkers, examiners, and inspectors, manufacturing	No related program
Truck drivers	No related program
Bartenders	No related program

Source: U.S. Department of Labor, Bureau of Labor Statistics, "Matching 1970 Census Based BLS National-State Matrix Occupational Categories to Office of Education Instructional Programs" (unpublished), 1974.

TABLE C.12

Enrollment in Vocational Programs per 100 Persons Employed in Related Occupations, 1970, and Projected Average Annual Rate of Growth in Enrollment, 1970-77, and Employment, 1970-80

Vocational Program	Enrollments per 100 Employed, 1970	Average Annual Growth Rate in Enrollments, 1970-77	Average Annual Growth Rate in Employment 1970-80
Agricultural production	22	-1.8	-4.4
Landscaping	9	7.8	0.2
Finance and credit	4	12.8	4.0
Food distribution	5	1.0	1.7
General merchandise			
Apparel and accessories	2	15.4	2.8
Hardware and building materials			
Industrial marketing	1	7.8	2.3
Insurance	3	0.5	2.4
Real estate	12	17.8	3.1
Recreation	5	41.8	4.4
Transportation	5	2.6	2.6
Nursing (associate degree)	4	15.5	3.7
Practical (vocational) nursing	16	9.7	5.6
Nursing assistants (aide)	6	11.4	3.7
Psychiatric aide			
Occupational therapy			
Physical therapy	4	28.4	6.1
Inhalation therapy			
Medical assistants	3	32.2	6.5
Care and guidance of children	8	32.8	3.6
Dressmaking			
Home furnishings equipment and service	8	16.0	1.1
Clothing management			
Food management, production and service	9	15.5	2.3
Bookkeepers			
Machine operators	17	6.8	2.2
Computer console operators			
Business data processing			
Scientific data processing	29	-0.4	3.7
Keypunch and coding-equipment operators			
General office clerks			
Filing, office machines, general office	35	2.0	3.5
Shipping and receiving clerks			
Stock and inventory clerks	1	-3.1	1.3
Interviewers and test technicians			
Personnel assistants	3	15.3	5.3
Secretaries			
Stenographers	16	6.9	3.6
Clerk typists			
Typists	57	5.6	2.6
Electrical technicians			
Electronic technicians	19	6.5	4.0
Mechanical technology	14	1.0	6.2

(continued)

(Table C.12 continued)

Vocational Program	Enrollments per 100 Employed, 1970	Average Annual Growth Rate in Enrollments, 1970-77	Average Annual Growth Rate in Employment, 1970-80
Air conditioning	22	28.7	5.2
Body and fender	7	28.8	0.8
Mechanics, auto } Agricultural mechanics	15	15.8	1.9
Aircraft maintenance	29	1.0	2.9
Interior decorating	11	15.6	3.2
Carpentry	5	19.1	0.9
Electricity } Electrical occupations	24	10.7	2.6
Operation, heavy equipment	N.A.	N.A.	1.8
Masonry	11	12.5	1.7
Painting and decorating	N.A.	N.A.	0.9
Plumbing and pipefitting	8	11.8	2.6
Drafters	35	5.5	3.0
Communications } Radio and TV	41	9.2	1.6
Foremanship	5	18.0	1.3
Printing-press operators } Lithography } Photoengraving	30	10.2	1.8
Machine shop } Machine tool operation } Metal trades combined } Sheetmetal } Electrical welding } Combination welding } Brazing and soldering	10	8.0	1.8
Cosmetology	8	10.8	2.3
Fireman training	55	17.6	3.6
Law-enforcement training	10	16.8	2.5
Cook/chef	2	17.9	3.7
Small-engine repair	8	24.1	1.8
Upholstering	11	27.6	1.8
Woodworking occupations	26	18.7	1.5
Occupations with No Related Vocational Program			
Assemblers	0	N.A.	1.2
Checkers, examiners, and inspectors, manufacturing	0	N.A.	1.6
Truck drivers	0	N.A.	1.4
Bartenders	0	N.A.	1.6
Total, all vocational programs and occupations included in study	11	9.2	2.1

Note: N.A. = Not Available.
Sources: Enrollment data—U.S. Office of Education; Employment data—U.S. Department of Labor, Bureau of Labor Statistics.

INDEX

adult programs, 23, 87
age factor, 22; in educational attainment, 12, 48, 112; in vocational education programs, 4; job opportunities, 31, 35; projection techniques, 107-08, 116
Air Quality Act, 31
Annual Manpower Planning Report, 126, (see also, Kentucky Department for Human Resources)
Assessing the Impact of Changes in National Priorities on the Utilization of Scientists and Engineers in the 1970's, 33
attrition, earnings power, 39; estimates, 7, 9, 25; job openings, 33, 37-38, 105-06

Bahl, R. (co-author), 35
Bureau of Labor Statistics, 7, 8, 24, 97, 98; Employment and Earnings, 15, 25; Estimating Occupational Separations from the Labor Force for States, 126; "Matching 1970 Census Based BLS National-State Matrix Occupation Categories to Office of Education Instruction Programs," 105; Occupation-by-Industry Matrix, 105; Tomorrow's Manpower Needs, 24, 43, 97, 106, 126; The U.S. Economy in 1985, 7, 24, 43, 95, 99 (see also, U.S. Department of Labor)

Bureau of the Census, Detailed Characteristics: U.S. Summary, 102; 1970 Occupation and Industry Classification Systems in Terms of Their 1960 Occupation and Industry Elements, 104 (see also, U.S. Department of Commerce)

career planning, 80, 92; women, 91 (see also, Educational Attainment and Occupational Training)
"Careers, Counselling, and the Curriculum," 95
Carnegie Commission on Higher Education, 50, 60
college, 2, 44, 50-54; age factor, 46; earnings, 54-57; enrollments, 13; geographic factor, 49-50; occupational representation, 7, 11-12, 46, 52-53; projection techniques, 97-98
Current Population Survey, for 1974, 17; projection techniques, 97, 104-05

Detailed Characteristics: U.S. Summary, 101 (see also, U.S. Department of Commerce, Bureau of the Census)
discrimination, by sex, 17, 73

earnings, economic growth, 10; educational attainment, 10, 16, 45, 50, 54-58; employment, 6, 9; job openings, 7, 37-43; Kentucky, 49; New Jersey, 49;

199

nonwhites, 10, 15, 65, 72, 73-76; projections, 41-43, 98, 115-20; role in program planning, 84-87; vocational training, 18, 20, 37, 58-59, 93; women, 10, 54, 65, 67, 70, 90

"Economic Problems of a Mature Economy," 33

educational attainment, 10-13, 45-60; age, 12, 23, 46, 115; distribution among occupations, 59, 46, 50-53; earnings, 10, 16, 59, 45, 50, 54-60; employment growth, 13; geographic location, 50; nonwhites, 75-78; occupational growth, 50; projections, 98, 112-15; women, 55 (see also, occupational training)

employment, distribution, 24-25, 82-84; due to vocational education, 18; earnings, 2, 9-10, 38-39, 43; estimates, 7, 20, 33, 35; growth, 6, 9-10, 14, 25-31, 33-39, 99; job openings, 55, 106; nonwhites, 15; projection techniques, 97-98, 107; region, 32-33; women, 15 (see also, women and nonwhites)

Employment and Earnings, 17, 23, 78 (see also, Bureau of Labor Statistics)

"Employment Data for Detailed Occupations, 1974," 17

enrollment, by sex, 20-23, 89; in occupational training programs, 80-84; in vocational education, 4, 18-20

equal employment goals, 17, 89; occupational distribution for women, 3

Estimating Occupational Separations from the Labor Force for States, 24, 126 (see also, U.S. Department of Labor, Bureau of Labor Statistics)

Evaluating Vocational Education—Policies and Plans for the 1970's, 20, 23

Freeman, Richard B., 13, 23, 60, 114

Garfinkle, S., 63
geographic factor, in educational attainment, 50; in employment growth, 32-33
Grubb, W. N., (co-author), 95
Gutmanis, I. (co-author), 31

high school, 1; age factor, 48-49; career planning, 90; dropouts, 45, 46; earnings, 45, 50, 54-57; geographic factor, 49-50; importance in work force, 12, 44; occupational training, 58-60, 86-87; projections, 12, 46-47

Inequality: A Reassessment of the Effect of Family and Schooling in America, 60
Inequality in Education, 95
inflation, effects on women, 63
inter-occupational mobility, 80

Jencks, C., 54, 60
job openings, 18-20, 24-43; as a result of attrition, 2, 8, 25, 37; as a result of employment growth, 2, 8, 25-31, 32-35; by region, 32-33; distribution of, 8-9; earning power, 7, 20, 38-43; factors contributing to, 7, 18, 19, 25; projections, 37; projection techniques, 37
Journal of Human Resources, 13, 23, 60, 95, 114

INDEX

Kellgren, Nils, 80, 95
Kentucky, 49; economic framework, 125; projections, 130-34; race indicator, 127; sex factor, 127; statistical reliability, 127
Kentucky Department for Human Resources, Annual Manpower Planning Report, 126

labor force, 6
Lazerson, M. (co-author), 95
Lecht, L. A., 20, 23, 31
Levitan, Sar (co-author), 12, 23, 60

Manpower Challenge of the Eighties, 126
Manpower Projections, 7, 24-37
Manpower Report of the President, 1975, 14, 23, 43, 60, 63, 78, 91, 92, 95
"Matching 1970 Census Based BLS National-State Matrix Occupational Categories to Office of Education Instruction Programs," 105 (see also, U.S. Department of Labor, Bureau of Labor Statistics)
median earnings, 3, 10, 16, 20, 24, 41 (see also, earnings)
Memorandum to the Secretary of Labor, "An Active Labor Market Policy," 95
men, educational attainment, 12-13; employment, 15; job opportunities, 14, 17; representation shifts, 35-36
minorities (see, nonwhites and women)
Monthly Labor Review, 78

National Science Foundation, 31
New Jersey, 49; economic framework, 125; projections, 130-134; race indicator, 127; sex factor, 127; statistical reliability, 127
New Jersey Department of Labor and Industry, Manpower Challenge of the Eighties, 126
New York Sunday Times, 60
nonwhites, 14; data and data sources for states, 126; earnings, 2-3, 10, 16, 65, 71-72, 73-75, 92-95; educational attainment, 76-77; employment distribution, 2, 16-17, 63-65, 71-75; equal opportunity goals, 14, 17, 62, 87-89; new entrants into labor market, 73-74; occupational training, 87-89, 92-95; projection techniques, 97-98, 104-05, 106-12; representation shifts, 7, 71-73; unemployment, 15, 31, 62

occupational shifts, contributing factors, 4-7, 17; educational attainment, 12; nonwhites, 63-64; women, 63-64 (see also, representation shifts)
occupational training, 13, 79-80; age factor, 46-49; assessing priorities, 80-84; data sources, 104-06; earnings, 58-60, 84-87, 92-95; enrollment distribution, 86-87; enrollment projections, 82-84; equal opportunity goals, 17, 18-22, 87, 89-92; federal funding, 79, 81, 86; importance of, 17, 44; job openings, 18-20; nonwhites, 87-89, 92-95; penetration rate, 80-82 (see also, vocational education)
1970 Occupation and Industry Classification Systems in Terms of Their 1960 Occupation and Industry Elements, 104

(see also, U.S. Department of Commerce)
"Occupations of Women and Black Workers," 78
Office of Education, 2, 82, 89
"Overinvestment in College Training," 13, 23, 60, 114

penetration rate in labor force, 80-82; earnings, 84-86
population, growth factors, 7, 32
projection techniques, age factor, 36, 107-09, 114; college graduates, 97; data and data sources, 101-03; earnings, 39-40, 88, 117-20; economic framework, 98-99; educational attainment, 98, 112, 117; employment growth, 37; for states, 130-34; job openings, 37, 105-06; nonwhites, 97; replacement demand, 37; selecting occupations, 100-01; sex factor, 106-12; women, 97, 98
Public and Proprietory Vocational Training, 95
Puryear, D. (co-author), 43

race factor, distribution of employment, 63-65; projection techniques, 106-12; representation in labor market, 71-73; unemployment, 62 (see also, nonwhites)
replacement demand, 2, 7-9, 27, 28, 29, 37, 68 (see also, attrition)
representation shifts, for nonwhites, 71-73; for women, 8, 67-70 (see also, employment and women)
Rosen, R. (co-author), 31

sex factor, data and data sources for states, 126; earnings, 54-57; enrollment in occupational training, 18-22; in distribution of employment, 63-65, 70-71; projection techniques, 106-12; representation shifts, 67-70 (see also, women and men)
socio-economic factors, affecting occupations, 4-7
Statistical Abstract, 60
stereotypes, of nonwhites, 71; of women, 71 (see also, discrimination)

Tomorrow's Manpower Needs, 24, 43, 97, 126

unemployment, 7, 15, 31, 62; due to educational attainment, 13 (see also, attrition and employment)
U.S. Department of Commerce, Detailed Characteristics: U.S. Summary, 102-03; 1970 Occupation and Industry Classification Systems in Terms of Their 1960 Occupation and Industry Elements, 104
U.S. Department of Labor, 6, 24, 50, 84; Employment and Earnings, 15, 23; Estimating Occupational Separations from the Labor Force for States, 126; "Matching 1970 Census Based BLS National-State Matrix Occupational Categories to Office of Education Instruction Programs," 105; The U.S. Economy in 1985, 7, 23, 24, 43, 95, 99; Tomorrow's Manpower Needs, 24, 43, 97, 106, 126
The U.S. Economy in 1985, 7, 23, 24, 43, 95, 99 (see also, U.S. Department of Labor, Bureau of Labor Statistics)
U.S. News and World Report, 10, 23

INDEX

U. S. Office of Education, 2, 18, 20, 100, 105

vocational education, age factor, 4, 22; effect on earnings, 10, 20, 39, 43; enrollment growth, 4, 13-20, 21; importance of, 2, 10, 18, 20, 37 (see also, occupational training)
Vocational Education Acts, 1968 Amendments, 18
"Vocational Education in American Schooling: Historical Perspectives," 95

Water Quality Act, 31
Wilensky, Harold L., 95
Wilms, Wellford W., 95
women, 14, 78; attrition, 2, 24, 25, 35-37; earnings, 2, 10, 54-57, 63-65, 67, 89-91; educational attainment, 55-57; employment distribution, 2, 7, 15-17, 21, 33, 35-36, 63-71, 92-95; employment growth, 15-16, 35-37; equal opportunity goals, 17, 87-89; new entrants into labor market, 69-70, 91-92; occupational training, 20-21, 89-92; projection techniques, 97, 98, 106-11; representation shifts, 8-9, 68-70; unemployment, 16, 31, 62 (see also, employment and job openings)

Work is Here to Stay, Alas, 12, 23, 60

ABOUT THE AUTHOR

LEONARD A. LECHT is the director of the Special Projects department of The Conference Board, a nonprofit, business research organization. Previously, he was director of the National Planning Association's Priorities Analysis Research, an organization concerned with policy-relevant research relating to the national economy and the development of human natural resources. Dr. Lecht has also served as consultant or expert witness for several government committees.

Dr. Lecht has written numerous books, articles, and papers, including: <u>Educating Vocational Education—Policies and Plans for the 1970s</u>, (Praeger, 1974); <u>Dollars for National Goals: Looking Ahead to 1980</u>, (John Wiley & Sons, 1974); <u>Manpower Requirements for National Goals in the 1970's</u>, (Praeger, 1969); "Manpower Needs, National Goals, and Research Priorities for Vocational-Technical Education," House Committee on Education and Labor, 1970; "The Socio-economic Framework and Technological Progress in Education," Designing Education for the Future, 1968.

Dr. Lecht received his Ph.D. in Economics from Columbia University in 1953, and taught at Carelton College in Minnesota and at the University of Texas. From 1954 to 1963 Dr. Lecht served as chairman of the Department of Economics at Long Island University; then in 1963 he joined the National Planning Association.

RELATED TITLES
Published by
Praeger Special Studies

*A FULL EMPLOYMENT PROGRAM FOR THE 1970s
     edited by Alan Gartner
     William Lynch, Jr.
     and Frank Riessman

IMMIGRANT PROFESSIONALS IN THE UNITED STATES:
Discrimination in the Scientific Labor Market
     Bradley W. Parlin

THE LABOR SUPPLY FOR LOWER-LEVEL OCCUPATIONS
     Harold Wool
     assisted by Bruce Dana Phillips

WOMEN'S INFERIOR EDUCATION:
An Economic Analysis
     Blanche Fitzpatrick

*Also available in paperback as a PSS Student Edition.